Remarkable Things

Deirdre Palmer

If fortune should her favours give
That I in better plight may live
I'd try to have my boy again
And train him up the best of men.
Anon.

Discover us online:
www.crookedcatpublishing.com

Join us on facebook:
www.facebook.com/crookedcatpublishing

Tweet a photo of yourself holding
this book to **@crookedcatbooks**
and something nice will happen.

To Michael, with love.

About the Author

Deirdre lives in Brighton, the city by the sea. Most of her working life has been spent in administration, mainly in the public sector, most recently at the University of Brighton.

When she began writing fiction seriously, she joined the Romantic Novelists' Association's New Writers' Scheme, and is now a full member of the Association.

In recent years she has twice been a major prize-winner in the Mail on Sunday Novel Competition.
Deirdre belongs to a thriving, ten-strong blog group called 'The Write Romantics'.

You can find out more about Deirdre Palmer at:
http://deirdrepalmer.com/
https://www.facebook.com/deirdre.palmer.735
https://twitter.com/DLPalmer_Writer
http://thewriteromantics.com/

Acknowledgements

This book could not have been written without the endless encouragement, inspiration and practical help of so many people.

My special thanks go to Maureen Stenning, Michael Wilson, Marion Cunningham, Angie Gough, Val Bunker, (the late) Ken Bunker, Penny Marler, Patricia Corby; fellow 'Write Romantics' Jo Bartlett, Helen Rolfe, Lynne Davidson, Julie Heslington, Jackie Ladbury, Helen Phifer, Rachael Thomas, Alex Weston and Sharon Booth; and of course to my nearest and dearest, Michael, Christopher, Luke and Kerry. My love to you all.

A big thank-you to Laurence and Steph Patterson at Crooked Cat Publishing for believing in this book enough to take it to market, and to my editor, Christine McPherson, for making it the best it could be.

And finally, thanks to The Romantic Novelists' Association and all who sail in her.

Deirdre Palmer

Remarkable Things

Chapter One

1960

Newcastle-upon-Tyne

My name is Catherine Mary Harte and I am a sinner.

I had but this one thought in mind as I was emptied from the front door of our house into the dark street and the waiting car. All else was wiped away.

Standing in this room, my suitcase furrowing the cheap carpet, I listened as Matron explained the rules; they are pinned up over there, on the back of the door. Then she sat me down on the narrow bed and told me that afterwards I would have six weeks in which to make up my mind while both of us knew that for girls like me there was no choice. That was the truth of it. Matron was quite kindly, though. I would not have expected that, had I expected anything. She called me Cathy.

He called me Cathy, too. He knows nothing of this, nor should he.

There are still two of the six weeks left but there is nothing to be gained by seeing them out. Better to have it over and done.

The water from the hot tap at this hour is never more than tepid. As I wash my face, my eyes are drawn to the wall above the basin, to the bright square of yellow paint where the mirror was until last week when the girl who shared the room wrenched it from its hook and smashed it against the boarded-over fireplace in a sudden frenzy. I didn't mind about the mirror. I know enough of the shame that possesses me; I have no need to witness it in the flesh.

I dry my face and hands and hang the towel on the metal rail. A utility chest of drawers stands beneath the window. I go to it and open the bottom drawer, lifting the linen inside to take out a leather-bound bible with my name in a seven-year-old's writing inside the cover, a narrow silver bracelet engraved with a twining rose, a pair of grey kid gloves, quite worn through in places, and a black poodle brooch with a red collar and a diamanté eye. Lastly, there's a cotton drawstring bag embroidered on one side with a circle of flowers, leaves and birds, and within the circle the letter *M* in dark blue chain stitch with a row of small red hearts underneath. I take the things over to the bed and lay them out on the counterpane, touching each in turn, just once, before picking up the bag and placing everything else inside.

I duck my chin and, using the nail scissors from the bedside table, snip at one of the buttons of my nightdress. The blades are blunt, the angle awkward. The thin material tears and a small, jagged piece comes away with the button. I add the button to the collection and draw the bag closed, then stand for a moment with it pressed to my cheek. It is damp when I take it away.

The baby stirs and whimpers, his eyelids fluttering briefly as I place the bag at the foot of the crib, next to the brown paper parcel of matinée jackets, rompers and bootees. They will come for him soon, the kind people with the blanked-out faces I see in my dreams. I told him so last night, whispering to him as he lay silently in my arms, eyes shining up at me through the darkness. I held him the whole night long, both of us drifting in and out of sleep, and when finally I placed him in his crib it was as if I tore away my own flesh.

Somewhere in the house another baby starts to wail. I take off my nightdress with its trailing cottons and, although it is nearly summer and the days are mild, I put on a woollen frock, stockings, brogues, and my winter coat. I look about the room as if there is something I might have forgotten. A wooden cross on a rope of beads hangs above the bed. I reach up, unhook it and place it around my neck, tucking the cross inside my coat, then drop to my knees beside the bed and pray, hard and fast, for forgiveness.

I go to the crib and lean in to kiss my boy one last time but, afraid of waking him, I pull back; I have already said goodbye. Leaving the door of the room ajar so they will hear when he cries, I let myself out of the house and walk through the dawn-damp streets towards the bridge.

My name is Catherine Mary Harte and I am a sinner.

All else is wiped away.

Chapter Two

2010

Brighton

'There's no mistake, Mr Albourne.' The solicitor lowered her spectacles and peered at Gus over the top of them. 'You are your aunt's sole beneficiary.'

'Yes, so you said, but I don't see how that can possibly be.' Gus's brain was struggling to cope with this turn of events. 'There are two of us, you see. Or there were. My brother, Robert, died in a road accident on the twentieth of July, 2008. This will was made before then, am I right?'

The solicitor nodded. 'Some time before, yes, but there are no conditions and no mention of anyone else. Miss Albourne's estate was always to go to you in its entirety. It's quite straightforward. Ah…'

The girl he'd seen on reception rattled into the room with a tray of tea. Gus smiled up at her. She blushed as she hurried away.

Drinking the tea gave him something to do while his mind turned over the growing idea that Aunt Augusta must have gone doolally before she penned her last will and testament. How else could she have forgotten about Robert? But surely he would have noticed if his aunt had not been up to speed in the marbles department? To his slight shame he hadn't visited her as often as he might have, but even so… No, it couldn't be. Even at eighty-seven, she was as sharp as a tack, right up until the last time he'd seen her when she'd been reproving a junior nurse for her hesitant reading of the blood pressure gauge. Augusta knew about these things, having been in nursing the whole of her working life.

The solicitor tinkled her spoon in the saucer and glanced at the clock. 'I knew your aunt slightly, Mr Albourne. I'd had some dealings with her over the years. She always struck me as a very determined woman, one who certainly knew her own mind and who would not necessarily be bound by convention.' She paused, raising her eyebrows questioningly at Gus.

He nodded thoughtfully. 'Yes, I see what you're saying, but I still don't understand why. She gave no indication, you see.'

The solicitor smiled. 'There was no obligation on her part to do that. Perhaps what you see as unfair appeared to her to be quite the opposite. Perhaps...' She rearranged the papers that lay between them on the desk, pulling out one of the sheets and turning it sideways.

'Yes?' Gus leaned forward a little, twisting his head and narrowing his eyes until the small print moved roughly into focus; his own spectacles lay, pristine and forgotten, in their case at home.

'It's none of my business, but since you seem a little confused... Augustus is your middle name, isn't it? Matthew Augustus Albourne.' She tapped a scarlet fingernail at the relevant line and looked at Gus. 'Were you named after your aunt?'

'You're saying I was her favourite?'

'It's one theory.' The solicitor sat back in her chair.

Gus had realised years ago that he'd been named after his father's sister but had never asked why and no-one had ever said. Why should they? It was just a name, one he had acquired, as he understood it, around the same time as he had acquired his new surname. His father had called him Gus for as long as he could remember, while his mother, his brother, and most of his friends called him Matthew. By the time he was seven or eight he'd become Gus to more or less everyone, until the only people who called him Matthew were his teachers, the doctor, and the reporter from the *Daily Express*.

'I really don't know,' he said, as it struck him that he never would now since there was no-one left to ask.

'We'll be in touch over the transfer of the deeds and so on,' the solicitor said as she showed him out a few minutes later. 'It shouldn't take long.'

Deeds? Yes, of course, the deeds to Aunt Augusta's house. Until today he hadn't even known that she owned the house, nor given it any thought. In fact, he knew very little about his aunt altogether except that she'd been a hospital matron, loved cats – he remembered her distress over the demise of an ancient tabby – and was an avid reader. She had given him a copy of *Oliver Twist* for his tenth birthday; a gloomy choice of reading matter, he'd thought at the time. It wasn't until some years later it dawned on him that it was also a pertinent one.

Gus walked home in a somewhat bemused state, his mental 'to do' list lengthening considerably with every step. At the top of the list was, irrefutably: 'Ring Elspeth'. Elspeth was Robert's widow. She had a daughter, Jenny, his niece. If anyone deserved to benefit from Augusta's death it was those two. Gus no longer had a wife, neither did he have children. His job as a property surveyor and manager of a letting agency paid well enough and was bolstered up by the rent from the maisonette that had once been his marital home. It wasn't a fortune but he'd never hankered after one; there were more important things.

His sister-in-law, on the other hand, lived in a sprawling thirties villa planted squarely in the middle of an equally oversized unmanageable plot. Robert had been forever tacking bits onto the house in the hope of adding value, but Elspeth would never sell up and move because of Jenny's increasing need for familiarity. The place was rapidly turning into a money-pit. It seemed that every time Gus called, Elspeth was surrounded by workmen putting right some aspect of Robert's handiwork which would have been better carried out by experts in the first place. Robert had been head teacher of a small, church-run primary school and although he would have made sure his family was provided for – Jenny in particular, because her needs stretched far into the future – such provision was hardly likely to be substantial.

Perhaps he should visit rather than phoning, Gus thought, as he strode up the hill towards his flat. He would have to tread carefully with Elspeth. Her pride, although admirable, was laced with a stubbornness he would have to negotiate before he could persuade her to accept a penny of Augusta's money. Selfless as she was, she was far more likely to break open a bottle and toast his good fortune. Yet persuade her he must, if justice was to be done.

Later, as Gus peeled off his trainers after his evening run, he began to realise that today's events had stirred up something inside him beyond curiosity and the sudden weight of responsibility. The handful of known facts surrounding his dubious start in life had been parcelled up long ago and stashed away in the vaults of his personal history – permanently, as far as he was concerned. Now, he felt as if a line had been thrown out and was drawing him slowly backwards, compelling him to follow. It wasn't the sanest of thoughts, he was well aware of that, but so far it was refusing to budge.

After supper he sat in the bay window with his Scotch and watched the trees in the darkening park being whipped into a frenzy by the March wind. His thoughts returned to Augusta's funeral, which had been something of a revelation. There being no family left other than himself and, indirectly, Elspeth, he had not expected the smaller chapel at the crematorium to be three-quarters full, and he'd been hard pressed to shake hands with everyone after the service. There were friends of Augusta's, mostly elderly, as well as people from the village, two middle-aged women from the mobile library and the young woman whom his aunt had employed in recent months to help her about the house. Colleagues from her nursing days were there, too, some as old as Augusta herself, others considerably younger. They had spoken about her with such warmth, such enthusiasm.

Yes, it had been a remarkable turn-out, all things considered. Augusta had in some way touched the lives of all those people who came to say goodbye to her and now she had touched his, and in no way lightly. He raised his glass in a silent toast.

Chapter Three

Unlike Gus who, in his father's words, 'ran through girls like water biscuits' until, to everyone's relief, he'd settled down, Robert only ever had one proper girlfriend, whom their mother instantly summed up as being 'a jolly good sort'. Sitting opposite Elspeth now, in a sagging wicker chair in her leaky conservatory, Gus was, as always, struck by the aptness of the description. Elspeth's green-eyed gaze was no less candid for the laughter lines that embraced it, the roundness of her figure no less reassuring for a certain softening around the edges, the chestnut curls, tied back in a red and purple cotton scarf, no less exuberant for a dusting of smoky grey. Her freckles still reminded him of the cinnamon his mother used to shake into cake mixture.

'Jenny, go and put the kettle on for tea, please, love,' Elspeth said.

Jenny's shoulders flounced in preparation for the well-worn script. 'Uncle Gus doesn't want tea. He wants a chocolate biscuit.'

'Jenny...' Elspeth's tone carried a gentle warning.

'Come on, Jenny, let's do it together.' Gus stood up. 'And then,' he said, his mouth close to Jenny's ear, 'perhaps we can find the secret biscuit tin.'

'Don't encourage her,' Elspeth said, laughter in her voice.

Placated, Jenny skipped in front of Gus. She had the same slight stoop about the shoulders as her father, Gus noticed. She was almost as tall, too. It was a pity Elspeth and Robert hadn't had more children but he supposed that after Jenny... The familiar wave of sadness swept through him. How Elspeth stayed so cheerful he couldn't imagine.

'I had no idea the old girl was so well-heeled,' Elspeth was saying, as Gus returned with the tea, Jenny prancing behind with the packet of chocolate digestives.

'She wasn't, not particularly. The house, well, cottage really, makes up almost the entire estate. There's a bit of money and some savings bonds, amounting to a few thousand, no more. I don't need the house. I could sell it and share the proceeds with you, fifty-fifty.'

Gus had already braved this suggestion early on; since it was the main purpose of the visit he had thought it prudent to get it out of the way. Elspeth, however, was being distinctly evasive. Not wishing to pressurise her, he gazed out of the window to where a battery of plastic pipes and sundry bits of kit lay abandoned on the grass. It looked like the site of a rocket launch.

Elspeth followed his line of sight. 'I'm having some of the guttering redone. It's leaky at the joints where Rob extended the kitchen. The pieces don't quite match, apparently.' She shook her head, smiling indulgently. 'But it's all right. These things don't matter, do they, in the great scheme of things?'

'No, I don't suppose they do. Look…'

'Where's your girlfriend, Uncle Gus?' Jenny said, spraying biscuit crumbs.

'Good question.'

'Is she pretty?'

'When I find her I'll let you know.'

He winked at Elspeth. She gave him a tight little smile and dropped her gaze to her mug of tea. Gus waited. Eventually she looked up.

'You keep the house and the money, Gus. Augusta left it to you, which meant she wanted you to have it, no-one else. I appreciate the offer, really I do, but it wouldn't be right. I have this place…' – she waved an arm – 'and Robert didn't exactly leave me high and dry. It would have been easier if he hadn't died right out of the blue, I grant you, but we're all right, so don't you worry. Just enjoy it, I say.'

She gave him a full-on smile but there was something behind it that made him feel distinctly depressed.

'Elspeth, I do wish you'd reconsider,' he said, after a moment. 'I'm certain Augusta would approve, if that's what you're worried about. It's probably what she intended all along. She just didn't get it down in writing where it counted, that's all.'

If only he could believe it was that simple he might be able to present a more convincing case instead of trying to further his cause with half-truths.

'I'm having cake for my birthday, Uncle Gus,' Jenny chipped in. 'Will you come?'

'Wouldn't miss it for the world.'

Elspeth turned to her daughter. 'Jenny, go and let out Spotty out into the garden, will you? In fact, why don't you go with him and throw his rubber ring? Here, put your parka on, and mind you don't fall over the pipes.'

Gus watched as the Dalmatian lumbered across the grass, Jenny cantering behind. 'She seems well.'

'Oh, she is, she is.' Elspeth watched her daughter and the dog for a moment, then turned to Gus. 'No, I won't reconsider, but thank you again. It's very generous of you.'

'I'm not being generous, Elspeth.' Gus was beginning to feel like a benevolent uncle who visited once a year for the pleasure of seeing his riches bestowed on those less fortunate. 'Robert was Augusta's proper nephew, her flesh and blood, and I really don't deserve...'

'Gus, you were no less a part of that family than he was. What is right is that Augusta's wishes are adhered to. Surely you can see that?'

He could, but it would make it a darn sight easier if he knew what had been in his aunt's mind. He was beginning to wish he had taken more interest in the affairs of his family but his parents had not been the kind of people to discuss things of any importance in front of the children. And later on, when he was grown up – or thought he was – there were more pressing matters to pursue.

'I always had the impression,' he said, 'that Augusta didn't like my mother. I used to think it was because she was German.'

Elspeth's eyes widened briefly. 'Oh no, it wasn't that. It was the other way around. It was Liesel who didn't much care for Augusta. She thought she was interfering.'

'Are you sure? Is that what Robert said?'

'Oh yes, quite sure.'

Gus thought for a moment. Understandably, his brother would have picked up on certain things that he, being eleven years younger, may have missed, but it seemed strange that Robert had never put him straight – unless he had, and he, Gus, had simply forgotten. He didn't think so, though.

His sister-in-law had a guarded look about her now, as if she was afraid he was going to question her further, although why that should worry her he had no idea. He looked through the window at his niece who was scrambling about in the long grass near the end of the huge garden, presumably looking for the dog's toy. Elspeth had quite enough problems of her own without concerning herself with his.

He thought about the legacy, wishing again that she would let him share it with her; she had been such a good wife to Robert. Resistance he had expected, but not point-blank refusal. He would leave it for now, though – Elspeth had given him no choice.

'Look, Gus…' she began, giving him a very direct look. 'It isn't pride, the reason I won't accept your offer. Not that.' She shook her head.

'You don't have to explain, Elspeth.'

'No, but I think it's only fair that I do. When I said your mother didn't care for your father's sister, what I meant was that she truly hated her.' Gus opened his mouth but Elspeth held up a hand. 'Hate is a very strong word, I know, but that's how it was. And because your mother felt that way, so did Robert. They were very close, mother and son, as you may remember. So you see, Gus, that is why I can't accept any of Augusta's money, and I never will. It would be a betrayal.'

Gus sat in the café at Somerset House and reached into his inside pocket for the envelope. It had arrived in the post yesterday while he was at work and, knowing what it contained, he had made an instant decision not to open it until he had time and space to give his thoughts free rein.

He had hardly read a word of his newspaper on the journey up. He'd glanced at the headlines as the train pulled out of Brighton and made a stab at the crossword somewhere around Burgess Hill, more for the diversion than the interest, but he'd spent most of the time with his eyes on the passing landscape while his mind replayed Elspeth's revelation.

She was right; hate was indeed a strong word, one which he never would have associated with his mother nor his brother. What circumstances could have motivated such feeling he couldn't imagine, not even when he scraped the recesses of his mind for forgotten clues. Now he thought about it, it was always his father, Henry, who took Gus to visit Aunt Augusta. He had put Robert's absence down to his being that much older, and had never questioned why his mother didn't join them on the trips to Hangburton. It had not seemed relevant.

If Augusta had been aware of Robert's opinion of her, which seemed likely, it might explain why she left him out of her will. What it did not explain was how that opinion arose in the first place. Several times during the drive home from Elspeth's he had considered turning the car round and going back to ask her what else she knew, but he didn't want to risk upsetting her by raking over old ground. It was three years since Robert's death but he could tell how much Elspeth still missed him.

Gus had then spent a restless night trying to make sense of it all. With so little to go on he had reached one dead end after another until, finally, he made up his mind that the only way was to begin at the beginning – the beginning being the contents of the envelope he now held.

Moving his coffee cup to one side, he adjusted his position on the stool and carefully peeled open the envelope. Fishing inside, he frowned as he found himself holding his own, returned, cheque. He unfolded the accompanying piece of paper which bore the logo of the Newcastle register office and a few handwritten lines. *Dear Mr Albourne*, he read. *We have been unable to trace the death record of a Catherine Mary Harte during the dates you specified. Please make another application if you wish us to search within further dates.* Below the signature it said: *PS. We have also checked alternative spellings.*

Gus strolled across the courtyard where a crew of young men in black t-shirts were noisily erecting staging for, according to the posters, a Cuban music night. Stepping over cables to reach the entrance of the Courtauld, he began to regret not opening the envelope last night. If he had, the mild shock and disappointment would have been over and done with by now, leaving him free to enjoy his day. Instead, a cloud had been cast over it, his own stupid fault for endowing a simple piece of post with such significance.

Every Thursday, if he could possibly manage it, Gus came to London. It was a throw-back from boyhood – the urge to be invisible, to go somewhere and not tell a soul where he was going or where he'd been. Back then, he had sneaked away to his secret den in the shrubs behind the cricket pavilion or to dangle his legs over the end of the pier and watch the men fishing, or he'd take the bus to a different part of the town and just wander round the streets. It wasn't that these places were necessarily out of bounds, it was the idea that nobody knew he was there that appealed. He was never gone long enough to be missed, but that wasn't the point. Escapism, he supposed you'd call it.

As a place to be invisible, London worked admirably and it was a darn sight more interesting. He took the same train up every week; his actual destination varied according to his mood, but one of the rules was that he wouldn't decide beforehand, unless there was something particular he wanted to see. He would wait until he arrived at Victoria and then, as likely as not, his feet would follow a route almost of their own accord. It might be the Kensington museums, an art gallery, or Borough Market and Southwark Cathedral. On a fine day he might simply head for green space and wander by the Serpentine or up Primrose Hill.

Of course, the irony these days was that nobody, except

possibly Elspeth, would be in the least interested in his whereabouts, but the spirit of the thing remained more or less intact.

Upstairs in the hushed gallery, he sat on a shiny bench opposite a favourite Cézanne and willed its vibrancy to entice him in. It wasn't working. He'd known before he set foot inside that it wouldn't, not today. Today, there was no escape; his mind refused to be tricked.

He thought about what he knew. He had known he was adopted ever since he was old enough to understand what it meant but it wasn't until he was approaching eleven that he'd begun to notice how this marked him out as different among his peer group. Curiosity aroused, he'd wondered what had happened to his real mother. Was she dead? If so, had she died during the act of giving birth to him? From his limited reading, mainly via school English lessons, and observing his adoptive mother's addiction to old films in which such tragedies abounded, he gathered there was a certain romance attached to this which might in some way reflect onto him.

Casually, he had put the question to his father while the two of them were playing French cricket in the garden. The answer came back equally casually. Yes, he understood she was dead, his father said, clocking the ball with the child-sized bat. He was told so at the time. She disappeared from the place girls went to have their babies, and by the time it was noticed and the search begun, there were certain signs indicating that she'd gone off the bridge and drowned.

The information caused Gus no more than a momentary spike of shock. For all she meant to him she might as well have been a character in one of Liesel's films. Catherine Harte was just a name on his birth certificate. At least that made her a real person, though, whereas his biological father wasn't even that, but there were kids at school without fathers and no-one seemed at all interested, not least the kids themselves. The absence of a father was neither here nor there, it seemed. Mothers were different.

After the cricket, Gus had gone down to the end of the garden, intent on smoking the stump of a cigarette he had in his pocket, and discovered Henry sitting on the old iron bench in the long grass. He was leaning forwards, bent double almost, his face buried in his hands, very still apart from the barely perceptible up and down movement of his shoulders. Gus had crept away before he was noticed. It seemed the right thing to do.

At times he had tried to imagine the desperation surrounding his mother's tragic end, purely because he thought he should, but he had been able to view it only at a distance, as if it was a stranger's story lifted from the archives of social history.

But Catherine Harte wasn't a stranger, not in the accepted sense of the word. He may not have known her as a person but he had been physically a part of her, and she of him. The pair of them had been sustained for three-quarters of a year by the same nutritional source. Perhaps he had underestimated the strength of such a tie; perhaps he had not recognised its existence at all.

Of course, it was possible that a mistake had been made in the records, the only explanation, in fact. He had joined one of those family history websites and carried out a perfunctory search but had soon become frustrated at the endless, eye-straining lists of entries and each click of the mouse sent him spiralling round until he arrived back at the same place and facing another screenful of advice and instructions. Far better to let the experts handle it, he had thought, and he had posted off the form and cheque with every confidence of a result.

Well, there was nothing more he could do about it. He didn't even know now why he had wanted his mother's death certificate. What would it have told him that he didn't know already? He had his own birth certificate, sent for when he was twenty-one, with a blank under 'father's name' and 'adopted' written in the margin, as well as some papers concerning his adoption, acquired two years ago on the death of Liesel. That was the point at which his story truly began – the day the Albournes took him in. His curiosity about Catherine had been aroused, it was true, but only because the news of the legacy had set him thinking about the past.

Meanwhile, his present predicament showed no signs of abating. What would he feel once he held in his hand the keys to the cottage at Hangburton? Guilt? Anger? Gratitude? A mixture of all three, he suspected, much as he had that day in the solicitor's office. Again, he thought of Robert and the little family he had left behind as the unfairness of it all struck a nerve.

After a while he got up from the bench and wandered on through the galleries. A moody Rubens landscape caught his eye. As he contemplated its moonlit skies, a memory flooded in, compelling him to stay where he was for several minutes to keep it in place; Aunt Augusta's hand, large and papery dry, encompassing his own small hand as she said goodbye to him after his visit, and the passing over of four or five sweets, a secret transaction. They were hard little mint things that he didn't like but would duly slide into the pocket of his grey flannel shorts as conspiratorial smiles were exchanged while his father pretended ostentatiously not to notice. She had seemed old to him even then, yet she could not have been more than forty or so at the time. He remembered asking his father what a spinster was after hearing his mother say it. It had conjured up a vision of a spider and he had wondered vaguely whether it had anything to do with Little Miss Muffet.

He thought about Elspeth. How could she have been married to Robert for all those years without knowing the cause of the rift in the family? Perhaps she believed she was protecting him by keeping it to herself. Well, he would just have to persuade her otherwise. He would wait a while for the dust to settle and then he would talk to her again. Meanwhile there was plenty to occupy him; like it or not, he was about to become the owner of a property in a sought-after South Downs village and was in the envious position of having to decide whether or not to live in it. On this happier note, Gus left the Courtauld and headed back through Somerset House, intent on crossing to the South Bank for lunch.

Halfway over Waterloo Bridge, he stopped to gaze at the river as it slid coolly beneath him. He thought of another river – alien, northerly, the claimer of innocent life. He pushed the thought away. Raising his eyes purposefully to the clutter of buildings and the sun strobing off a distant crane, he continued over the bridge at a faster pace. On the other side was a litter bin. Delving into his pocket for the envelope, he tore it into tiny squares and deposited it. A little piece of his cheque escaped the mouth of the bin. The breeze lifted the pale blue fragment and carried it, twirling, towards the river.

Chapter Four

Millie Hope stood by the window in the little back room that doubled as stock-room and kitchen. The clock said 10:23. Almost time... and here it was, the 10.19 semi-fast Brighton to Victoria, slowing as it approached Park Station but not stopping.

Fingers laced around her coffee mug, she felt the faint shudder in the fabric of the building as the carriages slid by. For a moment she thought he wasn't there until the familiar profile showed itself: strong chin, straight nose, dark hair receding slightly at the sides to form a devilish peak on his forehead. He looked to be wearing glasses, although she couldn't be sure. And again, the grey jacket, or it could have been a shirt, she couldn't tell from this distance. The only change, indiscernible yet certain, was the date on the newspaper that shielded him from his fellow travellers.

Voyeurism, her friend Charmaine called it. Curiosity, Millie said. Curiosity about people, their purpose, their routine. Especially routine, the lynchpin of so many lives and the saviour of hers at a time when she most needed saving. There was comfort in sameness.

She had a theory about the man on the train. He had a lover, a married woman who could only get away once a week, and they met every Thursday under the clock at Victoria Station, or perhaps outside Smith's, which wasn't quite so cheesy. She would wait inside, pretending to scan the three-for-two paperbacks, and duck out when she saw him striding across the platform. After a furtive embrace, they'd jump in a taxi and head straight to the hotel, no messing about, because after a week they'd be pretty desperate. The man himself wasn't married – at least, not in this week's version – but he and the woman were very much in love and she was on the verge of leaving her husband.

'You haven't been watching *Brief Encounter* again, by any chance?' Charmaine had enquired. They were in Charmaine's bathroom at the time.

'*Brief Encounter,* my backside. These two are much more advanced than that,' Millie had said, looking up at Charmaine in the mirror, then at herself wearing the rubber cap through which sprouted tendrils of hair copiously soaked in honey-blond bleach. At least there was less hair to contend with now she'd had it cut into a chin-length bob with a side-swept fringe. Charmaine said it made her look like Mariella Frostrup, but all Millie could see at that moment was the creature from the Black Lagoon. 'They did it on the first date, no messing about. This is serious sex, remember.'

'Okay, so after the serious sex he rings for Claridge's room service and they have a tasty little picnic in bed before they part, sobbing into one another's arms.' Charmaine was getting good at this.

'More or less, except it's not Claridge's. He only took her there the first couple of times to impress her. Now it's the Holiday Inn.'

The shop door bell tinkled. Millie tipped the dregs of her coffee into the sink and went through. Violet Mabey was flicking through the racks of cross-stitch kits, while outside her little dog strained at its lead and yapped crazily. Millie closed her ears to the racket.

Violet held up one of the kits as Millie approached. 'Have I done this one, Mrs Hope?'

'If it's the one with the boy, the dog, and the red postbox, then yes, you have.'

Violet sighed and replaced the kit in the rack. 'Never mind, I'll just take a few silks. I'm a bit short on the blue ones. Or was it the browns? I'd better take both, just to be on the safe side.'

Millie had already eased out the shallow wooden tray containing the blue embroidery silks, satisfyingly arranged from milky dawn to deepest midnight, each skein encased in its own little paper tube. She slid out the tray next to it, the browns and creams. Violet's long, pale fingers hovered and pecked until, eventually, three skeins from each section were delivered to the counter and the transaction completed.

The shop door closed with an indecisive click.

The rest of the morning brought a steady flow of customers. Three teenage girls from the sixth form college came in with vintage-style cloth bags which they filled with giant balls of brightly-coloured wool from the odds and ends basket, chunky knitting needles and a book of easy makes. The 'new knitters', Millie called them; those who had been inspired by stories in trendy magazines about celebrities who knitted between photo shoots. A young woman who wanted to make her own wedding invitations pored over the cards and embellishments and eventually called upon Millie to help her choose between the heart motif and the crystal-eyed daisies. Mr Tozer came for fresh supplies of canvas and tapestry wool for his invalid wife, and a couple of other regulars dropped in for buttons, reels of thread and a chat.

It wasn't until one o'clock when Millie closed the shop for lunch that she went through to the back and discovered two missed calls on her mobile. It was probably Charmaine… no, they both came from the same unfamiliar number, she discovered as she paged through the screens. A bolt of adrenalin sent her stomach into flight. She moved a couple of boxes and sat down, scrutinising the number again, then writing it down at the top of the puzzle page in the daily paper in case, by some act of ineptitude on her part, she managed to delete it. That would be disastrous if, by some remote God-given chance, it was Karen who had called.

Twenty minutes later, Millie clicked off the phone, retrieved a cigarette from the emergency packet she kept on the top shelf and lit it unsteadily. She had just had the most unreal conversation. Mark was dead. Her Mark, well, not technically *her* Mark – he hadn't been that for the last eight years – had passed away at three o'clock this morning following a massive heart attack.

Mark. Dead. She repeated the words in her head, waiting for them to make an impact, but nothing happened. Drawing deeply on the cigarette, she tried to examine this bizarre lack of emotion, realising that if she felt anything at all, it was gratitude, albeit on a small scale. She felt grateful to Irene for letting her know so soon after the event, while at the same time wondering why she had felt the need to do so. Millie hadn't known what to say except to offer clichéd words of sympathy which Irene had received with overt thanks and, Millie detected, some relief.

The conversation she'd just had with Irene was only the second time she had ever spoken to the woman, apart from the odd occasion when reluctantly Millie had sought to consult Mark over Karen or some domestic matter and Irene happened to answer the phone. The only other time she'd spoken to her directly was the day after Mark left when, armed with his new number, she had wasted no time in ringing to give Irene the full benefit of her opinion. The high point of the conversation, if you could call it that since Millie had not let Irene get a word in edgeways, had been when she'd accused the woman of being a tart. Even then, in full spleen-venting flood, she had not been able to think of a better, or worse, word than 'tart'. All things considered, this morning's exchange had been remarkably civil.

Millie stood up and quickly sat down again. The room seemed to have revolved around her; the walls had exchanged positions. Grinding her cigarette into a saucer, she opened the foil package of sandwiches but hunger had deserted her. She wrapped them up again and dropped the package in the bin.

Irene would write to her about the funeral arrangements, she'd told Millie in her gravelly East End voice. Millie had wondered why she couldn't just phone again but hadn't felt able to suggest it. Should she go to the funeral? Did she want to go? Irene had said she would be welcome and Millie grudgingly conceded that Irene's prior claim on Mark gave her leave to grant such permission, but it was too soon to know how she felt about it, except that Mark's funeral didn't seem to be anything to do with her.

That was another thing. What was her status now? Who

was she? She wasn't a widow, but then neither was Irene since Mark had not had the decency to marry the woman after Millie had gone to all the trouble of divorcing him. Before this morning she'd known precisely who she was; she was Mark's ex-wife. But how could she be an ex-wife if there wasn't an ex-husband? No, she wasn't an ex-anything now, or a current anything. There was no longer a term to describe her, unless she was an ex-ex-wife.

She knew full well what Charmaine's take on this would be: 'You are *yourself*, Millie.' And she'd be right, except there was no escaping the way society raised its eyebrows and expected some kind of added qualification from those above a certain age, women in particular, who announced themselves as merely 'single' – as if it was anyone else's business.

A train rolled past, coming into Brighton. Millie's thoughts automatically switched to her Thursday man. Perhaps he didn't have an illicit assignation at all. Perhaps he was caught in the clutches of unrequited passion and while, deep down, he knew that all that lay at the other end of the line was more rejection, it would never be enough to stop him from trying again next week. Whatever it was, a happy ending didn't seem to be an option, at least not today.

Millie sighed. Where was all this coming from? Sometimes she wondered if she was going quietly round the bend.

It was only as, ten minutes later, she leaned across the sink to dribble water into the polyanthus on the windowsill that the welter of feeling she had lacked earlier suddenly swamped her, feeling, she understood now, that had been deliberately held back. She sank into the chair, still clutching the little metal watering can, as the surge of emotion knocked the breath out of her. This wasn't just about Mark. She was sorry he had died – how could she not be? – and sad for him that his life had been cruelly severed before he'd even reached fifty. She felt sad for Irene, too, despite the past, but this wasn't about either of them. This overwhelming sense of helplessness and bone-aching loss was about her daughter. Karen would have to be told that her father had died. There was only one thing standing in the way of that: Millie had no idea where she was.

On Saturday evening Charmaine came to Millie's house in Star Street, bringing with her a bottle of Shiraz, a family-sized bag of popcorn, and a promise that between them they would 'sort this out once and for all'. Grateful though Millie was, she couldn't help feeling that her friend's optimism was a tad misplaced.

'Google,' Charmaine said, looking over Millie's shoulder at the notebook with the red spotted cover that she kept for the purpose.

'Tried it.' Millie pointed at the ticked-off item on the list.

'Try it again.'

'I did, last night. It gets thousands of results, literally. They should write that in the books on parenting. Give your children the most unusual names you can think of in case you ever have to track them down.'

'Okay, it might be a challenge but between us perhaps we could…'

'No, I've been through as many as I can but it's hopeless. She won't be on there unless she's done something particular, will she? And before you say Facebook, I've joined and looked up everyone with the same name. None of them are her, as far as I can tell.' Millie gave a little humourless laugh. 'Now that does feel like voyeurism, of the first degree.'

'Needs must, though,' Charmaine said. 'I know! What about the electoral register? That's on line now, isn't it?'

'It is but she's not listed. That's typical of Karen.'

Millie sighed. She reached out and switched on the lamp, pooling the room with soft light and casting the street outside into further darkness.

'I know you want to help, Char, and you do, just by being here, but I have to face the fact that Karen doesn't want me to find her. She could have changed her name or be using *his* surname. She might…' – Millie shuddered – '…she might even have married him by now, for all I know.'

Charmaine looked appalled. 'You don't really think she'd marry him, do you?'

'At one time I'd have said not a cat in hell's chance, even if he did manage to do something as normal as proposing. Still, after two years, who knows?'

'Is it really that long?'

Millie nodded, biting her lower lip. It would be two years ago next month since she'd stood in this room and listened to her daughter yell down the phone that she, Millie, was a 'lying, jealous old woman', she wanted nothing more to do with her, she wasn't coming home, not ever, nor would she be phoning again and if Millie didn't like it she had only herself to blame.

Then he'd joined in, Jack-the-lad, as Millie had grown used to thinking of him, except he had turned out to be not so much a lad as a hard-headed, criminally-minded lout. The words he had spat out at Millie had been bad enough but she'd been doubly mortified at the way Karen had stood by and let her so-called boyfriend fling insults at her mother.

But worse was to come because the following day, Jack phoned again, presumably when Karen wasn't there. He had all but threatened Millie that if she ever came near them again he would... Millie cut dead her train of thought. She'd re-lived that metaphorical earth-tremor too many times already. Even so, she had not for one moment regretted what she'd done. How could she? If she had any regrets at all it was that she hadn't made a better job of it.

'I assume you've tried all Karen's numbers again so we can discount those.' Charmaine drained the last of the wine into Millie's glass.

'Her mobile and so on, yes, and no joy. As for the rest on this list,' she said, flicking over the page, 'I went through those a couple of months ago. No-one's got any news and I can't keep making a nuisance of myself. I'll leave it a while longer before I try again. The house in Croydon's a dead loss. The phone just rings and rings and no-one answers. The last time I tried it wasn't even working. Anyway, whoever lived there when Karen did would have moved on by now. It was that kind of place.'

Run-down and full of strange smells. Millie had wanted to scoop up her daughter and move her out of there right away but at the ripe old age of eighteen, Karen was having none of it.

Millie had blamed herself, and still did to some extent. Guilt was an inescapable feature of parental territory, though perhaps not in Mark's case. She had written him a letter after it became clear that Karen had meant what she'd said, asking that if Karen got in touch would he please let Millie know. He had scribbled a note back to say that, yes, he'd do that, but Millie should remember that Karen was an adult now and could do as she pleased.

The throwaway line held a jellyfish sting. Millie had blamed Irene's influence at the time, not wishing to believe that Mark would ever stop caring about his daughter's welfare of his own volition. Eventually, though, she had to accept that she no longer knew the man she'd been married to. Perhaps she never had.

'I'd better go,' Charmaine said just after ten. 'John was up all last night with a dying patient. He'll want an early one tonight.'

As Millie stood on the doorstep, arms folded against the chill of the night air, Charmaine turned to her.

'Millie,' she said, carefully. 'You know how much I want you to find Karen, almost as much as you do, but supposing you don't find her yet and she doesn't come back for a long time, then–?'

'Then Karen won't know how much I love her.'

'And what about you? How will you feel?'

'I won't feel like me again, not until I find her and know she's safe.'

Millie waited all the following week for Irene's letter to arrive, then when it didn't she began to wonder whether this was a deliberate omission on Irene's part and she had no intention of letting Millie know when the funeral was. On Friday she nipped home at lunchtime and found the letter on the mat.

She stood in the hall, examining the Chelmsford postmark, the unfamiliar writing on the envelope, before taking it through to the kitchen and slitting it open with the cheese knife. A thick white card fell out. It had deckle edging, a black scroll in each corner and the funeral arrangements in black italics in the centre. The undertaker's details were on the back. How very Victorian, Millie thought.

Dear Mrs Hope, please find enclosed time and place of funeral which is later than expected as there had to be a postmortem and of course everything shuts down over Easter, the accompanying letter, on blue lined Basildon Bond, began. Millie read on. *I know it is not the proper way to be talking about money at this junction, but I am sure Mark would have wanted you to know as soon as possible. I think you knew we had sold the tea-shops. We sold out to a chain and they made us a very good offer. As you know, Mark and I were never married but I am left very well set up myself because of our successful business partnership and I have the house. Mark always intended you to have a share in his success and with my knowledge and blessing he made you a beneficiary in his will. It will take some time for probate to go through and you will be informed through the proper channels. In the meantime I am letting you know that you will receive the sum of £150,000. Sincerely yours, Irene Trevellyn. P.S. Karen not mentioned in will but I know Mark would want her to benefit too.*

'…with my knowledge and blessing'? Millie fought to control the sense of injustice that had risen to do battle with the overwhelming shock, reminding herself once again that Mark's affairs were Irene's province, not hers. Guilt money, that's what it was, and yet… one hundred and fifty thousand pounds! Did it matter why?

She read the letter again, allowing herself a little smile at Irene's use of the word 'junction'. And then she looked again at the amount in case she'd misread the number of noughts – she hadn't.

She had to find Karen now. She needed to let her know what Mark had done for them. Whatever his motives, clearly he had envisaged the way their lives would be enhanced by such a sum. She would be perfectly happy, should Karen agree, to spend it all on setting up a future for her, pay for her to take a childcare course, perhaps.

Millie folded the letter, put it back in the envelope with the card and tucked it inside her bag.

'I love you, Karen,' she said silently to the sky as she walked back down the hill to the shop. 'Please come home, baby.'

Chapter Five

Gus moved into his inherited property on the twentieth of April. It happened to be his fiftieth birthday, which might have been auspicious or not, depending on how he looked at it. In truth, he preferred not to look at all.

Augusta had not stipulated that he should make it his home but he felt it was what she would have wished, and the more he thought about it the more attractive a taste of rural life became. Besides, it made sound financial sense. For once in his life, heart and head were in perfect alignment. It made a welcome change.

The house stood in the middle of a row of red-brick cottages built in 1888 and optimistically named Prosperity Terrace. It had fared well over the years; Gus had carried out his own thorough survey and found nothing major amiss, then through his estate agency connections he obtained further advice from a structural engineer and a woodworm expert for no more than the price of a couple of dinners and several liquid lunches. Once the few essential structural repairs had been carried out and a new shower installed in the bathroom, he set to with the wallpaper stripper until the only evidence of chintz that remained was in his aunt's bedroom, the door to which he kept firmly shut.

The sitting room and hall floors were professionally sanded and varnished and he waxed the downstairs doors himself, having sent them away to be stripped of their sticky build-up of gloss paint. This gradual paring down was more satisfying that he could have imagined. It brought out the house's character, let in air and allowed it to breathe again. But even as he applied the final coat of off-white paint to the walls and buffed up the pretty Victorian fireplaces, the feeling remained that the house was not his for keeps, and he set out for Elspeth's one afternoon with an armful of presents for Jenny's twenty-ninth birthday and a selection of opening gambits to try out on his sister-in-law.

From the moment he arrived, however, it was obvious that it was pointless trying again to persuade Elspeth to accept a share of his inheritance. While she answered the door to him with her usual warmth, the look in her eye and the slight lifting of her chin issued a warning that he had better behave himself, as if he were a schoolboy with a tendency to lapse into naughtiness. Much as he respected Elspeth's wishes, or tried to, he wasn't about to let her get away scot-free, though; she could hardly object to a little questioning in another direction.

His opportunity came after tea, when Jenny and her friends had gone upstairs to play CDs, and he and Elspeth were left alone in the kitchen. He picked up a tea towel and began, slowly, to dry a plate.

'Elspeth, why do you think Henry and Liesel adopted me when they already had Robert?'

Elspeth's hands stilled momentarily in the frothy water.

'Now there's a question and a half.'

She flashed him a smile before moving away from the sink to dry her hands and wrap the remains of Jenny's cake with foil.

'There,' she said, keeping her back to Gus as she turned the cake round until she was satisfied there were no gaps. 'That'll keep it moist. I've left a piece out for you to take home.'

Gus waited. Eventually Elspeth turned to him. She was holding a pink candle in a rose-shaped holder, twisting the soft wax in her fingers.

'Did they never tell you?'

'No. I'm sure they would have done if I'd asked, but I didn't. It never came up.'

'And it's come up now?'

'Yes, in a way. Because of... you know.'

Elspeth nodded, letting a plum of silence fall. When she spoke again, it was in a considered kind of way.

'It's not that unusual, adopting as well as having your own

31

children. It's just another way of making a family. Perhaps Liesel couldn't have any more babies after Robert. I don't know if that's true, of course. Robert never said, but then it isn't something he'd be likely to know.'

'But there is something, isn't there? Something my brother knew…'

'Not really,' Elspeth said, dropping the candle onto the cake plate and turning to face Gus. 'All I remember him saying is that they found out there was a little boy wanting a home through someone they knew, presumably someone who was connected to the church or the mother-and-baby home – the home was run by the church, as they often were – and that was it, they took you. I think it was quite a shock to Rob at the time. Look, Gus,' – Elspeth reached out and closed her damp hand over his – 'you know you were as much loved and wanted as your brother… as Robert, don't you?'

And there, Gus thought, was the crux of the thing; the natural and adopted sons were equal in the eyes of their parents – he, Gus, had lived with the happy evidence of that all his life – so what gave their aunt the right to favour one above the other? Even if Robert did 'hate' her, as Elspeth would have it, he only did so out of loyalty to his mother and Augusta should have risen above it rather than punishing him for it, which was what it amounted to.

'Oh yes, I know I was. It's just…'

'Gus, it doesn't always do to go looking for reasons, try to put things into neat little packages. Not everything has a reason. Some things just *are* and that's that.' Elspeth released his hand and smiled. The smile held a note of finality.

Gus drove back to Hangburton in an even more distracted state than before. Despite what Elspeth had told him, he couldn't help feeling that Robert must have had some idea as to why his mother felt the way she did about Augusta. Perhaps his aunt had intended this to happen, that by giving him the house she was also giving him a reason to question his background, to search for truths he might never discover.

But why would she do that? Why complicate his life? A gift with conditions was no gift at all.

It seemed to Gus that the more information he gleaned, however insubstantial, the more the questions grew wings and beat themselves to the surface. He had no reason to dispute Elspeth's, and therefore Robert's, view of things, but why did the Albournes suddenly decide they wanted another baby just because someone had mentioned him to them? He couldn't have been the only one on the market; there wasn't exactly a shortage at the time, and if they'd wanted a second child all along, why wait until Robert was eleven before they acquired one, even if nature had let them down? His mother, he remembered, had a particular fondness for the little girls who lived next door – she used to make clothes for their dolls and let down her thick, pale hair and allow them plait it and tie it with ribbons – so why not a girl rather than another boy?

He should do as Elspeth suggested, accept the past as it was and not look for reasons, a concept that not so long ago he would have echoed with careless ease. But that was before a tragic unmarried mother – his mother – had innocently inveigled her way into his consciousness, and before he'd been ambushed by this sense of outrageous injustice. Now, he couldn't seem to settle at anything. Annoying lapses of concentration had him wasting time tracking down his own mislaid possessions, and at work he kept clients waiting while he searched for keys he had failed to return to their proper place.

At night he had only to close his eyes and he'd be back in the claustrophobic black heat of the sandy cave, his hands grazed and bleeding as he scrabbled at the rocky debris blocking the entrance, while Arthur, the friend he'd made on holiday, stayed quiet and stoical by his side. The recurrence of the cave dream disturbed him. It hadn't happened for a while and he had hoped it had gone for good. The lack of proper sleep wasn't helping.

Running helped to allay some of his anxiety, although it wasn't so easy in an unfamiliar place and he hadn't yet worked out a regular route. Even so, he set off each evening, afraid that if he stopped, the motivation would drain away. He'd noticed more than one twitching curtain as he jogged along. Not that he minded, but the pavements in Hangburton were narrow and tended to stop dead when you least expected or peter out into flinty tracks, and he wasn't ready to risk spraining an ankle and looking a fool in front of his new neighbours. It would make sense, he decided, to explore his new territory at a slower pace; he took some time off from work to do so.

One afternoon, after a muddy walk around the outskirts of the common, he emerged from the public footpath that ran alongside Saint Saviour's and found himself outside the village hall. Beneath the notice-board was a bench with *Harry loves Imogen* carefully carved along the arm. He smiled as he remembered the graffiti in the park opposite his old flat, where *Donna's got massif tits* was slashed into most of the available woodwork.

One of the notices on the board caught his eye. It was about a new project, an embroidered wall hanging depicting the history of the village. The first meeting, he read, was this afternoon – in fact, it was already in progress. It was the word 'history' that drew his attention. He had read a great deal about Hangburton's past; perhaps he would be able to offer some useful information.

The foolishness of this idea became apparent soon after he had ventured inside and slipped into the circle of chairs set out in the middle of the hall which smelt of sour milk and feet. From the talk that was going on around him, he deduced that such knowledge was already well-charted, not only in books but in the fabric of the village and the minds of its inhabitants, including this diverse bunch. When an eventual lull came in the discussion, Gus took the opportunity to introduce himself. The women – they were all women – regarded him with ill-disguised but not unfriendly curiosity.

'I don't suppose you can sew,' one of them said in a throwaway manner, as if she already knew the answer.

Yes, as it happened, he could, he said. He would even go so far as to say he was quite accomplished with a needle. An astonished silence followed this admission, during which the women glanced from one to the other as if some secret code passed between them while Gus wished he could re-call his words like an email he hadn't meant to send.

Another of them spoke, the pretty, dark-haired one with a jolly-hockeysticks ponytail. Early forties, he thought; he couldn't pin it down any closer than that.

'How did you learn?'

Her tone and its accompanying enquiring smile seemed to imply genuine interest without any sexist implication.

His father had been a tailor, Gus replied, and had taught him the rudiments. This was the truth, but only part of it. He had spent his twentieth year in a turbulent live-in relationship with a girl called Poppy, during which he had tried to balance out her complete disinterest in all things domestic, not only by doing all the cooking but by sewing curtains and cushion covers to brighten up the dingy bedsit. He even made Poppy a ra-ra skirt that she'd worn with Lycra leggings, then had to make three more after she'd told her friends.

The eldest of the women now leaned forward in her chair, introduced herself as Sidonie Rayment and, addressing Gus as if he was a child, or simple, or both, explained that each person invited to take part in the project would complete a panel on a given theme. The panels would then be sewn together and finished off with a border and the village coat of arms.

'I thought we hadn't decided about the border.'

The woman who had asked Gus if he could sew looked around the circle for assent.

'No, we hadn't,' asserted another, 'and I don't remember anyone mentioning a coat of arms either.'

'Nobody ever *listens*. I distinctly said the coat of arms should go at the top.' Sidonie drew herself up and thrust her bolster-like chest forward. Gus immediately thought of pigeons. 'And of *course* there has to be a border. How else will the thing hang together?'

The discussion continued along these lines for a further five minutes to no obvious conclusion until Gus, struck by a sudden boredom, stood up and said he may as well leave them to it. They looked up at him as if they'd forgotten he was there, then Sidonie thanked him for coming and said would he mind very much if they didn't decide there and then.

'This is Jessica, my daughter,' she said, indicating the pony-tailed one with a nod of her head. 'She'll be in touch.'

Jessica ripped the corner off a sheet of paper, blushing slightly as she passed it to him with a pen. Gus scribbled down his phone number and escaped.

Two days passed with no phone call and he was beginning to think he'd been let off the hook when he came home from work to find a note from Jessica on his doormat. He shouldn't be surprised – of course they would know where he lived; they probably knew the colour of his underpants by now. They would be delighted to have him join their group, the note said, and gave the details of the next meeting.

Resigned to his fate while at the same time feeling quietly pleased at this small breach of his outsider status, Gus duly turned up as requested, sat down, and awaited instructions. An hour or so later, he had acquired responsibility for not one but two of the panels and he walked home wondering, not for the first time, what on earth had possessed him to get involved in the first place.

He had taken to calling in at the Dog and Trumpet on a couple of evenings a week and on his next visit he noticed a fair amount of eyebrow-raising accompanying the bonhomie among the men he now numbered among his new acquaintances, although nothing was actually said, at least not in his hearing. There was no malice in it, of course, just a mild, unobjectionable curiosity. Some of them, noting he lived alone, probably thought he was gay. Not that he cared what they thought.

Being the only man among a bevy of women didn't bother him in the slightest. He liked women in general. He liked the way they moved, the way they laughed, the way they used paints and powders and brushes to effect their sly transformations. He liked sewing, too, the peace of it and the sense of creating something worthwhile. It reminded him of his father, Henry, glasses half-mast, bent over a suit jacket as he hand-stitched the lapels while Gus sat on the stool beside him and attempted to create an even seam along a left-over piece of serge. The shop was still there, the one Henry had bought when

36

he'd moved the family from Newcastle to Brighton just after they'd taken Gus, but now it was owned by a Chinese family who took in alterations.

He hadn't done any actual embroidery before but sewing was sewing, wasn't it? Not so, apparently; you couldn't just stitch away and hope for the best. Although he had been given the freedom to create whatever pictures he liked within his allotted themes – Hangburton Manor and a minor medieval battle that had been fought, allegedly, on the common – the stitches had to be identifiable. He had admitted his ignorance, in private, to Jessica and she had given him a book on basic embroidery stitches, a spare piece of material and a wooden hoop to stretch it over, but his first efforts looked distinctly amateurish. Clearly, he had quite a journey ahead.

On Sunday afternoon, thinking he could do no worse than he had already, he sat down at the table with the intention of starting work on Hangburton Manor. Feeling fairly satisfied with the design he had come up with, he picked up a pencil and began to draw the outline onto the fabric, just as the phone rang. Tutting, he took off his glasses and went to answer it, the pencil still in his hand. It was Jessica, wanting to know how he was getting on and reminding him that if he was stuck at any time he had only to ask and she would come straight over. He barely had time to answer when her china-teacup voice instructed him to 'hang on a sec' and while he waited he heard muffled whispering, quite urgent in tone, presumably between Jessica and Sidonie, her mother, although he couldn't make out the actual words.

Jessica came back on the line. 'That was just Mum saying why don't I invite you round for supper some time but I told her you'd be far too busy.' She gave a shrill little laugh.

Oh God. 'Well, yes, I am quite busy at the moment but please thank your mother for me,' he said, and clicked off the phone.

Back at the table, Gus wondered if, in his haste to end the conversation, he'd been unnecessarily sharp. He hoped he hadn't offended Jessica. She had, after all, gone out of her way to help him but the idea of spending an evening with mother and daughter in their house just didn't appeal, not at this stage. Stage? Was he at a 'stage' with Jessica? There was a definite attraction there – on his part, certainly, and, if he was not mistaken, on hers, too. He acknowledged this with a mixture of delight and alarm; the whole thing had a ring of gloomy inevitability about it. But still... Perhaps he'd ask her out for a drink one evening, just as a thank-you. Somewhere away from the village, though.

Returning to the task in hand, he finished drawing the outline of his design then sat back, pencil between his teeth, to consider his options. The parterre in front of the Manor with its little squares seemed relatively straightforward; he would have a go at that before tackling the house. He snipped off a length of forest green silk, divided it into three strands as the book said, and moistened one strand with his tongue before threading the needle. He would use cross-stitch, which was easy enough provided you didn't miscount the threads, but he was short of green silks and it wouldn't do to use the same shade throughout.

The haberdashers in the village would be closed today but he could pick some up tomorrow. There was that little craft shop in Brighton, near Park Station; he'd noticed it the other day when he went to value a nearby property. He would be anonymous there, a stranger passing through. The idea appealed immensely.

Chapter Six

Millie had a date. Not a *date* date, at least she would not describe it as such, although Jet, with his irritating tendency to live in a dream-world, probably would. They had replayed the charade many times, Jet asking Millie out as if it was the first time he'd asked her, Millie refusing on principle, Jet giving her his puppy-eyed 'Ah, go on' plea and Millie saying yes, all right, anything to shut him up.

This time, though, she'd tempered the play-acting a bit. Jet had been so sweet over Mark, encouraging her to talk when she needed to or simply letting her sit in silence for ages, her hands round a mug of tea. Jet owned the skateboard shop next door to Millie's and was constantly on hand – a mixed blessing, but one Millie had lately come to appreciate.

Sometimes Millie felt guilty at the ambiguity of the relationship because of the dissatisfaction she knew Jet felt, but she didn't see what else she could do, other than avoid giving him false hope that there could ever be more than friendship and affection. Besides, it wasn't just about Jet, it was about herself. She wasn't looking for a serious romantic liaison with anyone. Time did not heal; it simply cast a blanket over everything, a blanket soft enough for the spikes to poke through when you were least expecting them.

Jet's playful advances at the end of the night were also part of the ritual but he knew better than to expect more than a goodnight kiss. Millie had nearly slept with him once, last year, after a particularly good night out at a mightily expensive restaurant where they'd enjoyed excellent food and unprecedented quantities of wine, thanks to a large order for in-line skates Jet had received from a street sports initiative and a one-main-course-free voucher cut out of the local paper.

Pressed into the squeaking depths of Jet's leather-look sofa in his flat above the shop, she had felt the after-haze of the wine begin to lift just as Jet hooked surprisingly expert thumbs beneath her bra straps. He had taken the rejection remarkably well, all things considered. The incident had never been referred to since, except obliquely, by way of a knowing twinkle in Jet's eye every time Millie placed a firm hand over her wine glass. She'd behaved shamefully that night; she flinched every time she remembered it.

Jet was not his real name; she suspected that forty-nine was not his real age, either. She had never found out what his proper name was but Brian or Colin would deserve an each-way bet. She could see 'Jet' now, in emerald green letters adorning the pallid no man's land between the end of his hair and the beginning of his shirt as he orbited the salad cart, bending intently over the contents as if what he chose was a matter of supreme national importance.

Charmaine had turned up her nose at the Harvester as a venue for a hot date, however tongue-in-cheek, but Millie didn't mind where they went as long as it was neither too far afield nor too often. Actually she quite liked it here. It demanded minimum debate over what to wear, you got more or less what you saw, and the food was cheap and cheerful. Not that Jet didn't always offer to pay; he was most chivalrous about that. He was equally chivalrous about caving in when Millie insisted on paying half.

Tightly settled now in their allotted booth, they talked of the forthcoming release of the 1911 census records. Jet was researching his family history and awaited this momentous occasion with gleeful anticipation. Millie, too, had followed the family tree on her mother's side and could appreciate Jet's enthusiasm, although her own searches had not extended as far as second cousins thrice removed.

If only it was as easy to find the living people as it was the dead ones, Millie thought, watching butter from Jet's corn-on-the-cob drip onto the snake's head emerging from his shirt-sleeve while he related with relish the tale of a great-great-uncle who'd been a gravedigger at Highgate cemetery.

Sipping her last glass of wine, Millie felt her mind begin to drift. She recalled, as clear as day, Karen sitting on the kitchen worktop, the heels of her red Converse high-tops drumming against the cupboard door, declaring that she didn't believe in inheritance and neither did Jack. What had brought this on Millie couldn't remember now. Nothing probably, knowing Karen; she was given to throwing out random statements purely to provoke a reaction.

'Well then,' Millie had answered coolly, not pausing in her vegetable chopping. 'I shall have to give some serious thought as to which charity gets the house and the business.'

Karen's feet stopped drumming. 'Oh, I didn't mean...'

No, I bet you didn't, Millie had thought, hiding a smile.

What would Karen make of her father's legacy? Would she refuse to have anything to do with it or had her high principles dulled down with the weight of a few more years of experience? Panic suddenly engulfed Millie, heating her face, taking her breath away. How could this be, this totally impossible situation in which she had no idea as to how her own daughter was living her life, what she thought, what she cared about, who she was with, what she saw, every day? Did she walk in the sunshine, happy and unafraid, or did she creep along in the half-dark, seeing and knowing all kinds of horrors, drawn there by Jack and his kind? She couldn't bear it, couldn't live with the fear any longer...

'Millie?' Jet's voice came, a distant hum like a plane passing overhead.

'I'm all right.' Millie reached for her glass of water, took it to her lips with a shaky hand.

'No, no, you're not. Let me take you home.' Jet was half out of his seat.

'No, really.' Millie smiled. The panicky sensation was passing. She drank some more water then set the glass down steadily. 'It's just... Karen, you know? It hits me like this sometimes. I'm fine now, really.'

'As long as you're sure.'

'I just want to look after her, Jet. That's not too much to

ask, is it?'

'Course it isn't. And you will do, sooner than you know it. I can feel it in me water.' Jet waggled his eyebrows.

Millie laughed out loud – his intention of course. She felt better now, she really did, except that she wished the other feeling would go away, the feeling that she lacked identity and definition. Instead it dragged along behind her like a sticky trail of something nasty she had trodden in. It was not only because of Mark dying; she knew well enough she should have stopped thinking of herself as his ex-wife long ago but it had simply never occurred to her to stop. No, it was also about being a mother. Millie had always believed that having a child made you a mother for life, but if that child deliberately severed the ties, what then? How could she be a mother if Karen wouldn't let her be one? It had come as something of a shock to discover that parental status was, to some extent, a matter of permission.

Later, in the taxi home, her head resting companionably against Jet's shoulder, Millie allowed her thoughts to wander again, settling first on Mark then, inevitably, on Karen, and then, suddenly and inexplicably, the man on the train. Who was he, and what was he doing now?

The following morning, Millie was in the back room of the shop unpacking a box containing a brand new line – kits to make patchwork bags with printed cotton squares in red, white and blue and pale wood handles. Very New England, very trendy. She was so engrossed in examining her new stock that it was a minute or two before her brain registered the tinkle of the shop doorbell.

'Sorry to keep you… oh!'

The exclamation escaped unchecked as she stopped halfway between the stock room door and the counter. Her customer was standing in the middle of the shop, hands linked loosely behind his back, gazing up at the shelves of knitting wool.

'Mm?' He turned towards her, his smile polite but distant, as if his mind was elsewhere.

Millie recovered herself, swallowed the knot in her throat

and stepped out from behind the counter. 'Is there something particular you're looking for?'

'What? Oh, yes.' Again the smile, this time not at all distant but very much in the moment.

Millie felt the heat travelling up her back, reaching her neck. It couldn't be him, her Thursday man, could it? No, of course it couldn't. And yet, seeing him standing there, sideways on, as she had come through to the shop, the straight, largish nose, firm chin, distinctive widow's peak... she could take up a pencil right now and draw that profile from memory.

'Embroidery thread. Silks. Where do you keep them?'

Grateful to have something to do, Millie tugged out a couple of trays from the cabinet. 'There you go. They're in colour order.'

'So they are.' He cast her an amused look, ducking his head as if he was peering over the top of invisible spectacles.

Blushing slightly, Millie pressed her lips firmly shut in case she was tempted to make any more inane comments, and went behind the counter. The substantial slab of mahogany that now divided them was reassuringly protective, although what she needed protection from she hadn't a clue. She just knew that since she'd clapped eyes on this man, she'd been all at sixes and sevens. It *had* to be him. If it wasn't, the likeness was uncanny. She watched as he stooped over the trays and made his selection, carefully sliding each tray back into place as he went. Finally he brought a handful of skeins over and dropped them on the counter.

'I don't suppose you've got any more of the green ones? I could do with some different shades, if you have them.'

Millie wondered who the silks were for. His mother? His wife? The hand that was now holding a wallet was ringless but that that didn't mean anything. Not that there had to be a woman involved. Plenty of men made use of a needle. Several came into the shop, in fact, but they tended to be all of a kind and certainly not of this kind; none of them had an unassuming assuredness, a ready smile that laughter lines only enhanced and a directness of gaze that made Millie feel he could see right through her.

Rapidly she regrouped, aware that she'd been staring. 'I should have. You're right, there isn't a full range in the tray. I meant to do that this morning. Wait there, I'll go and see.'

'It doesn't matter. I can always come back another time.'

'No, no, it won't take a sec.'

Well and truly flustered now, Millie dived through the door to the stock room, dragged out the step-stool and launched herself onto the top of it, striking her elbow on the corner of a box that was sticking out and sending the whole thing crashing to the floor.

'Are you all right in there?' she heard him say. Then, before she could reply, he was there, beside the step-stool, bending to right the box.

'I'm fine, just being clumsy. Leave that, I'll do it later.'

He carried on stuffing the spilled contents back into the box. Oh well, if he really wanted to help…

'Here, take this, would you?'

She handed down the box of embroidery silks. She didn't have far to reach; he must be all of six feet tall. He took it from her, deep-set brown eyes showing amusement as he smiled up at her, but not, she understood, at her expense.

'Gus Albourne,' he said, dropping the box on the floor and extending a hand.

Both Millie's hands were already occupied, one pushing back another box into place, the other maintaining a grasp on the nearest shelf.

'Do come down from there. You look a bit unsteady.'

That was one word for it. Millie came down, wiped her perfectly clean hands on her jeans and held out her right hand, which Gus took in his. Enquiring eyebrows were raised.

'Oh… I'm Millie. Millie Hope.'

'Gus,' he said, still holding her hand in a light but firm grasp.

'Yes, so you said.'

'I'll take this through, shall I?' He relinquished her hand, took the box through and set it down on the counter. 'I expect you're wondering why I need these.'

'Not really,' Millie lied.

The eyebrows went up again.

'Well, all right, I am a bit. I like to take an interest.'

Millie was aware that she sounded defensive. She hadn't meant to.

It was close on one o'clock, time to turn the sign round. Another few minutes wouldn't hurt.

Millie went home for lunch the following Monday. Gus was waiting outside the shop when she came back. As soon as he saw her approach he abandoned his position by the shop window and stood in the middle of the pavement, smiling a welcome.

'I wasn't sure what time you re-opened. I forgot to look the other day.'

Millie returned the smile but said nothing. The certainty that Gus was the man on the train had crept up on her, working its way into her consciousness until it had become indisputable fact. It put a different complexion on things, added an edge to what should have been an ordinary return visit by an ordinary satisfied customer; she wasn't sure how she felt about it.

The keys already in her hand, she unlocked the door and switched the sign round. He followed her inside and stood gazing at the shelves, hands behind him, as he had the first time. She asked him if he wanted to buy anything today and he said no, but if he could perhaps take her up on her kind offer to show him a few stitches, if she had the time, that would be just the thing.

Had she said that? She supposed she must have done. Goodness knows why – she had enough problems of her own without taking on someone else's. Noticing her hesitation, Gus was already starting to apologise for having turned up unannounced.

'No, it's fine. Now's as good a time as any. Come on through.'

He followed her through to the back and, at her invitation, settled himself at the table while she fetched needles, silks, an off-cut of fabric and a hoop. He seemed to take up a disproportionate amount of space in the little room.

'I've already mastered cross-stitch,' he said, setting about a rapid demonstration.

He held up the row of red stitches for her approval. She hardly liked not to give it but he was here to learn.

'You've got the wrong thread on top in a couple of places.' She pointed with a needle. 'They all have to go the same way, the right-facing stitch first, then the left one over it.'

'Ah, I knew that was too good to be true. Here, let me have another go.'

The bell indicated the arrival of a customer and Millie went through. By the time she returned, Gus had achieved a perfect row of cross-stitch.

'Better?'

'Much.' Millie smiled. 'But those are the easy ones.'

Gus regarded her closely for a moment, as if he was searching for something. His glasses had slipped down a bit. He pushed them back into place. 'I think I'm ready to go up a class.'

'Have you ever heard the expression "Don't try to run before you can walk"?'

'Heck yes, my father used to say it all the time.'

'My mother did, too,' Millie said, 'but I never took any notice then so we won't do now. Let's crack on, shall we?'

It occurred to Millie later, as she left Gus to create a mini-sampler from the stitches she'd shown him while she attended to matters in the shop, that it might have been wiser to have kept him on the other side of the counter until she knew a little more about him. She wasn't normally this free and easy with the customers but this one seemed to have slipped through her invisible safety barrier almost without her noticing.

It wasn't that she felt threatened in any way – she liked Gus, the little she knew of him – it was more the sense of having lost something that could never be regained, something she had relied on. Her over-active imagination was to blame for that, of course. She had spent weeks spinning a mystery around this man and now he had partially solved it before she was ready. Stupid though it seemed, she felt almost resentful.

Thursday turned out to be one of those days when nothing seemed to go right. It didn't help that her bones ached with tiredness. Last night, as she was getting ready for bed, she noticed that her sapphire engagement ring that she sometimes wore on her right hand was missing from the glass dish. It was well past midnight by the time she found it wedged down the dusty back of the chest of drawers and restored it to its rightful place. Then, just as she'd settled down, she thought she could smell burning and had to go back downstairs to satisfy herself she'd left nothing on. Consequently, she had woken this morning half an hour after the alarm had gone off, feverish and fretful, with Karen's name on her lips.

Hurrying to make a cup of tea before she turned the shop door sign to 'Open', she crashed the mug clumsily against the tap as she rinsed it and the handle cracked in half. Later, she was serving one customer while another waited, and at the same time the postman brought a parcel requiring her signature. Consequently she missed the ten-nineteen going through and she had been particularly anxious to catch sight of Gus today. His unscheduled arrival in her shop – in her life – sent shockwaves of adrenalin pulsing through her every time she thought about it, and while they brought with them the welcome message that she was truly alive, seeing him returned to his default position on the train would, in a way she could not explain, have made her feel safe.

The parcel, once she had the chance to unpack it, turned out to contain embroidery fabric in more eleven and sixteen thread-count than you could shake a stick at but none in the fourteen she'd ordered weeks ago and for which she had several customers waiting. Before long they'd be off to the big haberdashery shop in Brighton or to one of those out-of-town discount places and she would have lost them for good. She called the suppliers, only to find the number permanently engaged, and the website was shut for maintenance.

The morning continued in the same frustrating vein and Millie hardly had the chance to sit down, let alone check the personal ads in the daily paper which waited virginally in the back room. At one o'clock, once she had managed to shoo out the remaining customer, she turned the sign round with a sigh of relief and went through to the back but scanning the paper over her coffee and sandwich only brought further disappointment. Her ad wasn't in, despite the dent in her credit card and the promise of the woman on the phone. No, hang on, here it was. Millie had turned the page to where the personals continued. *Would anyone knowing the whereabouts of Karen Harp (last known place of residence 16 Albany Road, Croydon, Surrey) please contact...* Millie's phone numbers followed.

Harp? Oh, for heaven's sake! Was it a requirement of these jobs to have nothing between the ears? She wouldn't mind but she'd spelled out the name more than once, and the voice on the other end had sounded English. Just as well she hadn't shelled out for a boxed job. As it was, this one was squeezed into a corner between ads for incontinence aids and a children's party entertainer, making it highly unlikely that anyone would spot it in any case.

Millie worded an alternative advert in her head, a full-page, budget-busting spread in all the dailies: *Would Karen Hope, aged twenty-one-and-a-quarter, please phone home as her father has popped his clogs and left her a fortune.* That would get her going. Come to think of it, it would get all the Karen Hopes in the country diving for their mobiles. Millie sighed. It wasn't a laughing matter, was it? Karen was about to miss her own father's funeral and Millie could do precious little about it. There was, of course, the remotest possibility that Karen was in the Chelmsford area and had seen the announcement in the deaths column of the local paper, but that was about as likely as Millie's car not needing a shove and a bump-start on a damp morning.

She made another coffee, more for the comfort of wrapping her hands around the mug than a need for the drink itself. She felt chilled to the bone, had done so all morning. Sun in April promised so much yet delivered so little. Sitting down with her coffee, she considered the wording of another kind of notice, the one to go on the shop door next Monday when she closed for the funeral. Ordinarily, Charmaine would have covered for her but she had insisted on driving her and Millie had accepted

48

her kindness with relief and only a token protest.

Peeling a square of paper from the block, she wrote: *Shop closed today due to family funeral. Apologies to all my customers.* No, that wouldn't do. All she'd get for the rest of the week would be solicitous enquiries, and she could hardly go to the lengths of explaining that the deceased wasn't family at all, just someone who used to be. *Sorry I am closed today due to bereavement.* Even worse. Her brain seemed to have frozen along with her fingers. Several attempts later, she settled on: *Shop closed today due to unforeseen circumstances. Open tomorrow as usual. Apologies, M. Hope.* She found a bigger piece of paper and wrote it out neatly in black felt tip before she changed her mind again.

Last night, the stack of photo albums had caught her eye as she'd gone to the wardrobe in the back bedroom, Karen's room, for her smart grey dress and fitted black jacket with the velvet collar; she didn't want Irene to think she had no sense of style or occasion. She had hung the dress and jacket on the wardrobe door, then, without thinking too much about it, dragged out the earliest album and sat on the bed with it on her lap, peeling apart the pages at random. The wedding photos, stagey and full of hats and fixed smiles, left her unmoved, as did the self-conscious pictures taken outside their honeymoon caravan in the Isle of Wight. A few pages on and there he was again, her Mark, young, tall and resplendent in his navy blue railway uniform, standing on the steps of the house where they'd had their first flat. On impulse, she had run downstairs in her dressing gown and snapped him as he left for work. He'd laughed and kissed her, told her she was silly, but he'd been so pleased at her pride in him. She would have been... four, perhaps five months pregnant at the time.

She had stared at the photo until the image of Mark began to blur and something inside gave way. Letting the album slide to the floor, she had drawn her body into a foetal curl and sobbed her heart out.

Chapter Seven

'Are you sure you want to do this, Mill?' Charmaine asked, as she steered the car between the tall iron gates.

'No, but I'm going to.' Millie snapped down the mirror and gave her face and hair a final check. Perhaps she should have worn a hat. People didn't so much now, though, and it wasn't as if she was one of the chief mourners.

The road wound on endlessly towards the crematorium chapel, row upon row of chalk-white headstones marching impersonally into the distance on either side. The building itself, when they finally approached it, was even less prepossessing, having been seemingly fashioned from a single enormous slab of grey concrete, relieved only by a row of arrow-slit windows and a tall, undisguisable chimney rising apologetically at the back. Still, Millie thought, she didn't suppose there was much choice in these matters.

Throughout the mercifully short service, Millie's eyes were fixed either on the service sheet or straight ahead, affording her a direct view of the back of Irene's gingery-brown head which had clearly been freshly coiffed for the occasion and sported a kind of Alice band with a bit of black net and a couple of feathers attached. A fascinator, Millie supposed; she had always associated those with weddings, not funerals. Of course, she didn't know for certain that it was Irene's head she was looking at. She only guessed it was because of the lack of other likely candidates in front pew position. There was no sign of Karen. Millie had known she wasn't here almost without looking as soon as she'd walked in.

It was not until the final music started up – a classical orchestral piece, not the sentimental crooning Millie would have put money on – that she made herself look properly at the oak coffin on the plinth. She thought hard about Mark for a few moments and sent up a little prayer, then, swallowing the lump in her throat, filed out of the back row into the glare of midday.

She hung back as the other mourners took a dutiful turn around the red-brick wall that held the flowers, slipping into the queue at the last moment to satisfy herself that her own tribute, a simple, raffia-tied spray of white narcissi and grape hyacinths, had arrived. Then she and Charmaine stood aside from the chattering groups and waited.

Irene glanced in Millie's direction several times before she approached, hand outstretched, neutral, enquiring smile in place as if she were greeting a lesser-known acquaintance of Mark's rather than the woman she had stolen him from.

'Millie.'

'Yes.'

Millie put forward her own hand, at the same time executing a swift appraisal of Irene who was, undoubtedly, doing the same to her. Faultlessly applied Boots No7 served well to disguise a modicum of puffiness around the eyes and faint lines of strain around the mouth, both of which were understandable, given the circumstances. Taller than Millie had imagined, and thinner, too – but round enough in the right places, she conceded – Irene exhibited a sartorial restraint only a little spoiled by a too-short skirt and one piece of jewellery too many. These failings struck a chord and Millie felt surprisingly disposed towards giving her a hug. She suppressed the feeling and launched instead into a repetition of what she had said on the phone, that she was sorry about Mark and what a shock it must have been. Irene agreed that, yes, it had been a terrible shock, but she was bearing up remarkably well, considering, and if it was one thing bereavement did it was keep you busy, and what a blessing that was.

Then she said, 'Your daughter couldn't make it, then.'

'No.' Millie straightened her shoulders and met Irene's gaze.

Irene gave a little knowing nod. 'Little minx.'

Millie's body tensed as the heat crept rapidly upwards and

set fire to her face.

'Oh, I'm sorry,' Irene said, looking anything but. She stretched out a gloved hand and patted Millie's arm. 'None of my business, I'm sure.'

Millie took a deep breath. She had set out this morning with one purpose in mind, to say goodbye to Mark, privately and with dignity, detaching herself from everything else. The last thing she'd intended was to allow Irene to rattle her but now that she'd shown her hand so easily, she might as well turn the situation to her advantage.

She forced a smile. 'It doesn't matter. Actually, Irene, I wanted to ask you, had Mark heard from Karen at all? Or have you?'

'No.' Irene shook her head. The fascinator bobbed like a pecking bird. 'Why, haven't you?'

Wasn't it obvious? 'Karen doesn't know about her father yet and I'd like to break the news myself if I possibly can. I'm sure you understand…'

'Oh, I do…'

'… so if she does happen to get in touch I'd be ever so grateful if you could try and get her number or her address, anything, and let me know straight away?'

Millie knew she sounded desperate but she didn't care. This woman didn't matter. Only Karen did.

'Of course.' Another pat on the arm. 'Have no worries on that score.'

Millie murmured her thanks as Irene was swallowed up by a group of besuited men. Mark's friends? Business associates? Members of the bowling club, perhaps? The revelation during the funeral address that Mark played bowls, apparently rather well, had caused Millie to wonder briefly whether she was at the right funeral; he had always said bowls was an old man's game. Whilst she didn't care who these people were, it was strangely disconcerting not to know. She felt suddenly, unaccountably, very alone.

Charmaine, who had melted away when Irene approached, was now back at Millie's side. Millie gave her a grateful smile and the two of them linked arms as they walked towards the car park. They were almost there when someone said Millie's name. Unhooking herself from Charmaine, she turned, and found herself facing a balding, bespectacled man with a mouthful of teeth reminiscent of the surrounding tombstones. She looked at him enquiringly.

'It is Millie, isn't it?' He brought his face quite close to hers; focussing seemed to be something of a problem for him. 'Ralph Hitchin. Cousin of Mark's, on his father's side. Saw you at the wedding. Well, I would have done, seeing as you were the bride.' He laughed, spluttering a bit. Millie took a step back.

'Ralph, yes, I remember.'

Only because he had told her, Millie thought, mentally comparing this man to the slimmer, wavy-haired version with the twinkling blue eyes who had danced with her at every opportunity at their reception in the Co-op Hall, leaving his own wife marooned on the hard chairs with the contingent of elderly relatives until Mark had, politely but firmly, reclaimed her.

'And Marion? Is she here?' Millie glanced about.

'No, no. Sadly not.'

Ralph bowed his head but offered no clarification. She'd had little news of any of Mark's family for years, not even when she was still married to him, and the Hopes had never been big on get-togethers. Weddings and funerals, that was about the sum total of it. She racked her brains as to when she had last seen Ralph. He answered the question for her.

'Auntie Joan's funeral, wasn't it, the last time?' Joan, Mark's mother. Yes, it would be. 'Not what you'd call a close family.' Ralph smiled ruefully, again echoing Millie's thoughts. 'Too many of us to fit in one front room, probably.'

'Is there anyone else here from the family? I didn't spot anyone. It's been a long time, of course...'

'No, no. A few of them wanted to come but it's the distance. Old ones too dodgy on the pins, or gone altogether. Kids not interested. You know how it is.' Ralph's eyes strayed away from Millie, one shiny-toed shoe scuffing the gravel.

The eyes returned, meeting Millie's head-on. 'This is a bit tricky and I'm not sure if I should be saying but, talking of kids…'

'What is it, Ralph?'

He was going to ask about Karen. He'd be wondering why she had missed her own father's funeral. You and me both, pal. Millie began to frame a reply in her head, something non-committal. It wasn't as if Ralph was likely to be that interested; probably just mildly curious, as she herself would be.

Ralph looked even more uncomfortable. 'I spoke to her, you see. Your Karen.'

'*What*? You spoke to Karen? When? Where? Ralph?'

Why would Karen be speaking to Ralph? She didn't even know him, not above the level of the obligatory exchange of Christmas cards. Millie glanced at Charmaine then looked back at Ralph.

'She asked me not to say anything,' Ralph said. 'Didn't see that as a problem. We were hardly likely to bump into one another, were we? Me in Maidstone, you in Brighton. The divorce and everything.' He gave a little embarrassed shrug. 'But now I see you here…'

Millie's head felt swimmy. She gave it a shake in an attempt to clear it. She mustn't let go of this, mustn't let Ralph get away before she'd squeezed every drop of information from him.

Charmaine cupped Millie's elbow, a supportive, guiding gesture. 'Look, there's a bench over there,' she said. 'Why don't the two of you have a sit down and a chat?'

Millie threw her a grateful look. Ralph gave a little nod, trotted resignedly over to the bench and sat down, revealing several inches of hairless white leg between his socks and his turn-ups. Millie sat in the middle, not too close to Ralph, with Charmaine on her other side.

She took a deep breath to relieve the tightness in her chest and turned to Ralph. 'You've got children, daughters, haven't you? Christine and… Heather, isn't it?'

Ralph smiled. 'Yes, yes, that's them. Both married now, Christine for the second time, but there it is. All worked out for the best.'

He seemed to relax slightly, hoping perhaps they were just

going to have a quick family catch-up before he was let off the hook. Millie felt almost sorry to disappoint him.

'And do you see much of them, your girls?'

'Oh yes. Phone calls. Visits. When they want something usually.' Ralph smiled, raising his eyes. 'Not so much Heather these days. Up in the Midlands. Kiddies of her own. Busy, busy. She'll be down though, when she can.'

'Then you'll know, Ralph. You'll understand when I tell you that I haven't even spoken to my daughter for two years, let alone set eyes on her, and why I'd do anything, *anything*, to find her and make things right again.'

'Ah, yes. I did get the impression there'd been, shall we say, a falling-out. Not that she gave any details and I didn't ask. No, no. Nothing to do with me.'

Ralph shook his head and looked longingly in the direction of the car park.

'It doesn't matter. Look, Ralph, I don't know what you promised Karen but I really do need to find her, or at least know where she is and if she's all right. Please tell me, when did you speak to her? Do you know where she is?'

Ralph fell into silent contemplation. Millie's nerve-ends shrieked. How long was he going to make her wait for a simple answer to a simple question? He must remember, surely. She grimaced at Charmaine, who made a face back.

Eventually, Ralph spoke. 'It was last August, the sixteenth. Could have been the seventeenth. Got a phone call from Karen, out of the blue. Couldn't think who she was at first, then it dawned. She didn't beat about the bush. Wanted a job, or rather a leg-up to get one.'

'A *job*? But why? Why would she contact you, I mean?'

Ralph continued as if Millie hadn't spoken. 'She remembered I was in the travel business. Asked me if I still was. Yes, I told her. Area manager.'

Area manager? Ralph had done well, Millie thought. The apparent incongruity between Ralph and the travel industry had always surprised her. The tortoise and the hare. She felt it afresh now. How old would he be? Sixty-five, sixty-six?

'Retired a few months back, as it happens,' Ralph said.

'Still there at the time, though. How could I help? I said. And that's when she asked me. Karen.'

'Yes, what did she say?' Millie fidgeted impatiently beside Ralph who, having given up all hope of an early escape, was now the essence of composure.

'She said she needed a job, one where she could get away, make a fresh start, but she wasn't having any luck. Like I say, she needed a leg-up. Had to admire her, phoning me on spec. Showed gumption, I thought.'

Get away? Fresh start? Get away from whom, her mother? She'd already done that, surely? Unless she meant get away from him, Evil Jack. A tiny light went on inside Millie's head. Perhaps things weren't as bad as she'd feared. She wished Ralph would get on with it, though.

'Ralph, please, do you know where Karen is? Did she leave an address, phone number, anything?'

Ralph looked crestfallen. 'No, sorry, she didn't. Said she would phone me back in a couple of days.'

'And did she?'

'She did. I'd pulled a few strings by that time. Got her to the top of the list. The recruitment list. Holiday reps.'

'Holiday reps?' Millie gazed stupidly at Ralph. Her brain seemed not to be working at full tilt.

'Yes, you know, in the resorts, looking after the package tourists. Popular job with the young ones. Damn hard work though. Long hours for not much pay. They don't realise. I don't think Karen realised, or perhaps…' – he looked at Millie – 'she didn't much care.'

'You mean she was that desperate to get away?' Millie asked, quietly.

Ralph offered a kind smile. His heart was in the right place, Millie thought. And then she knew that he wouldn't hide anything from her. All he would tell her today was, truthfully, all he knew. She mustn't be too hard on him.

'Ralph, look, I'm sorry to have put you in an awkward position. If… *when* I find my daughter, I won't mention you had anything to do with it, but please, what else do you know? Did she get a job, my Karen?'

Ralph nodded slowly, his eyes on his shiny shoes. 'She did, yes. We – the company – took her on as a trainee holiday rep. I had no contact from then on, you understand. Not my remit, but they took her on the basis on my verbal reference.'

'That was extremely generous of you under the circumstances,' Millie said, wondering exactly how much Ralph had been told about Karen's working life that had suffered more ups and downs than the escalator in Selfridge's.

Karen was bright; she'd done well at school. She had the knack of passing exams even when she'd barely opened a book beforehand; an enviable skill in itself, Millie had always considered. But after sixth form she had not, as Mark would have put it, knuckled down. She didn't want to go to university and Millie had known better than to try and persuade her. Instead, there had been much indecisive drifting, starting one thing, giving it up, starting another. The only career in which Karen had expressed more than a whisper of interest was looking after children. She loved them, seemed drawn to them. She even started a course at the local college but then she met him, Jack the lad, and her whole world tipped on its head. At least that was how it seemed to Millie.

Ralph shrugged. 'Blood's thicker than water. You look after your own. My old mum taught me that.'

'So if Karen works for the travel company, they'll tell me how I can reach her, won't they?'

'They might not,' Charmaine interjected. 'It's the Data Protection Act. John gets it all the time at the surgery, people asking after other people and their medical goings-on. They're usually well-intentioned, of course, but you don't dare let anything slip, not these days.'

'I'm afraid that's right,' Ralph said. 'And as I say, I've retired now, and even if I hadn't, I wouldn't have had access to that kind of information. All strictly controlled. Has to be.'

'I see.' Millie thought for a moment. Her hopes had suffered a setback, but not an irretrievable one. There must be a way out of this.

'Ralph, do you happen to know where Karen was sent, originally? If it was only eight months ago she'd still be there, wouldn't she? In the same resort?'

'I only know where she asked to be sent. No guarantee she got there. Or stayed there, come to that.'

'So where was that?'

Ralph's eyes levelled with Millie's. 'Sydney. Sydney, Australia.'

Chapter Eight

Three weeks had passed since Mark's funeral and Millie had made two important decisions. The first was that she would stop racking up her phone bill with fruitless calls to complete strangers on both sides of the world in an attempt to track down her daughter. The second was that she would not touch a penny of Mark's money until she had found Karen. The obvious conflict between these two notions was not enough to shift her from either cause.

Travelbugs UK had turned out to be one of those companies that operated entirely on-line, which meant there were no brochures with useful phone numbers in shouty fonts. Millie would have much preferred to skim the brash promises of a holiday brochure with her feet up on the sofa than spend hours glued to the computer screen. There was something more trustworthy about the printed word. The pertinent page could be marked by the turning down of its corner, the relevant phone number obtrusively ringed in biro, and there it would remain until Millie was ready. Saving the webpage to 'Favourites' was not the same, not by a long chalk.

It occurred to her later that this sudden pickiness over available research methods was linked to fear as much as to personal preference. Fear that she would not find Karen.

Fear that she would.

She felt perversely thankful that Ralph had said Sydney rather than somewhere like Spain to which she might have been tempted to book a flight, there and then. The long-haul hotel options on the Travelbugs website were limited, which seemed a blessing until she began to make the calls. The Sydney hotels used by the company all belonged to one group and were linked to the same number, necessitating painstaking questioning as to which reception Millie was actually speaking. Having to make the calls late at night to allow for the time difference didn't help either, as Millie was not at her best, but she soldiered on, notebook at hand, just in case some useful information should be imparted which, by and large, it wasn't.

The law prevented free speech from the Australian end and most of the conversations had been conducted almost in code, frustrating not only for her but, Millie sensed, for the people she managed to speak to. But if her interpretation was correct, the message was clear enough. Karen's name rang no bells. She wasn't working as a rep at any of the hotels in the city and, as far as Millie could tell, she never had. The calls she'd made to the British end of the company had been equally stunted by regulations. The outcome of the whole exercise was at worst, negative, and at best, inconclusive. It was all so disheartening.

Charmaine sweetly tried to divert Millie's mind by arranging outings and activities for the two of them that had nothing whatsoever to do with errant daughters. It helped, up to a point, but, strangely enough, the thing that helped most was seeing Gus on the train. Routine again, Millie thought, as she stood at the back window and watched him glide past; a regular happening that took no account of weather or events or circumstances, unless you counted the vagaries of the railway networks, which Millie didn't since the train had been no more than seven minutes late in weeks. If only the rest of life could be as reliable.

Millie gave herself a few days' grace, then sat down after supper one evening and resumed her search. Having exhausted the travel company angle, for now at least, she retreated to well-trodden terrain and worked her way through her precious collection of Karen-shaped phone numbers, having first copied them onto a clean, new page of her notebook where they sat looking fresh and decidedly more hopeful.

The outcome, however, was depressingly familiar. Two of Karen's friends and the mother of a third informed Millie, kindly but regretfully, that they had no more idea of her whereabouts than they had before. The bistro where she'd waited table for a while had changed hands and there was nobody left who remembered her. The bar staff at the pub where she'd worked for longer still hadn't heard from her, and neither had the two girls Karen had been friendly with at the children's nursery where she'd obtained work experience.

And so it went on, until she reached the last number on the list – the house Karen had shared with friends and then with Jack. But again, the high-pitched hum which assaulted her ears proved, once and for all, that the number had been disconnected.

Millie sighed, got up and went to the kitchen to fetch a glass of wine. When she returned, she sat for a while, sipping her drink while she gathered her thoughts. Ralph, Mark's cousin. She could phone him, couldn't she, now that a respectable amount of time had passed since the funeral? She didn't doubt that he would have been in touch if he had any news, but he wouldn't mind if she were to gently refresh his memory. His number was still in the handbag she'd taken to the funeral. She ran upstairs to fetch it.

Ralph answered straight away, sounding pleased to hear from her, listening carefully as Millie updated him on her abortive Travelbugs enquiries after as little small talk as she could decently get away with.

'Not surprised,' Ralph spluttered, bringing Millie a mind-picture of wet lips stretched around conspicuous molars. 'Not surprised at all. Shame, though. Sorry about that.'

'Don't be,' Millie assured him. 'You've been more help than anyone. I just thought I'd ring, you know…'

'As it happens, there is something,' Ralph cut in. 'It's not much, so don't get your hopes up.'

'No, no, I won't,' Millie replied, not quite truthfully. 'Go on.'

Ralph began to explain, annoyingly slowly but Millie held back on trying to hurry him along. Apparently he'd been invited to the company reunion, an annual bash at a hotel for current and ex-employees alike. If last year's was anything to go by, the buffet table would stretch from here to Timbuktu and the wine would flow like nobody's business which more than made up for the self-congratulatory company film show that would have to be endured. There was more in this vein before, eventually, Ralph homed in on the purpose of this revelation. The point was, he said, that there were bound to be holiday reps there, some of whom would have been working for the company at the same time as Karen.

'I'll do the rounds,' Ralph promised. 'See what I can find out. It's not for a while yet, this do, but I'll get back to you if anything comes of it. Scouts' honour and all that.'

When Ralph ended the call, Millie found herself smiling into soft evening light that filled the room.

The rest of the week seemed to race by, carrying Millie along on a rising trajectory of renewed optimism and imbuing her with welcome sense of purpose, although she wasn't sure where it was leading, until on Sunday morning, she woke up knowing precisely what it was she needed to do. Fixing to the dashboard her personal sat-nav – a bunting of sticky notes with road numbers and landmarks written on – and pausing only to check and double-check that she hadn't left the gas on or anything electrical unnecessarily plugged in, she jumped in the car and pointed it towards Croydon.

Albany Road was quiet, empty, the only sign of habitation a faint trickle of music from somewhere inside. The car door, when Millie closed it, sounded over-loud and intrusive. Ahead of her as she walked, the heat melded road and pavement into one indecisive blur. She almost passed number sixteen without noticing, so changed was its appearance since she had last been here. Gone were the stringy curtains, the lick of green slime on the wall from the leaky guttering, the grimy front door with a hole where the letterbox should be, over which someone had roughly taped a piece of cardboard cut from a Weetabix box. Instead, all was clean and bright, the house obviously having been thoroughly renovated and, according to the doorbell plate, divided into three flats.

Millie stood at the bottom of the litter-free steps, gazed up at the splendour of the plastic window-frames and brand new paintwork and felt almost affronted. But what had she expected? That the house Karen had once called home existed inside a bubble, immune to the rush of development? Of course she had known, deep down, that Karen wasn't here, that nothing of her daughter remained in this nowhere street in this anywhere suburb, but she'd had to see for herself, seal off in her mind this particular facet of the search. That was why she had come.

The house to the left had received the same treatment as number sixteen; there would be recent occupants in the upper flats, and the basement was empty and had a 'For Sale' sign attached to the gate. The house on the other side, though, looked relatively untouched. There was no harm in trying while she was here. Millie went up the steps and rang the bell. The olive-skinned young woman who came to the door – not English; Italian perhaps – held a small baby to her shoulder while a wide-eyed toddler clung to her skirt. Yes, she told Millie in answer to her question, she had lived here before they made the flats next door but she knew nothing of the people who had lived there and didn't remember anyone who looked like Karen.

'So many people. They come and go.' She smiled apologetically and nodded at the photo. 'Pretty girl. I wish you find her.'

Millie asked the same question of a young man propped in a doorway, smoking, and received only an indolent shake of his head in reply. There were shops on both corners at the far end of the street, a newsagent's and a take-away burger place. She walked along and made enquiries in both but no-one recognised Karen from her photo. Even so, as she retraced her steps she felt a sense of mild satisfaction, a subtle easing of her mind.

Yes, she had drawn a blank, but perhaps now she could allow the pictures to fade, the freeze-frames of Karen bounding up the steps of number sixteen, long blond hair swinging, putting her key in the lock of that scruffy front door, coming home to goodness knows what.

Millie sat in the car for a while, breathing deeply, letting her shoulders subside, before starting the engine. There was a Tesco on the corner by the roundabout; she'd noticed it as she arrived. She might as well nip in there and pick up a few things. It would save bothering when she got back to Brighton.

Why was it that paying a simple visit to a strange supermarket was such a disorientating experience, Millie wondered, as she negotiated the unfamiliar layout with her basket. She'd picked up a Sunday paper at the entrance and managed to locate the bread, milk and cheese, but so far the section with the ham had evaded her and the hanging signs seemed to be designed to deliberately mislead.

Turning yet another corner, she saw ahead of her in the otherwise empty aisle a uniformed assistant bent double over a case of something as he replenished the shelves. She would ask him; he must be used to fielding stupid questions. He straightened up as she approached, and immediately Millie was struck by a sense of familiarity as she watched the long body unfurl, the arm in its too-short sleeve reach easily to the top shelf. Her feet stalled on the tiles, the basket a ton weight in her hand as the blood rushed to her face. The young man turned towards her, and Millie found herself staring into the coal-black eyes of Jack O'Brien.

Charmaine had been incredulous when she discovered that Millie had never heard of the O'Brien family, whose members regularly troubled the benches of the magistrates' court as well as keeping the journalists from the local rag in shoe leather. Millie's protestations that she didn't read the local paper or take heed of gossip had been summarily dismissed.

'They're notorious, the O'Briens,' Charmaine had proclaimed. 'The eldest brother – there are six of them, can you imagine? – has just finished a prison sentence for arson and the rest make careers out of petty crime. The father's absent most of the time and only comes back when he wants something, the mother's been done for shoplifting, and when they're not being arrested they're causing havoc at the surgery, or they used to.'

'They're John's patients?'

'Not any more. The eldest have gone their own way and the council moved the rest of them so they're out of his area

now, thank goodness. I didn't tell you that, of course. Millie…'
– Charmaine had been all concern – 'Do you really want your
daughter going out with one of the O'Briens?'

No, of course she didn't, once she knew what they were
like, but Karen was over eighteen and there wasn't a lot she
could do about it other than try to keep a watchful eye.
Anyway, Millie preferred to look on the bright side. Perhaps
Jack, the youngest of the brothers according to Charmaine, was
the one who broke the mould. Who was to say that he wasn't a
perfectly wholesome, well-intentioned boy?

Millie had tried not to feel, or look, too dismayed when one
day Jack turned up at Star Street looking nothing close to
wholesome. She had answered the door to find him leaning in
the doorway, arms outstretched, hands heeled against the
brickwork, his rangy body engaged in an impatient, unrelenting
swing. His sallow skin had seemed in need of a good scrub and
his eyes – she would never forget those eyes, the darkest she
had ever seen – issued their piercing challenge beneath a wildly
curling, greasy fringe. It was depressingly easy to see how this
untamed individual with the faint but unmistakeable whiff of
potential danger would appeal to her daughter.

Millie had come face-to-face with Jack a few more times,
although she had never managed to get anything out of him
other than an off-hand grunt, and then he and Karen had fallen
out and parted, and Millie had breathed a sigh of relief. Shortly
afterwards, she read in the paper that Jack had been handed a
suspended sentence for possession of drugs.

With Millie's blessing – what else could she do? – Karen
left home after the break-up, firstly to a flat share in Brighton
and then to Croydon where she had friends and the dubious-
sounding promise of a job in a pet shop. Millie missed her but
conceded Karen had to lead her own life. It wasn't as if she was
far away, and she did ring home for a nice long chat at least
once a week.

It was some months before Millie discovered that Karen
had not only been reconciled with Jack but had let him move in
with her.

Millie knew as soon as she'd dashed across the supermarket car park, jumped in the car and roared off, that she'd made a mistake. She couldn't believe that, after all the searching, the heartache, she had come within inches of the very person who might know where her daughter was and had turned tail and run. She should have spoken up, dismissed her pounding heart and wobbly legs as meaningless symptoms of Jack-phobia. Instead, she'd been cowardly, put her own needs before those of her daughter's. *How could she have done that?*

But it wasn't phobia, was it? The fistful of fear that lodged, insoluble, inside her at the mere thought, never mind the sight, of him, wasn't irrational. Jack knew where to find her, always had. Just because he hadn't so far turned up on her doorstep didn't mean he never would, and now that he'd seen her, she'd be in the forefront of his mind. He might not have recognized her, of course – he'd shown no signs of doing so in the few seconds she'd stood before him – but it seemed logical to assume that he had.

Karen swam into her mind. He'd changed her, Jack. She was no angel – Millie wasn't that blind – but he'd switched on something in her, a devil-may-care grittiness that Millie didn't like. How dare he do that to her daughter? *How dare he?* Millie clung to the steering wheel as her body threatened to lift itself clean out of the seat. She should turn round now, go back and confront him. But even as she thought it, she carried on.

A car hooted from behind as she changed lanes a bit too sharply. Snapping her concentration into place, she raised an apologetic hand. It wasn't until she'd gained the straight stretch of road heading for Brighton that she allowed Jack to enter her mind again. Even if she had stood her ground and asked him what he knew of Karen's whereabouts, he wasn't likely to come right out with it, was he? And supposing they were still together? Millie's instincts told her it was unlikely after all this time, but perhaps that was just wishful thinking. Jack would tell Karen her mother was on the trail and any chance there might have been of reconciliation would be thrown to the wind. Karen's perverse nature would see to that.

No, she couldn't do it; confronting Jack O'Brien would be

foolhardy in the extreme. Yet, deep down, there was still a part of her that believed that until she conquered her dread of him and all he represented, Karen would be lost to her forever.

Chapter Nine

Gus had felt unusually ill at ease among the crowds at Covent Garden, as if the spotlight was on him rather than the accomplished young opera singers performing in the square. Irritated with himself, he'd cut his losses and headed back early to Victoria.

He shouldn't have come. He hadn't been in the mood for London today but neither had he wanted to stay in the house he still thought of as Augusta's, no matter how many times he told himself that number nine Prosperity Terrace was his and he was free to do as he wanted with it. Because he wasn't, was he? He couldn't do as he wanted. He couldn't sell up, give his sister-in-law half the proceeds and move back to Brighton because of some ancient feud between his mother and his aunt that he knew nothing about and, by the looks of it, never would.

Of course, he could always sell the house and stash away the money until Elspeth came to her senses, or simply move out without selling but neither notion sat easily with his conscience. Someone had to be there, guarding the house, until justice could be done and his brother's rightful place in the family hierarchy regained, and that someone had to be him; despite the trouble she had caused him, he had made that promise to Augusta, not in reality but in his heart, and if that made him a sentimental old fool then so be it.

There was half an hour until the train. He stood glumly against a pillar as the minutes ticked slowly by, the crowd flowing purposefully around him making him feel even more adrift. Clearly, he needed a plan for the rest of the day, something active to lift him out of his broodiness. For a start, he'd go for a run, then he could ask Jessica round. On the other hand, they had seen a lot of one another recently so maybe it wasn't such a good idea; he had the distinct feeling that the spectrum of the Hangburton spotlight had broadened specifically to include him and all his activities.

His first invitation to take Jessica for a drink, intended purely as a thank-you for her help with the embroidery – at least he told himself this at the time – had been received without surprise and with a girlish eagerness that had brought Gus a soupcon of anxiety. Their second outing – calling it a date had seemed somewhat premature – had been to Hangburton Manor which Gus really ought to see for himself if he was to achieve any kind of realism with his embroidery panel; Jessica's words, not his. By the end of the afternoon, he was left in no doubt that she had in mind a great deal more than casual friendship. He supposed that at his age he should be flattered, considering that Jessica looked to be at least ten years his junior. And at first he was, until he tried to see beyond her obvious charms towards, hopefully, something deeper.

Jessica lived with her mother who, to outward appearances, was fully fit and able. Gus found this a bit odd, until it became apparent that she didn't have a job, so he supposed the arrangement was one of financial practicality. She used to be a receptionist at the Old Grange Hotel out on the Cowfold road, she told him, but having been 'bored witless' for the whole time she'd been there – a very short time, if Gus understood correctly – she'd upped and left. Before the receptionist job, she appeared to have flitted from one thing to another, giving up for no evident reason other than her unwillingness to over-tax herself. None of this augured well, but he had no right to occupy the higher ground and maybe he should stop being so damned arrogant and just get on with it. It wasn't as if he was looking for a life partner.

An old mill house stood in the grounds of Hangburton Manor, some distance from the house and partly concealed by trees. He would not have noticed it if Jessica hadn't casually taken his hand and led him, laughing, away from the formal garden, through the meadow and down to the stream. Never had ancient, creaking wood received such tender attention from white, pink-tipped hands, nor the smooth surface of the millstone been so appreciatively caressed.

And there, in the dust-filled sunlight with the smell of aged chaff clogging his nostrils, Gus kissed Jessica or she kissed him, he couldn't remember now, but kiss followed kiss until her lipstick was smeared around her mouth as if she'd been eating cherries, which made him want to kiss her more, and then, somehow, his hand found its way inside her bra.

He had instantly regretted it; all of it, not just the bra thing. Why couldn't he control himself for once and let his brain do the talking? It was pathetic that at his age his reactions were as primal as those of a randy, acned teenage boy. Clair had always joked that he was regressing. Perhaps she was right.

Things with Jessica had moved on apace since the mill incident. Having scored an easy defeat over his conscience and given himself up to the natural order of things, he could not help but admire her openness. If sex was what she wanted, why shouldn't she be honest about it? There was nothing wrong with that. Gus had not lived through the Summer of Love for nothing, even though he was only thirteen at the time.

'I think it would be best if we kept our relationship to ourselves,' he'd said one evening as Jessica lay back, spent and naked, against his sofa cushions.

Her eyes had flashed surprise. 'Keep it a secret, you mean?'

'As far as we can, of course,' he had replied, thinking it was probably too late for complete secrecy since no-one could have failed to notice the way she sidled up to him in public and placed a proprietary hand on his arm at every opportunity.

She shrugged. 'If you like. My mother's really pleased. She thinks you're the bee's knees.'

Gus sighed. He was right; that particular horse had already left the stable.

'I'm not used to everyone knowing my personal business, that's all.'

Jessica had pouted a bit. 'Mum's not everyone.'

No, but she might as well be, he'd thought. Jessica understood perfectly well what he meant, of course. Her deliberate obtuseness irritated him, and although the night was yet young he'd had the sudden urge to spend the rest of it alone. He had passed her clothes to her with almost indecent haste.

Gus strode purposefully across the platform at Brighton. It wasn't a run he needed, and it wasn't Jessica either. No, he knew precisely what he had to do. He drove back to Hangburton only just on the right side of the speed limit, made a quick sandwich, then went upstairs and, hesitating for only a moment, opened the door to Augusta's bedroom.

He had been in here before, of course, but only to check that all was well before resolutely closing the door again. His aunt would have fully expected him to change the room to suit his requirements, as he had done with the rest of the house, and he wasn't clear in his mind why he hadn't touched this one, except it had felt right to leave it a while and let the proverbial dust settle – a mark of respect, perhaps. Now, though, it seemed the time had come.

The room was at the back of the house. The bedroom he had made his was at the front and overlooked the through road that connected with the village high street. The road wasn't generally noisy, the majority of its traffic passing through first thing in the morning and coming to life again for the afternoon school run, but the back room was slightly larger, overlooked the garden and had a pleasing tranquillity about it. He might move in here and turn the front bedroom into a study. If he was destined to live here for the time being, he may as well make the most of the space.

He looked around. Three walls were painted in a green that made him think of broad beans while wallpaper dripping with blancmange-pink flowers covered the fourth. A single divan with a broad bean velour padded headboard was backed against the blancmange-papered wall. The bed linen had been removed and a blancmange candlewick bedspread thrown over the mattress. A piano stool topped with faded tapestry crouched in front of a dressing table, a chest of drawers stood beneath the window and a double wardrobe hugged the alcove. Several framed prints adorned the walls, their subjects leaning surprisingly towards the sentimental; Gus would never have associated his aunt with all these wistful children and solemn dogs.

He unhooked a Helen Allingham cottage print and turned it over. On the back was the printer's label and the price, ten-and-six, in pencil. He propped the picture against the skirting board; he would leave the others for now.

The dust that had settled in here was not only of the proverbial kind; he could have written his name on the polished surface of the dressing table. He went back downstairs and fetched a duster, the spray polish and a rubbish sack. The first item to go into the sack was the dried flower arrangement that sat behind the grate in the little cast iron fireplace. It crumbled to dust as he lifted it out and most of it ended up on the floor rather than in the sack. The chest of drawers and dressing table contained only a few worthless odds and ends, Augusta's clothes having been taken to the charity shop by the woman who used to help in the house. Most of her jewellery was of the costume sort and had gone to charity along with the clothes, but Gus had in his possession a marcasite-encrusted silver heart on a chain, a vintage pearl necklace, and a pretty gold ring with a blue stone.

A clutch of empty hangers from the wardrobe went into the sack, along with two pairs of well-worn shoes, a shamble of stockings in a carrier bag and a battered portable radio. That would do for now; at least he had made a start. The carpet would have to come up at some stage, of course. Beside the bed, a new-looking pink flowered rug added extra comfort. It was no use to him but someone might like it, Jenny, perhaps.

Stooping to roll it up, he thought he may as well check under the bed. There was a box of some sort. He knelt down and pulled it out. It was a large, flat, cardboard box which, according to the faded label, had once held yellow velvet curtains, probably the ones that used to hang in the sitting room. Blowing some of the dust off the top, he lifted the box onto the bed and removed the lid, releasing an unpleasant musty smell.

It was stuffed with papers of all sorts. A perished rubber band struggled to contain a sheaf of birthday cards written to his aunt, mainly from people whose names he didn't recognise although he did find one in his father's writing which said: 'With best wishes from Henry, Liesel, Robert and Gus'. There were old postcards, auction catalogues, theatre programmes, instruction leaflets for various appliances, three envelopes full of old stamps, and dozens of receipts, some dating back twenty years. All of these he put in the sack, along with a booklet titled 'A nurse's guide to the sanitary handling of bedpans' and a yellowing timetable for Newcastle buses which Gus could only think had been kept for sentiment's sake as Augusta had moved south around the same time as he and his family.

He sat back on the bed and rubbed his hot forehead with a hand grubby from his exertions. He was tired now, and bored. He might just as well have shoved the whole box in the recycling and had done with it, but he was nearly there. He took out an old road map of Sussex that was disintegrating along the folds, a street-map of Brighton and Hove, equally out of date, and one of Newcastle and surrounding district.

On impulse he opened this up and spread it on the candlewick, then rather wished he hadn't as he found himself looking at the pale blue snake of the Tyne. He shivered involuntarily as a chill ran through him. It was his own fault; he should have left it alone, but even now he could not bring himself to fold up the map and put it aside. He traced the course of the river with his fingertip, drawing it across the folds of the various sections, and then his eye caught on a small cross made in pencil, marking a spot on a street not far from the river. *Saint Christopher's Road*, he read.

Saint Christopher's House in Saint Christopher's Road, Newcastle-upon-Tyne – the place where he was born.

He lifted the map and moved it aside. There was one more item in the box, a long, brown official-looking envelope addressed to Augusta. Gus's hand shook slightly as he slid out the paper inside and unfolded it. It was a certified copy of a birth certificate: *Catherine Mary Harte, born on the twentieth day of September, 1938.*

But why? Why would his aunt have a copy of his natural mother's birth certificate? What had it to do with her? His parents, Henry and Liesel, may perhaps have wanted to acquire such a document in the interests of discovering the pedigree of the boy they were about to give a home to, but why Augusta? Unless she applied for it on his parents' behalf and somehow it never ended up in their possession. Yet the copy was dated December 1959, four months before he was born. If he had understood Elspeth correctly, the Albournes had not known of his existence until afterwards.

He stared at the paper in his hand, trying to understand. Catherine was only twenty-two when she gave birth to him; he hadn't known that. In the eyes of the law she was an adult, but still it seemed so young. Such a waste of a life.

Gus went to bed that night full of sadness, for Catherine, for Robert, for himself, for all of them, but especially for Catherine.

It seemed to Gus that every television schedule featured a programme about people attempting to unearth long-forgotten or hitherto unknown ancestors and generally forage about in the vaults of their past. Fleshing out the bones of the family tree had suddenly become a national obsession – unless it had always been so and it was his present frame of mind that brought it to his attention; he couldn't be sure.

The national press, too, especially the magazines that came with the Sundays, had picked up on this trend and carried stories of women who had spent time in institutions such as the one he was born in, and of the babies themselves and what became of them. Gus felt an irresistible compulsion to read these articles, which he did virtually at arm's length with a tumbler of Scotch on standby, but no matter how harrowing the content, he did not read of any of the mothers having brought themselves to an untimely end. Most of them seemed to have gone on to lead fulfilling and relatively happy lives, despite the secret regrets that never left them. Some had even been reunited with the children they thought they had lost forever.

Clearly he had too much time on his hands, he thought, as he grimly logged onto the internet for the fourth evening in a row and sought out even more of these sorry sagas with which to torment himself. This wasn't like him at all, and yet he couldn't seem to stop, probably because a part of him believed that by cramming his brain vicariously with the experiences of strangers he could in some way begin to understand Catherine's motives in her double abandonment of him.

Yes, that was how he felt. Abandoned. At his age. He cursed his own stupid self-pity in bringing the word into his mental vocabulary but here it was all the same, in billboard-high neon letters, parading itself tauntingly before him.

And what was Augusta's part in all of this? He now knew that Catherine Harte had been known to the Albourne family before she gave birth to him – the date on the copy certificate gave evidence of that – unless it was only Augusta who knew her at that time. Elspeth had mentioned that the home where he was born was connected to the church, as its name suggested. Augusta had once been a churchgoer, not here in Sussex but back in Newcastle. It suddenly came to him that he knew this.

The small, black-and-white photograph of Augusta, the only one he'd found, now lay face down in its frame on top of the bookcase where his heavy hand had slammed it, the glass shamefully split from corner to corner. Why, if his aunt had seen fit to leave him all her worldly goods, had she not also seen fit to talk to him instead of letting him inherit a load of guilt and unanswerable questions along with the rest of her estate?

All these thoughts, and more, provided a relentless, discordant backing-track to his days and nights until one morning, unable to contain his frustration any longer, he rang the agency to say he wouldn't be in, then wrenched the car into gear and headed for Elspeth's with the copy of his mother's birth certificate in his pocket.

He arrived, in his eagerness, far too early. It was only five to nine when he swerved into the crescent off the main road where the house was. The minibus that took Jenny to the day centre didn't arrive until half past and he wasn't planning on gate-crashing breakfast. He sat in the car for a few minutes with the engine running, his fingers drumming the dashboard, then executed a smart u-turn and headed back down the main road to a café where he whiled away a tense half hour with a mug of tea and the daily paper before driving, as slowly as he could, back to his original destination.

'Gus!'

Elspeth greeted his arrival with alarmed surprise and immediately he felt guilty for not having phoned first.

'Sorry, yes, I know it's early but can we talk, please?'

'Well...'

Oh Lord. She was going to say no, send him away empty-handed. He wasn't sure he could cope with that.

'No, it's only that I'm on my way over to Mum's,' Elspeth said, seeing his expression. 'The bulb's blown in the hall light. She hasn't got a spare and she has to have it on all day otherwise she can't see diddly-squat, so she says.' Elspeth raised her eyes. 'You could always come along for the ride. We wouldn't have to stop long.'

We? Couldn't he wait outside in the car while Elspeth did what she had to, or stay here until she came back? It seemed churlish to make either suggestion, though, since Elspeth herself obviously wasn't going to.

Fifteen minutes later, Gus levered himself out of the passenger seat of Elspeth's ancient hatchback, relieved at least that they'd left Spotty at home and he wasn't barking his head off behind the dog-guard, as he was apt to do. Following his sister-in-law through the main entrance of Whitefriar Court, he felt the sting of adrenalin as he found himself facing the clamped steel doors of the lift but Elspeth hurried past, took out a key and let them into the noticeably day-lit hall of one of the ground floor flats.

'Elspie? Who's that with you?' Gus heard, as Elspeth's mother, Rose, made slow but upright progress out of the sitting room and peered myopically at them over the top of a pair of stylish, metal-framed spectacles.

'It's Gus, Mum. Robert's brother. You remember?'

Unlikely, Gus thought, given that the old lady suffered from vascular dementia.

'Of *course* I remember him! He gave me that lovely red scarf one Christmas.'

'She must be having a good day,' Elspeth hissed at Gus over her shoulder. 'We'll have to stop for a bit. You don't mind, do you?'

It would be all the same if he did, Gus thought glumly, as Elspeth flicked the switch in the hall and the overhead light added a purposeless gleam to the brightness angling in from the adjacent rooms.

'Nothing wrong with the light, Mum. You couldn't have turned it on properly. I'll leave the spare bulb here, look, by the phone, in case it does go. But get the warden to do it. Don't start climbing about, for heaven's sake.'

Even more glumly, Gus watched Rose enter the kitchen and swoosh water into the kettle. The certificate was burning a hole in his pocket. If he didn't talk to Elspeth soon, he'd be a sure-fire candidate for the next available flat in this development, if not a stage on from it, but she didn't seem to notice his discomfort.

The seat of the cottage-style sofa on which he was invited to sit extended nowhere near the length of his thighs and Elspeth on the matching chair was faring no better, but the room was on the poky side, necessitating this paring down of furniture size. The sizeable black face of the flat-screen TV assumed cinematic proportions by comparison.

Elspeth's mother lowered herself into the only comfortable chair and emitted little 'ah' sounds as she sipped her tea. Eventually, she put down her cup and saucer and gazed at Gus. Immediately he could see Elspeth in the slightly dulled but spirited green eyes, the wispy grey curls with a pale hint here and there of the red-gold they used to be, and the square determination of her shoulders. Faced with the claustrophobia and pointless optimism of old age, Gus was ashamed to have been feeling sorry for himself. He must remember never to grow old.

'What've you been up to then, Rose?' he asked, narrowing his eyes. 'Still paragliding?'

The old lady's eyes twinkled back at him. 'Of course! That and the sky-diving.'

She laughed naughtily as Gus grinned and flashed his eyes

at her.

He glanced at Elspeth. She was drinking her tea while staring absently out of the window; she looked exhausted. He should try and do more for her but she wouldn't let him, he knew that. If only she would take the money, she could have someone in to do the garden and the cleaning, buy a decent car... He remembered why he had sought her out today, the reasons for which now seemed incredibly selfish.

Rose was talking to him, he realised. Her voice had acquired a hoarse fadedness and it was a strain to catch all the words, especially as someone had started up an electric lawnmower outside.

'You should never have left them. It was wrong, so wrong. Oh yes, I know she told you to go...' – Rose nodded vehemently – '...but that was only in temper. Marriage has to be worked at. You should have stayed put, for the boy's sake if not for that German wife of yours.'

Gus leaned forwards abruptly, almost toppling the small table holding his tea.

'Boy? What boy?'

'*Your* boy! Robert! Haven't forgotten him already, have you?'

Rose was eyeing Gus now as if he was the devil incarnate. He frowned and looked at Elspeth who had peeled her eyes away from the window and was now regarding her mother with growing alarm.

'She was the last person you should have run away to, that sister of yours.' Rose was warming to her theme. 'Holier than thou, that's what Robert says. What's her name, Elspie? I can't seem to think.'

'Augusta.' Elspeth almost spat out the name, leaving Gus even more perplexed. She turned to him. 'Don't worry. She's getting you muddled up but it'll pass in a minute.'

'That's it. Augusta.' Rose sat back, satisfied.

'What does she know about Augusta? What does she mean, *that sister of yours*?'

'Gus, leave it,' Elspeth stage-whispered. 'I told you, she's getting you muddled.'

'Did more harm than good, I always thought, leaving Robert like that, arguments or no arguments. Eleven's a tricky age, neither one thing nor t'other.'

'Yes, Mum, but it all worked out in the end, as well you know because Robert told you. Anyway, it's all in the past so let's leave it that way, shall we?'

Beneath Elspeth's placating tone was an edgy nervousness she couldn't conceal. Gus felt a distinct rise in his anxiety levels. He faced Elspeth, not caring whether Rose could hear or not.

'Who does she think I am?'

He had already worked this out but he needed Elspeth to say it. She sighed.

'Henry. She thinks you're your father. It's no good arguing with her. Doesn't get you anywhere. Just humour her, Gus, please?'

A note of desperation had crept into Elspeth's voice. Gus shifted position a bit, turning slightly away from her and further towards her mother.

'I really don't remember much about this, Rose,' he said evenly. 'As Elspeth says, it's all in the past, but I would never have hurt them deliberately, not… Liesel, or Robert.'

Rose squared her shoulders and turned accusing eyes on him.

'I don't expect you did, but all the same Robert never forgot the time you went off and left him and his mother. Upset him terribly. He told me all about it when we were having a heart to heart, just after he married Elspie.'

Gus swallowed the knot in his throat. The whine of the lawnmower had thrust itself painfully inside his skull. He could sense Elspeth willing him to let this go, but he couldn't. It was too good an opportunity to miss.

The old woman jabbed a gnarled forefinger in his direction. 'That girl was no better than she should be, of course, the one you were carrying on with. She takes half the blame, I'll give you that.'

Carrying on with? His heart thundered beneath his ribcage. Elspeth had both hands pressed to her face. Her eyes were closed.

Rose's mind, however, had seemingly snapped back to the present. She smiled warmly at Gus.

'More tea, dear? And a slice of pork, perhaps? No, I don't mean pork. What do I mean, Elspie?'

Elspeth came back to life. 'Cake, I expect. No, Mum, thanks. We've got to get going.'

She stood up and wedged a firm hand under Gus's arm, giving him no choice but to stand up and follow her out of the flat, into the grass-scented sunshine.

Gus could not bring himself to speak on the way back to Elspeth's house. It was all he could do to breathe. Elspeth clutched the steering wheel as if it might leap out of her hands at any moment, and only when they pulled up outside her house did she glance in his direction and throw him an almost-smile.

It was clear by the way she stood in the middle of the pavement, the door keys bunched tightly in her hand, that she didn't want to ask him in. They would just have to do this out here then. Surprisingly, he felt almost calm now. He leaned against the side of Elspeth's car and folded his arms as if he had all day, which, in fact, he had.

'So what was that all about?'

Elspeth glanced skywards. 'I know. Mum's a bit of a basket case at times.' She gave a humourless little laugh, then briefly covered her mouth. 'I shouldn't laugh but it's better than doing the other thing.'

No. He wasn't going to let her play the sympathy card.

'Basket case or not, it didn't come from nowhere, what she said about Robert and our father.'

'No, it came right out of her head, the same as the other things she says when she's being as mad as cheese. I could make us a sandwich, if you're staying.'

Gus didn't move. 'What do you know about my father leaving home, running off to Augusta? Because sure as eggs are eggs, you know something, that's blindingly obvious.'

'Or an omelette. I could do us an omelette…'

'*Elspeth.*'

'Look, Gus, I don't know what it is you think I'm not telling you but I was not part of all that. I wasn't there when you were children, was I? And if you think Rob told me everything that ever happened in the family then, yes, he probably did at some point but don't expect me to remember all the details now. Just don't. All right?'

Her eyes had clouded over. Gus wanted to say sorry but the word refused to leave his lips. Yet if anyone was sorry, he was. Sorry he had ever been left a house, sorry he had ever seen it as anything other than a pile of bricks, and sorry he had ever turned around, looked back, and been frightened at what he saw.

He gave a grim little nod, pushed himself away from Elspeth's car and stepped backwards towards his own, his gaze fixed on Elspeth's all the while, until she gave him a solemn half-wave, turned on her heel and went indoors.

It wasn't until he was halfway home that he remembered the certificate was still in his pocket.

Chapter Ten

Gus absently traced the line of Jessica's shoulder blade with his tongue, his body setting itself in motion as if it was attached to a remote tuning device. His preoccupation wasn't fair on her, he knew that, but the more he tried to stay focussed, the faster his thoughts tumbled through his brain like water through a sluice-gate.

He refused to believe his father had had an affair; there was no question about it. He wasn't the type, and besides, his parents' marriage had been as solid as the Himalayas. It was nonsense, all he'd heard yesterday; the ramblings of a batty old woman, no more. And yet Elspeth's reaction to her mother's admonishment of him and her behaviour towards him even after they had left the flat, as if what had happened was his fault, was beginning to cast a shadow of painful uncertainty.

It suddenly hit him that the hurried acquisition of a new baby might have been by way of mending the split, if it existed, between Henry and Liesel, since his arrival occurred so soon afterwards. His mother, when talking to him openly about his adoption, had always insisted that they chose him to be their son and that made him special, but wasn't that the standard recommended approach in such cases? He had read it often enough in those articles he'd been poring over. Great. Now he felt not only abandoned but non-specific, like some commodity picked off the shelf at random as the supermarket was closing.

An irresistible pressure was building up in his loins. His movements quickened of their own accord, seconds before the warm explosion. He opened his eyes. Jessica was gazing up at him, her eyes liquid with desire as she ground her hips beneath him in spasms of unrequited lust. She caught hold of his hand

and placed it between her legs. It seemed to take an age until she let out that irritating little yelp of hers before she nuzzled his ear and covered his face with butterfly kisses, her customary ending to proceedings.

They were in, or rather on, his bed, the duvet having been jettisoned over the edge early on. This location was something of a novelty considering Jessica's predilection for sex anywhere but the bedroom – not that he was complaining but his back definitely had been. He had taken her out to dinner tonight, to a Tudorbethan, fairy-lit establishment that she had been hinting about for a while now. He hadn't minded shelling out an extraordinary amount of money for food that was pretentious and not at all exciting, but as the place was twelve miles away he hadn't even been able to indulge in enough alcohol to anaesthetise the experience.

He flopped onto his back and they lay side by side in sated silence. After a few minutes, he turned his head and stole a look at Jessica, at the delicate bone structure of her face, her hair coiling over the white pillow like chocolate icing, her small, neat breasts, the nipples shining from his attentions – a triumph of a girlfriend, it could be said, and yet...

'Sorry,' he said, half to himself.

Sorry he couldn't give her more, sorry that this was as good as it was ever going to be, because he could never fall in love with her.

Her eyes flicked open in surprise.

'Don't say that. It was lovely and you were fantastic. Like always.'

A languid hand came to rest on his thigh.

Gus inhaled deeply and let the air escape slowly through his mouth. Now he felt even more of a heel. He couldn't go on like this. If he'd learned anything from his tentative re-entry into the world of dating, an experience which had felt alarmingly like starting from scratch, it was that relationships never worked unless both parties were equal and wanted the same things. Jessica, although nothing had been voiced directly, had expectations that he was neither willing nor able to fulfil. Besides, he was too distracted at the moment with all his other problems to give her the attention she deserved.

Regretful though it was, he would have to stop seeing her, and soon. It wasn't going to be easy.

It was two weeks since Gus had accepted his final deposit on a lovers' paradise up four flights of greasy stairs with no space for a washing machine and a bathroom shoehorned into a cupboard. The move to Hangburton had been pivotal in more than one respect, as if one major change demanded another. He'd toyed for a while with the idea of leaving the agency and freelancing as a surveyor. The work might not be as regular, but the small risk involved was part of the attraction and so far he had plenty of work lined up via his mate Tom at the agency and his other contacts in the business. Yes, a good decision all round, Gus thought. He felt free and enlivened, and therefore better able to face whatever trials were to come, the most pressing of which was the problem of Jessica.

Since he'd decided to stop seeing her, they had been for a Sunday morning walk across the Downs during which he had tuned out her chatter whilst his mind formulated the words with which to deliver his bombshell. But the right moment failed to arrive and Jessica went home clutching his elicited promise to ring her later if he wanted her to come round.

He had not rung but that had not deterred her from ringing him. He felt slightly ashamed that he had lied outright and told her he had succumbed to a stomach bug. After that he ignored her texts and brushed off her phone calls with further lame excuses in the hope that the message would hit home without his having to make an issue of it.

He could not, of course, avoid contact altogether because of the close-knit village environment and the embroidery project, but he made sure that whenever the group met he did not pay any more attention to Jessica than to the other women. Since she clearly thought they were still an item and he was just being extra discreet, this didn't have any effect, and one evening after the group had met at Jessica's own house, she came dancing out of the front door after him, flung her arms around his neck and kissed him passionately in the shadow of an overhanging tree.

Gus responded to the kiss in the most perfunctory way possible, then, tucking the bag containing his needlework under his arm, took hold of her hands, detached her arms from around him and placed them firmly by her sides.

'What?' Her smile was bemused, uncertain.

He took a deep breath. 'I don't want to see you any more.'

'You see me all the time.' She waved a hand vaguely about her while she struggled to keep hold of the smile.

'That's not what I meant,' he said patiently, ignoring her deliberate pretence of misunderstanding.

A moment passed before Jessica spoke again.

'You meant you don't want us to, well…'

She tilted her head coquettishly, reached out and stroked his face so lightly it was as if he had walked into a cobweb. His insides contracted as he fought to stay in control.

'Exactly. I'm sorry. I've been having a few problems lately, family things that I have to deal with, and I just don't have the time or energy for anything else at the moment. I'm sorry, Jess.'

He hadn't meant to apologise once, let alone twice. Saying sorry for calling time on a relationship had the tendency to land you right back where you started, and over-explaining often had the same effect. It was best he stopped now and give her a minute or two for it to sink in.

'Is there someone else?' Her voice faltered slightly as she asked the obvious question.

'No, there's no-one else. I would tell you if there was.'

He gazed over her shoulder towards the village green and the timbered cottages huddled around it, the last strings of light fading above the chimneys. The poignant perfection of the scene made him long for a pylon or a petrol station roof. He looked back at Jessica, expecting to see appealing eyes, a bitten lower lip, even the threat of tears, arrogant sod that he was. But instead he saw an expression of unwavering normality, her weight subtly shifting from side to side the only sign that anything was amiss.

'Well, if that's what you want,' she said, brightly. 'It's fine with me.'

'Right, if you're sure…'

He hadn't meant to say that either. Why couldn't he just stick to the script?

'It's fine, I told you.'

Jessica's voice was slightly raised, her smile wafer-brittle. But she backed away from him, still smiling, and stood halfway along the path to her front door.

'See you, then.'

She waved, and was gone.

Gus walked home with a feeling of unease in the pit of his stomach.

Two days later, he ran – literally – into Sidonie, as he emerged from the post office just as she was going in.

'Sorry,' he said, retrieving the parcel he had knocked out of her arms and handing it back to her. 'I wasn't looking where I was going.'

'To an art exhibition with my daughter, I believe.' Sidonie winked at him and offered a red-painted smile. 'That's where you're going, isn't it?'

Gus frowned. 'No...'

But Sidonie had already pressed past him and joined the queue at the post office counter.

Art exhibition? Gus hurried home, forgetting he had meant to go to the bakery, and found a message on his answer machine from Jessica asking him to pick her up at two. A fuzzy feeling crept down his legs. He checked his mobile. Sure enough, the same message. He sat down, sent a text back – *Not free today, must have got wires crossed* – and waited. Sure enough, the landline phone rang.

'It's the new exhibition by that landscape painter we like. It opens today and we said we'd go, remember? It's in Horsham and the parking's deadly so we don't want to leave it too late.'

'But, Jessica,' Gus breathed, 'we aren't going out any more, not like that. Whatever we said we'd do, we aren't now. That's how it has to be.'

Silence. He was beginning to think she'd cut him off when she spoke again.

'Come on, Gus. I thought you'd have got over all that. We had fun, didn't we?'

Her tone was superficially cheerful but bore the hallmarks of a violin strung too tightly.

'We had fun, yes, with the emphasis on *had*, Jess. It's over. Nothing's changed. Take your mother to the exhibition. I'm sure she'll enjoy it.'

He rang off. Amazingly, Jessica did not ring back.

The front door knocker clattered the next morning. What time was it? About ten, he thought. The postman, then. Or Jessica. Gus went on slowly drying himself, sleep still stealing through his veins, despite the shower. He had been in Brighton last night, at the Foundryman with Tom, Mike and Andy from the agency, an excellent night it was, too, discounting the stomach-lurching taxi ride all the way back to Hangburton because he'd missed the last train to Haywards Heath.

The knocker banged twice more. He climbed unsteadily into his cords, went to the bedroom window and twitched the curtains apart, reeling back as the sun made painful contact with his eyeballs. Blinking, he peered down. He couldn't see who was at the door because of the porch, but Elspeth's car was parked a few yards along. Dragging a t-shirt over his head, he took the stairs two at a time and opened the door. Elspeth cast him a meaningful glance and walked past him, along the hallway to the kitchen, Gus padding behind.

'I had to come,' she said, leaning against his sink. 'I couldn't stand it any longer.'

Gus felt weak with relief. He hadn't been able to stand it either, not knowing whether any of what Rose had said was based on fact, worrying that he had put too much pressure on Elspeth. He had wanted to talk to her again straight away after the last time, but afraid of upsetting her further, he had, reluctantly, decided to leave her alone. And now here she was. He held out his arms. Elspeth stepped warily into them.

'You're damp,' she said, when they'd exchanged a tentative hug.

Gus switched the kettle on, slung tea bags into mugs, and

dropped on to a chair. His pleasure at seeing Elspeth was already dissipating; she had not come simply to make friends again. He scraped the other chair out from the table. Speech seemed be eluding him. Elspeth hesitated for a moment before sitting down. She leaned forward, resting her forearms on the table and regarded him seriously.

'Whatever I've told you or not told you before, it was all with the best of intentions. I was worried – more than worried; a bit frantic, actually – because I think the world of you, Gus, and I didn't know what to do. I didn't want to be responsible for starting you off on a path that could only make you miserable.'

'Shouldn't I be the judge of that?'

'Yes, you should. I realise that now. That's why I'm here.'

Gus sealed his lips together in a straight line and waited.

'I expect you wondered why Robert discussed his family's private business with my mother in the first place, especially as it all happened so long ago, and normally he wouldn't have but he was very fond of Rose. They took to one another like ducks to water from the moment I took Robert home.' Elspeth gave a little laugh. 'Sometimes when they got into one of their conversations I'd feel quite left out. Silly, really…'

Gus wished she'd get to the point. He stood up and made the tea, brought it back to the table.

'So it was true then, all that Rose said.'

Two pink spots appeared on Elspeth's cheeks beneath the freckles. 'More or less. They did split up, briefly, your parents. Your father left home for a while after your mother rumbled him and I don't imagine he had any choice in that, no matter what my mother thinks. It wasn't long before they sorted things out, though – three or four weeks at most – but to a young boy it seemed a lot longer. Robert was a sensitive boy, a sensitive man, too.'

So, his father did have an affair – what an awful, cold word that was – and his mother found out and kicked him out of the house. Not the end of the world. And yet it was, wasn't it? The end of *his* world, a world built upon the security and consistency and truth of the first sixteen years of his life. Well, now he knew. He had not been the special one, the child chosen for himself. He had been a sticking-plaster baby – as if being abandoned by his first mother wasn't enough.

The sins of the fathers... And of the mothers, come to that. It altered everything, even now, as he sauntered into middle-age. Especially now.

He looked at Elspeth shifting awkwardly in her chair as she waited for him to speak, but what did she expect him to say? He gazed around the kitchen at the bumpy, white-painted walls, the greasy cobweb looped across the air vent that he kept meaning to wipe away, the limp cotton curtains that he had not got around to replacing, and something in his mind shifted and rippled, like sand beneath the tide. It *was* just a house. Like it or not, it had been left to him alone, there wasn't a damn thing he could do about it and he wasn't even sure if he cared any more.

Through the door to the sitting room, he could see on the corner of the bookcase the envelope containing the copy of his natural mother's birth certificate. He wasn't going to show it to Elspeth now, ask her what she thought it meant, because he didn't want to know. He didn't want to know any of it. All he wanted was to be left in peace to get on with his pot-luck, uncomplicated life. If he stopped dwelling on the past and let it be, as Elspeth had suggested in the first place, it should be possible.

'Augusta knew about it, you see. She knew her brother had been seeing someone and she kept his secret. When Liesel found out – Robert never knew how – she couldn't forgive Augusta for knowing before she did and keeping quiet. She saw it as condoning what he'd done, and you remember how proud she was. She must have hated an outsider knowing their marriage was less than perfect, even her own sister-in-law...'

Gus held up a hand, pushed back his chair and stood up from the table.

'No. No more, Elspeth, please.'

'You don't want to talk about it?'

'Not any more. You were right, it can't do any good, but thank you very much for coming. I do appreciate it.'

Gus tried to temper the unintentional formality of this little speech by reaching over Elspeth's shoulder and closing his hand briefly over hers but he couldn't manage a smile. He hoped she understood.

Elspeth left soon after. When she'd gone, Gus reached into the cupboard for the Nurofen and threw back two capsules, gulping them down with the untouched tea. Its stewed lukewarmness, accompanied by the chemical taste of the plastic-coated capsules, brought a fresh wave of nausea. He would liked to have gone back to bed for a couple of hours but knew that in his wired-up state he wouldn't be able to sleep. He needed something to calm him down. A drink. No, it was still only ten to eleven. Even he had not yet sunk to those depths. Besides, he suspected that beneath the layer of unspecific emotion fizzing away on the surface of his brain, his hangover still lurked. The hair-of-the-dog idea had never appealed.

He drank some water, then paced randomly about the house, taking large strides which made the walls of the rooms seem ridiculously close together. As he marched through the sitting room for the second time, his eyes alighted on his embroidery panels and sewing paraphernalia. He stopped, and gingerly straightened out the first panel depicting Hangburton Manor. It didn't look too bad, all things considered. Even Sidonie had praised his efforts the last time she'd seen it. He sat down, fastened the material in the wooden hoop, threaded a needle, and began.

He stitched and stitched, filling in the entire roof of the manor house with passably realistic tiles, adding detail to flowers and trees and sky, and as he stitched, he felt his shoulders gradually subside, his stomach settle, his breathing regulate. He worked for so long that when eventually he did look up and glance out of the window, he was surprised to see that the weather had changed completely. The sky was awash with cloud, and plump drops of rain spattered the hydrangeas.

Tomorrow was Thursday. He would go to London. He hadn't been for the last few weeks but tomorrow he would go, and on Friday he would make a long overdue visit to Millie Hope, always assuming she had not forgotten who he was.

Chapter Eleven

Millie arranged the blush pink carnations in an old enamel jug she found under the sink and placed them on the windowsill where they sat looking self-conscious. Gus had brought them, he'd said in answer to her question, as a little thank-you for all the help she'd given him. And would continue to give, Millie thought ungratefully, trying to push back the disproportionate pleasure she felt at the gesture.

She had seen him yesterday, on the train, for the first time in four weeks. It had made her smile. Her talisman was back; all was right with her world. Well, it wasn't really but Millie's natural optimism had acquired a special gleam as if she'd taken the silver polish to it. It had occurred to her later that the sighting of her 'Thursday man', as Charmaine insisted on calling him, might signify that she would not be seeing him again in person. The irrationality of this idea had not escaped her but there was another clue in the fact that he had not come back to the shop when he said he would. Then again, they hadn't made firm arrangements; rather it had been a vague suggestion on his part, followed by vague agreement on hers. Even so, on the afternoon in question, when Gus had said he might pop in, the kettle had been brought to the boil three times and Violet Mabey as the first customer of the afternoon had found herself the unwitting recipient of a certain degree of snappiness. Well, the woman would dither so.

Millie had been in the middle of a stock-check this morning when the phone rang. She'd answered it distractedly, at the same time adding another item to the list in the notebook with parrots on the cover that she kept for the purpose.

'It's me. Can I come and see you this afternoon?' Gus had

said, getting straight to the point. 'Short notice, I know, but it took an age to find the number because I couldn't think what the name of the shop was. I knew it was something Knits and then I remembered the Preston bit. Why is it called Preston Knits? It's a bit old-fashioned, isn't it? Apart from the obvious connotations when you say it out loud...'

Millie had been shaking with laughter by the time he ran out of breath.

'If you let me get a word in edgeways,' she managed, 'I'll tell you why it's called that. It's because it's the original name and the elderly lady I took the shop over from didn't want it to change. She still owns the building, as it happens, and the one next door that sells skateboards.'

'It's just that when you say "Preston Knits" it makes me think of lining up at school waiting for the nurse to check our heads for livestock.'

Yes, I got that, Millie thought, raising her eyes as if Gus could see. He had the cheek of the devil, assuming she'd be instantly available whenever he chose to put in an appearance. Why hadn't he phoned before to let her know he'd been busy? If he had time to swan off to London, he had time to pick up a phone.

'Yes, do come. I'll be here,' she'd said.

Gus stood staring out of the window now, hands behind his back, his embroidery as yet unpacked. A train hooted as it rattled past.

'You can see right inside,' he said, turning to Millie as if he hadn't noticed before. 'You wouldn't think that.'

'Yes.'

Millie fiddled with mugs and tea bags. She wasn't going to admit to her voyeuristic tendencies; she felt guilty enough as it was.

'Doesn't it get on your nerves, the vibration and the noise of the trains going through all the time?'

'No, I like it. We had it all the time when I was a child. We lived just up the hill from here and my dad was a train driver. My ex-husband worked for the railway, too.'

Why had she said that?

92

'*Ex*-husband?' Gus turned round, his face alert with interest.

'Was. Mark died, only recently as it goes.'

'Ah. Not sure what to say there.' Gus nodded thoughtfully. 'Do I say sorry or what?'

'Not much else to say. Don't feel obliged.'

'I'm sorry.' He adopted an expression of solemnity that didn't quite work. It made Millie want to giggle.

Gus pulled out a chair and sat down. After a moment he said: 'My wife died. Clair, that was her name.'

He spoke so matter-of-factly that it took Millie a moment to assimilate what he'd said.

'Oh,' she said, dropping into the other chair. 'Oh Gus, I'm so sorry. When... how long ago?'

Why was it never easy to find the right words? Gus, however, seemed unfazed.

'It's nine years ago now, nearly ten. She got bone cancer, galloped through her like ninepence. There was nothing they could do in the end.'

'How dreadful,' Millie said quietly. 'She must have been so young.'

'Thirty-nine. We'd only been married for four years, no children.'

'Oh, these *things*... why do they have to happen?' Millie said suddenly, throwing up her hands.

'She was an amazing person.' Gus smiled, but there was sadness in his eyes. 'When I first knew her I never thought she'd give me the time of day, let alone that I'd end up marrying her. But it turned into a standing joke that she'd had designs on me for ages and I hadn't noticed – she was an architect, you see, a very good one as it happens... But there,' he smiled again, 'I try not to dwell.'

'No, no, of course not.'

Millie's mind was buzzing, with questions, with things unsaid that ought to be said, or possibly not. She hadn't expected this. A divorce, perhaps, or a split from a long-term lover; a man so likeable, so strikingly handsome – Millie winced as she thought this – was bound to have history, but she'd never imagined anything so tragic.

He must have read her expression. 'It's fine.' He laid a light hand briefly on her arm. 'Well, not fine, obviously, but life does go on. I didn't believe that, of course, not at first, not for a long time. Turns out it was true.' He widened his eyes as if he still didn't quite believe it.

Millie thought about Mark but without knowing where the thought was heading. Again Gus read her mind.

'If ever you want to talk about him, your ex, with it being so recent and everything, I'm a good listener, or so they tell me.'

'No, you're all right. But thank you.' Millie smiled. 'If that tea's gone cold I'll make some more.'

They been working in easy silence for a while, Gus on his panel, Millie on a tapestry cushion she was making for Charmaine's birthday, when she stilled her needle and looked across at him sewing away, his eyes narrowed in concentration.

'You have a real talent for this, don't you?'

While she worked, she'd been watching out of the corner of her eye as he drove the needle confidently in and out with a natural artistry that could never be gleaned from any outside source.

'I'm not sure about that. My father was a master tailor. He taught me to sew but I wouldn't go so far as to say there was any talent involved, not on my part anyway.'

'There you are then. It's in the genes.'

'He was my adoptive father.'

'Oh, I see. Sorry.'

'It's okay.' Gus gave a reassuring smile. 'You think this is all right then?'

Millie looked at the panel he was holding up, the better for her to see.

'Of course it is. I love it.'

'I never want to start this,' Gus said, 'but once I do it takes me away, you know?'

'We all need something that does that,' Millie replied, a shade too quickly.

94

She felt the heat of Gus's questioning gaze. Avoiding his eye, she picked up the scissors and snipped off her thread. 'I don't think I know who I am any more.'

'That's something else we have in common then.'

He came again the following Monday. Millie tried not to act either too surprised or too pleased, but suspected she failed on both counts. She rather liked knowing he felt at ease about dropping in unannounced and, she noted with some amusement, empty-handed. Embroidery, apparently, was not on today's agenda. Unfortunately, his ease extended to his lifting the flap in the counter and marching straight through to the back room where her latest attempts at wording a newspaper ad were strewn across the table, along with Karen's photo.

'Want to tell me about it?'

Millie felt no pressure from Gus's directness. She could tell him or not, as she wished, and nothing would have changed. His lack of pretence was one of the things she liked about him. She knew scarcely anything about this man, and yet suddenly she felt she could trust him with her life.

When she had finished her story, Gus said, 'It must be so hard to live with, day after day.' He seemed to be talking as much to himself as to Millie.

She swept up the frayed sheets from the notepad with their hesitant words and myriad crossings-out and shuffled them into a pile with the photo on top. Several times she had envisaged the photo, fuzzy and much enlarged, on a poster, like the ones outside police stations, but she knew it would never happen. To declare Karen publicly as a missing person would be to change her from the person she was into someone entirely different. *Missing.* It sounded so hopeless, so final. She picked up the photo and tucked it into her handbag.

'I don't even know if I'm going to put another advert in. I was only doing this because I can't just sit back and do nothing.'

'Karen's boyfriend, ex-boyfriend, this Jack,' Gus said carefully. 'The way you speak about him, it's as if he's really got to you. Forgive me if I'm wrong, but it's more than disapproval, isn't it?'

Millie leaned back from the table and wrapped her arms around herself. 'Is it?' Then: 'Yes, okay. The truth is he scares me rigid but I'm the fool to let him, aren't I?'

'Not at all. We can't necessarily predict our reactions or control them. There's always that element of surprise, the thing that grabs us by the hand and won't let go.' Gus smiled, a little sadly. 'That's what I've learned, anyway.'

Millie waited for Gus to elaborate. Instead he said, 'Jack seems to be the stumbling block here. Am I right?'

Certainly he was. Although Millie had not put it into words, it was becoming increasingly clear that Jack must be dealt with in some shape or form before she could move a step closer to finding Karen. She had given Gus the censored version of the Jack O'Brien story – she couldn't bear to give voice to the rest, not now – but he was astute enough to deduce that it wasn't just a classic case of mother opposes unsuitable boyfriend.

'Stumbling block? Yes, that's one way of putting it.' She smiled ruefully.

'Millie, do let me know if there's any way I can help, although I can't at the moment think how.'

'You're very kind, but I'll sort it out, somehow or other. Now, let's get that kettle on, shall we?'

Chapter Twelve

'Fear is a luxury, a diversion. It stops you knowing what's real, doing what you're supposed to do.' Gus sprinkled salt on his chips, picked one up with his fingers and ate it.

'That's very deep,' Millie said, 'and very true, although I've never thought of it that way before.'

'I can be deep when I want to.'

'Yes, I'm sure you can. I didn't mean…'

Gus smiled. 'I'm just joshing.'

Millie blushed a bit, or it could have been the heat from the fish and chips. He liked it when she blushed, not that she did it that often but it gave him a kind of inverse pleasure to know that he had the power to make it happen. It was Saturday evening and they were sitting at his kitchen table. He had been surprised to receive her phone call but pleased that she'd come straight to the point, saying there was something she would really like his opinion on and would he mind coming to her house rather than the shop as it would be easier without interruption.

Gus had immediately jumped one step further and invited Millie to Hangburton; it was high time somebody came other than Jessica – preferably a woman, preferably an attractive one. And besides, if she came to him, he wouldn't need to curtail his alcohol consumption which on a Saturday night was pretty much unthinkable.

Millie had not hesitated about accepting his invitation, which was refreshing in itself; he'd grown tired of the game-playing that many younger women indulged in. He admired the way she was obviously enjoying her food, too, and she was eating the batter round the fish instead of fussily picking it off and making an unholy mess of the whole business, as Jessica had. Neither had he felt the need to apologise for the meal not being the fruits of his own labours but those of Christos at *The Cod Plaice* down the road.

'The annoying thing is,' Millie said, reaching for the vinegar, 'I'm not normally this indecisive. I can usually make up my mind without turning to all and sundry. Oh, not that you're all and sundry…'

Gus laughed. 'I'm flattered you came to me but, like you, I don't really know what's best. If you did manage to speak to Jack, though, there's no guarantee you'd get anything out of him and then you'd have gone to all that trouble for nothing.'

Millie sighed. 'I know. It's just that the other day, when you said he was the stumbling block, that's exactly how I feel, that I have to do something about him and stop ducking the issue.'

'Self preservation isn't ducking.'

'No, but it's not me I should be thinking about, it's Karen. Oh Gus, he's such a low-life. I hate saying that about somebody but in his case it's true. How could she have got mixed up with a boy like that? What does she see in him?'

'Ah, now you've got me.'

'It's all right,' Millie said, brightening. 'I don't expect an answer to that. I think I just needed to talk about it, to someone different, and now I've done that I feel so much better. Charmaine's lovely – she's my friend I told you about – and Jet's been a rock, but they've heard it all before, too many times, probably.' She pulled a face.

Gus couldn't help feel a whisper of jealousy at the mention of Jet, the bloke from the skateboard shop with whom he sensed Millie shared a certain closeness. He pushed the feeling away. He wished he could say something to help but the truth was he felt as much at sea as Millie did, more so, because he couldn't help feeling she hadn't told him the full story. This fear she had of Jack had its roots buried far deeper than she'd admitted but he wasn't going to push her to tell him more. He might upset her and that was the last thing he wanted. She'd come to him, as far as he could work out, to seek his approval of her plan to track down this Jack character and cross-question him, probably because her other friends had not given theirs. They had a point, but Gus was unwilling to commit himself; he didn't know enough about the situation and the people concerned, and whatever he said could turn out to be entirely wrong.

'All I will say, Millie, is that you shouldn't take any risks with your personal safety. I could always go with you, if you do decide…'

He tailed off, feeling suddenly embarrassed at his presumptuousness, but Millie gave him an engaging smile and said, 'Let's talk about something more cheerful, shall we?'

She got up from the table and cleared both their plates away. That was another thing Gus liked, the way she seemed so comfortably at ease being here in his house, even though they had never before met beyond the confines of the shop.

'Cheerful? Like what?'

'Like you, for instance?'

Gus had felt sorry to disappoint Millie. There seemed very little that was cheerful about him at the moment. He hadn't meant to say anything, hadn't wanted to steal Millie's moment because the evening was for her, and that was how he'd intended it to stay. But once they had moved through to the sitting room, out it had all come, all the worries about his birth mother, his adoption, his damn-fool inheritance. If Millie was surprised by his sudden outpouring she didn't show it. Instead she gave subdued little nods as his narrative unfolded, interjecting only when he needed encouragement to continue. Gus felt relieved and grateful, and all the more disposed towards wanting to protect her. He must be going soft in his old age.

Had Millie said she thought it was high time he put all this behind him, he would have readily agreed with her, but she didn't. In fact, she said the opposite, that life had a habit of catching up with you just when you thought you were safe, and even though thoughts were just thoughts and not all of them true, it didn't necessarily mean you could make them go away.

'Now who's being deep?' he had countered, and they'd laughed.

99

He had shown her the copy of Catherine's birth certificate, handing it to her almost reverently as though it was the most precious thing in the world. Perhaps he had felt that way because it was the only link he had to his birth mother's life before he intruded so disastrously upon it. More likely, though, it was the mood of the evening which, together with the wine, had heightened his emotions and made him feel weirdly apprehensive, as if he was on some sort of precipice.

Millie had no more idea about the certificate than he had but apparently she'd researched her own family history and knew how to go about these things if Gus thought it would help. He couldn't immediately think how it would but he thanked her all the same.

He had thanked her, too, for offering to help him sort out Augusta's bedroom, once he had admitted there was still some kind of internal barrier preventing him from getting on with it. Millie was a demon with a paintbrush, she told him, smiling. He could well believe it. It was an attractive proposition; with Millie working alongside him, merrily slapping emulsion on to walls, he might be able to keep his maudlin thoughts at bay and possibly even enjoy the job. But even he was enough of a gentleman to realise that it was too much to ask.

He would go and see her again soon, ask her how she was and if she'd made any progress in her search for her daughter, whom he had cursed many times in private for putting her mother through such purgatory. He would, however, stay off the subject of his own personal drama if possible. At least then he might be able to stop all this pointless rumination.

'This is all right, still, isn't it?' Millie wrestled with her end of Augusta's fawn bedroom carpet, yanking the corner from beneath the chest of drawers and wrinkling her nose against the escaping dust. 'Say if it's not, because we can stop and I'll toddle off home.'

Clutching his end of the carpet, Gus looked up sharply. 'No, please don't go.'

Aware of the neediness in his voice, he wondered yet again what he was turning into. He ran his grubby free hand through his hair. 'What I mean is, I'm fine to carry on and I'd be grateful if you'd hang around a bit. I wish you'd concentrate on tea-making, though, and leave the heavy stuff to me.'

Millie blew upwards, sending her corn-coloured fringe into a Mexican wave. 'No chance. I'm stronger than I look. You stand still and I'll start rolling.'

'We'll roll together.' Gus stepped onto the strip of wooden floor already exposed, skirted the bed and took his place beside Millie. She smelt of dust and roses.

'What's happening about the shop today? Did you close it?' Gus tried not to pant as the two of them, plus carpet, lumbered towards the middle of the room. Millie's face was pink but otherwise she seemed as fresh as when she'd arrived whereas he was already flagging.

'Charmaine's doing this morning and Jet's taking over after lunch. He shuts Wednesday afternoons.'

Gus mentally cursed himself. Of course Millie wouldn't close the shop in the middle of the week and sacrifice a day's business just for him. He felt a prickle of unease at the mention of Jet; judging by the shadowy impression he'd gained as he'd peered through the skateboard shop window while pretending to inspect the offerings on display, he didn't seem at all the type of person to be dispensing ribbon and baby wool.

Gus pulled a length of thick string from his pocket and double-tied it round the rolled-up carpet before manoeuvring it into an upright position by the door. The floorboards were in fair condition. All they would need was sanding and sealing; the people who had done the downstairs floors could do that.

'What are you going to do with the furniture? Are you keeping any of it?' Millie plumped down on the bed, shook off her shoes and flexed her bare feet.

'The bed's definitely going. I don't know about the rest. It isn't exactly beautiful, is it?'

'Circa 1950 doesn't tend to be. Real wood, though, not veneer, at least I don't think so.'

Millie stood up, went over to the dressing table and rubbed at a mark on the top with her finger, then opened a drawer and peered inside.

'A second-hand shop might be interested, or a charity. You could ring round.'

'Or I could just take a hammer to the lot,' Gus said, thinking Millie's suggestions sounded like far too much bother.

She laughed. 'You'd enjoy that, wouldn't you?'

'You know me so well.'

Millie paused in her inspection of the dressing table, her hand stilled on the drawer handle, and looked into the spotted mirror, meeting Gus's gaze. There was something in her expression he couldn't fathom… It was gone.

She smiled, turning round to face him. 'So what's next? Shall we take the rest of the pictures down and stack them somewhere?'

'We could, I suppose.'

As Gus looked around at the wreckage of his aunt's bedroom, her face swam across his line of vision; not the sunken, undefined face he'd last seen framed by stiff NHS cotton but the firm-jawed, keen-eyed version he'd known as a child. His father's face appeared alongside, eyes kindly behind wire-rimmed spectacles, smile indulgent, and Gus felt a great wall of sadness engulf him, sending him lunging across the room to the window. Forcing up the casement, he stood clutching the frame, shoulders heaving, fighting to take in air.

'Gus?'

Millie was beside him, tentative fingers warm on his bare arm. After a moment he peeled himself from the window.

'Sorry. I felt a bit weird. I'm all right now.'

'Perhaps it was too soon after all,' Millie said gently. 'Why not give it a rest now?'

'In a minute. I'll just do these.'

He took down the remaining pictures and stood them with the Allingham print he had removed when he'd first come in here, then clambered onto the bed to detach the lightshade, coughing as a shower of dust came down with it. Millie was right, they'd done enough for one day. The curtains were down, the carpet up, the surfaces cleared, the drawers emptied, the cardboard boxes filled.

He didn't know what he would have done without Millie

today. Nothing at all, he suspected. Idly he picked at a seam in the blancmange-flowered wallpaper. It should come off easily enough, but that was for another time.

'What about this? Is this going?' Millie was examining the dark-wood piano stool that stood in front of the dressing table.

'Why, do you think I should keep it?'

'I would. The carving on the legs is ever so pretty and the tapestry on the seat is in quite good condition. If you look closely, the colours are lovely. They'd come up beautifully if it was cleaned.'

'Would you like it?' Gus asked, on impulse.

'Me? Oh no, I couldn't. It should stay here. This is where it belongs.'

'It's only a stool. It doesn't know where it belongs. Not my kind of thing, anyway.'

'Well then, I'd love to have it, but if you change your mind you must promise to tell me and back it comes. Promise, go on.'

'I promise.' Gus bowed his head in mock solemnity, then they both laughed.

Millie knelt down and lifted the lid of the piano stool. 'Better see what's in here first. Might be the family silver.'

'It's only old sheet music and stuff. I already looked,' Gus said, but Millie was pulling out the contents, glancing at each piece of paper before stuffing it into the top of one of the boxes.

'Music, like you said. What happened to the piano?'

'She got rid of it years ago. I don't ever remember her playing.'

'Look at these old knitting patterns.' Millie held one up for Gus to see. The wide blue eyes of a plump baby in a white knitted romper suit stared back at him. 'They're all baby patterns. Funny place to keep them. Your aunt didn't have children, did she?'

'No, but I expect she knitted for other people's. Robert and me, for instance.'

Gus's voice caught in his throat. He was starting to feel a bit odd again. Millie was still rooting about in the piano stool, lifting out layer after layer of discoloured tissue paper until she held in her hand a crumpled piece of off-white material. She shook it out and he could see that it was a bag with a drawstring, like the one his mother had made for his school plimsolls with his name embroidered in chain stitch. Pulling apart the top, Millie peered inside for a long moment, then sat back on her heels and glanced meaningfully up at him.

'I think you'd better look at this.'

Not plimsolls, then. Gus sank down on the floor beside Millie. He took the bag from her and held it in both hands. The rough cotton felt like cheap sheeting against his skin. He could feel things inside, small things, soft things, and something bigger, a book perhaps. For some reason he was afraid to look.

'What's in it?'

'I don't know. Do you want me to. .?' Millie offered.

'No, it's all right.' Gus opened the top of the bag fully, tipped the contents out on to the floorboards and laid the bag next to them.

'The embroidery on this is beautiful,' Millie said softly, putting her hand out to it but not touching. 'The stitches are so fine.'

Gus looked at the circle of yellow flowers and pale green leaves that embellished one side of the bag, each delicate petal and leaf perfectly constructed. Tiny, bright blue birds nestled amongst the leaves, and within the circle was the letter *M* in darker blue, underlined by a row of small red hearts.

'Does it mean anything to you, the initial *M*?'

'My name's Matthew. Matthew Augustus.' Gus forced himself to smile, although his heart was pounding. 'How's that for an old-fashioned moniker?'

'And the rest?' Millie indicated the contents of the bag.

Gus began to pick them up, one by one. There was a slim, silver bracelet engraved with a rose design, expandable but still only child's size, and a pair of shabby grey gloves made of feather-soft suede material, kid, he thought. He'd been right about the book; it was a bible, bound in dimpled dark green leather, its pages tissue-thin and gold-edged. He opened it. There was writing inside the cover in faded black ink: *Catherine Mary Harte, 26 Harper Crescent, Newcastle.* The painstaking line of script wobbled and dipped at the end, the last letters squashed together to fit.

Gus frowned over the next item, a torn piece of washed-out flowered cotton attached to a plain white button. He looked at Millie but she merely returned his look, her eyes offering encouragement. Lastly, there was a cheap brooch in the form of a poodle, black, with a red collar and a diamanté eye.

He stared at the pathetic little collection of mundane objects, hoping for a sign, a message, anything to help him make sense of this, give him the truth he needed, but nothing came.

'I've never seen these things before. Why are they here? I don't know what they mean, whose they are.'

Help me.

'Except the bible. We know whose that is. Was,' Millie said, quietly.

Gus nodded slowly. 'Do you think the other things were hers, too?'

Millie didn't reply at once. She sat very still, biting her lower lip, choosing her words.

Gus sighed and briefly closed his eyes. If Millie had something to say, which clearly she did, he wished she'd get on and say it because he sure as hell didn't know how much longer he could go on carrying the weight of all this... *feeling*.

'I may be wrong, but...' Millie began. Gus waited. 'Years ago, there were institutions where mothers could take their babies if they were in such desperate straits they were simply unable to keep them. It was a way of ensuring they were properly cared for, the only way in most cases. An act of pure, unselfish love, when you think about it.' Millie gave an emphatic nod. 'The babies would be sent in with little tokens. Some were just a scrap of material with a prayer or the child's name embroidered on, or a button or a strip of lace from the mother's own clothes, things that were worthless in themselves but precious nonetheless. They were used as a means of identification if the mother should ever go back to reclaim her child.'

Millie paused. She picked up the button attached to its

shred of cotton and ran her finger slowly round its rim before setting it down again.

Gus swallowed. 'Go on.'

'I know this isn't the same, but perhaps Catherine left these things as her way of letting you know who you are, and who she was. And to tell you that she loved you.'

'You really think that?' Gus asked quietly.

'I do, possibly because I want it to be true, for your sake, but it makes a kind of sense. It does to me, anyway.' Millie spoke tentatively, as if she was afraid of misleading him, but at the same she was convinced she was right. He could see it in her eyes.

'But why did it take all this time for me to find out about them? If it is true, and these things were always mine, why did my aunt hide them from me? Why did she even have them in the first place? I can't see what any of this has to do with her.'

'I don't know, Gus. That's a part of the mystery that might never be solved, now she's gone. She may not have hidden the things deliberately. The bag wasn't that well hidden, was it? Perhaps she just put it away at the time and forgot about it.'

Gus couldn't speak any more. He picked up the silver bracelet, tracing the engraved twining rose with his fingertip, noticing for the first time that it was bent slightly out of shape. He imagined the innocent chafe of metal against the slender blue-veined wrist of a young girl, the girl who became his mother and whose image, ghostly and insubstantial, existed only inside his imagination, for he had no way of knowing what she looked like, which of his traits and physical attributes he had inherited from her. Nor would he ever know.

'*No.*' The bracelet dropped to the floor with a clatter. 'You're wrong. None of this is anything to do with me. It's just a bag of scraps, that's all.'

He heard his own voice, vehement, echoing in the almost empty room. But despite its loudness, Millie didn't seem to be listening. Instead she was deep inside her own thoughts.

'Remarkable things,' she said, so quietly he barely heard. 'That was sometimes how they referred to the tokens. Remarkable things.'

Chapter Thirteen

'I'll be off home now,' Millie said, getting to her feet. 'You'll be better on your own. You know where I am if you need me.'

A warm, meaningful hug, a perfunctory kiss on his cheek, then before Gus had time to gather himself together and see her out, she was down the stairs and away.

The careful click of the front door resounded through the house, leaving the silence that followed to creep through the rooms like smoke. Gus came out onto the landing and, without looking back, closed the door on Augusta's room and went quickly downstairs, jumping the last few steps. Somewhere to the right of his peripheral vision dangled a great iron ball of sadness that threatened to demolish him with one almighty swing if he so much as stopped to think. He must keep moving, attack the rest of his day as if were a military operation. It was the only way.

Change bed; scrub bath; put washing in; take washing out; hang up. Finish digging out roots of old shrubs, add to mountainous pile at end of garden (mental note to find out local laws on bonfires); sweep path. Go for a run before dinner (had he had lunch?); watch news; pour small drink; not watch new crime drama; pour larger drink; sit in dark for hours trying to think of nothing in particular; bed.

He slept surprisingly soundly throughout the whole of what constituted his night, having eventually crawled upstairs at around three-thirty and woken just before midday. But instead of feeling refreshed after this marathon of unconsciousness, his mouth was as sour and furry as a decomposing lemon, his legs felt as if they'd been soaked in embalming fluid, and a high-pitched whistling sound accompanied his every move which, upon investigation, appeared not to be coming from anywhere outside but from within his own head.

Thursday. He'd planned to go to an open-air exhibition of sculpture in Regent's Park. It was too late now, and today was the last day. Still in his night-time attire of t-shirt and boxer shorts, he stomped downstairs and snapped the kettle on. Flicking open the lid of the bread bin, he surveyed the uninspiring contents – half a rock-hard baguette and two stale currant buns – and let the lid fall shut with a bang.

The doorbell sounded. Raising his eyes to the ceiling, he loped to the front door and opened it, to be confronted by Jessica wearing several tubefuls of cherry lip gloss, a pair of eye-wateringly tight denim shorts and a white lacy smock top, obviously with nothing underneath since he could see her nipples through the holes in the lace. All of this, to the untrained eye or otherwise, conspired to look fairly desperate.

Remembering his state of undress, Gus's hands flew to cover the fly of his boxer shorts.

She laughed. 'Nothing I haven't seen before.'

Flashing her eyes at him, she walked in, closed the door behind her and, standing coquettishly, and unnecessarily, on tiptoe, fastened her lips to his as one hand grasped the back of his head and the other delved beneath the waistband of his boxers. Gus recoiled as if he'd been shot, unplugging her mouth from his and forcing the hand to withdraw with a snap of elastic but failing to detach her from his person altogether. She merely approached from a different angle, flung both arms around his neck and began nuzzling his ear.

'Jess, please. Get off me, will you?'

The arms fell away. She stepped back, doe eyes gazing balefully at him. Oh God, she wasn't going to cry, was she?

She sniffed, seeming to recover herself. 'I only came to talk to you.'

She could have fooled him.

He lifted his hands. 'What's there to talk about? Look, I'm not in the mood and if you must know I'm feeling completely crap, so can you go now please.'

It wasn't a question. Nevertheless, Jessica seemed to be

considering her options. While she did so, she wandered into the sitting room and parked herself on the sofa. Gus followed, but remained standing, a few feet away.

'No, I don't think I can,' Jessica said, her forefinger dimpling her chin.

'Can what?'

'Go. Now.'

'Well, I'm asking you to. Actually no, I'm not asking, I'm telling.'

Gus was having enormous difficulty remaining upright but sitting down, next to her or anywhere else, would be tantamount to giving in. The room swayed around him. He squeezed his hands into fists, digging the nails into his palms.

'That's not very nice.' Jessica pouted, making full use of the doe eyes again.

'Well, I'm not very nice, not nice at all in fact, and the sooner you realise that the better it'll be for both of us.'

'I don't agree. That you're not nice. You always were before.'

Gus threw up his hands and rocked back on his heels. 'And that is the problem, isn't it? We get together for what... all of five minutes? and you think you know who I am and what I am and you're wrong, you're *so* wrong, because whatever it is, was, that you saw in me it's all in your imagination and I am so not the person you thought I was, because nobody ever is! *Do you understand?*'

Gus heard his own voice rising as hysteria threatened. What on earth was he rambling on about? He really had no idea. All he knew was that he had to get her out of here and, short of bodily removing her, for which he doubted he had the strength, he couldn't see how he was going to achieve it. His little speech, however, seemed to have had some effect because Jessica stood up, looking understandably confused now as well as upset, and was making for the door. The straps of the smock top had come adrift somehow, the neckline drooping perilously low and sideways, exposing almost the whole of one breast. She hauled bad-temperedly at it, wrenching it round and causing the thin material to rip below her armpit.

109

'Now look what you've made me do!'

She was near to tears. Gus wavered, but only for an instant. He really didn't like her much any more and, astonishingly, didn't even fancy her. Safe in this knowledge, he took a step closer and softened his voice. The least he could do was try to be kind.

'Don't upset yourself over me, Jess. I'm not worth it. I'll see you around, okay?'

'But...'

'No. No buts. I'm sorry.'

He padded out to the hall, ushering her along with him. At the front door, she stopped and looked moistly up at him.

'You do know I'm in love with you, don't you?'

Gus didn't answer. He opened the door and, miraculously, Jessica went through it. Closing it behind her, he leaned against it for a minute, breathing heavily, then climbed tiredly upstairs, consoling himself with the thought that she would calm down eventually.

Perhaps it was his fault for avoiding her since the art exhibition episode. It hadn't been easy. Everywhere he went – the deli, the little supermarket, the museum café – Jessica seemed to have got there first, as if she had second sight and knew his movements before he did. He'd become shamefully expert at doubling back or switching direction and picking up speed. The closest he'd come to an encounter was when he'd seen her waving at him from the other side of the high street. He'd waved briefly back before engaging in conversation with the landlord of the Dog and Trumpet who'd conveniently come out to water his hanging baskets. By the time he glanced furtively back, Jessica was flouncing away down the street like a sulky teenager.

Sidonie hadn't been overjoyed at his missing two embroidery group meetings in a row and had greeted his vague apologies with grudging acceptance but for the time being it was best if he steered clear. It would all settle down, in time. Meanwhile, he'd have to be on his guard in case Jessica decided to spring any more surprises.

He didn't feel comfortable about any of this; he felt

cornered, and resentful that Jessica had given him something more to worry about on top of his other troubles.

A car stopped outside. Seconds later, he heard its door close. Hurrying to the bedroom window, he looked down, hoping it was Millie. He'd half-expected her to come back today, or perhaps that was wishful thinking. But of course it wasn't her, just the district nurse for the old man two doors down. Gus sighed. If there was anyone he wanted to be with right now, it was Millie. She was so easy to talk to, so non-judgemental; she seemed to have a stabilising effect on him. It was probably just as well she hadn't come, though, considering recent events. The thought brought a smile to his face as he stripped off and stepped into the shower. What would she have made of Jessica, had she witnessed that little display? He couldn't begin to imagine, except that Millie Hope didn't have an unkind word to say about anybody – unless they thoroughly deserved it, like that Jack character.

After his shower, Gus dressed quickly then pushed open the door of Augusta's bedroom and stood on the threshold for a tense moment before going in. The window gaped open as he had left it and a lungful of muggy air daydreamed into the room. He went to close it, the newly-naked floorboards complaining beneath his weight. Beside the dressing-table, the piano stool stood at a careless angle, its lid uplifted, the drawstring bag and its random contents spread out at its claw-shaped feet as if they were left over from some bizarre ritual. He stooped to pick up the bible, bracelet, gloves and brooch, and placed them inside the bag. Lastly, he picked up the button clinging to its sad floral fragment, pressed it briefly to his lips and dropped it inside.

Suddenly it occurred to him that there might have been more, other things more meaningful, like a photograph or a letter, something he could have understood; he didn't know why he hadn't thought of it before. These things had passed through other hands, made other journeys, as he had. There was no way of telling if they had survived intact, been preserved down the years without interference, well-meant or otherwise. In any case, if it was true and they were intended for him, why had he never been given them and why did Augusta have them and not his adoptive parents?

He thought about Augusta, the power she'd exerted over him, using legal declaration as its justification. How easy it was to manipulate, to fashion the lives of others by actions that could never be called to account. But then, wasn't that precisely what his birth mother had done?

Screwing the bag tightly in his hand, carrying it down low by his side, he went to his own bedroom and tucked it away at the back of the shelf inside his wardrobe beneath a pile of jumpers.

Chapter Fourteen

'She wanted the best for me, didn't she?'

Gus couldn't bring himself to say the word 'love' in connection with his mother, even to Millie; it felt embarrassing and self-pitying. Besides, he was still unconvinced that this was the message implied by the piano stool find.

'Yes, I'm sure she did.'

'And yet she...' Gus clutched the phone more tightly.

'Perhaps she thought that removing herself completely *was* the best thing she could do for you, in which case you could say it was an act of heroism,' Millie said. 'Or she may not have made a decision at all. She may have acted on a terrible impulse while her mind was disturbed. There could be any number of reasons. Gus, you aren't blaming yourself for what happened to her, are you?'

He hesitated. There had been a dark moment when he'd felt responsible for Catherine's death, but it was only a moment – the irrationality of it had soon struck home. There were plenty of other culprits: her parents, religion, society in general, or – he had to force himself to think this – the shadowy figure of the man who had fathered him.

'No, I'm not blaming myself, but if she wanted to cut herself out of my life completely why did she leave me those things? Why bother?'

If she did leave them; it was only a theory, after all. He didn't say this to Millie. She seemed so convinced.

'Because she knew she was putting you up for adoption and she had months to plan for it,' Millie was saying. 'She would have gone into St Christopher's well before you arrived. The mothers always did.'

'Yes, of course. I'm being stupid.' His brain cells seemed to have felted together like a boil-washed woollen jumper.

'You're confused, that's all.' Millie paused, then she said carefully, 'Gus, how did you know Catherine died that way, in the river?'

'My father told me because I asked him. I think that was one reason I tried to get the death certificate, to see it written down. Now I'm not sure why I wanted to, though.'

'That was very honest of him. I'm not sure I could have done that.'

'No, well, that's the kind of man he was. Open, straightforward.'

Gus flinched inwardly as he realised what he'd said. Straightforward? That hardly fitted the bill now, did it? Millie, thankfully, didn't pick up on it, but then she wouldn't, would she? She would never put anything into his head that was likely to cause him additional distress, not if she could avoid it.

Millie was speaking again. 'Do you ever wonder about your natural father? You've never said.'

'That's because I don't wonder,' Gus said, a shade vehemently. 'If he didn't hang around long enough to be named on my birth certificate, let alone do the decent thing and stand by her, then what's there to wonder about? The chances are he never even knew I existed.'

'Or he did and he was just as terrified as she was. He might have been young, like she was, and subject to parental pressure, too.'

'Yes, well, I'll never know now, will I? To be honest, I don't even care.'

There was a little silence, then Millie said, 'Sorry Gus. I didn't mean to hit a raw spot. I won't mention it again.'

She sounded subdued. Gus hoped he hadn't upset her. 'No, look, I'm sorry. I didn't mean to snap. You all right?'

'Of course.'

Gus could hear the smile in her voice. He waited a moment, then: 'So what do I do next?'

'What do you want to do?'

'I don't know.'

'Talk to Elspeth again?'

'I thought about it. Not a lot of point.'

Millie didn't speak again immediately. Gus could imagine her expression, very still, as it always was when she was thinking hard about something. He thought he heard a train rumble past.

Then she said, 'Okay, how about we do a bit of digging?'

'How d'you mean?'

'Catherine might have had siblings. If she did, and they're still alive…'

'They might be able to tell me something about her, something that would help?'

'Yes, but you'd have to be ready to hear things that might be a bit difficult, things that might not make you feel better. You know what I'm saying?'

'Yes, yes.' Gus grabbed at this suggestion and held on fast. After all, it was, at the moment, the *only* suggestion. Besides, he couldn't feel worse than he already did. 'So how do we do it?'

'I could do it for you if you'd like me to. I'd need her birth certificate, if you're all right to part with it for a while, or you could get a photocopy.'

'No, you have this one. I'll drop it in tomorrow.'

Gus ended the call on a riptide of relief and exhilaration, the intensity of which far outweighed the circumstances, he realised, but he didn't care. Something was happening, that was the important thing.

His buoyancy didn't last. Gus tried to relax and let some of Millie's sweet optimism rub off on him but it wasn't working. Even if she did find out that Catherine had siblings and they managed to track them down, then what? If Catherine was typical of girls in her time, those who had 'got themselves into trouble', she would have been ostracised by her whole family; her parents would have made sure of it. It was kind of Millie to concern herself with his problems, especially when she had enough of her own, but Gus was convinced now that it was a pointless exercise, and before long he felt as despondent as before.

It wasn't helping that somewhere in the back of his mind the unresolved question of Jessica still remained. Not that she'd given him any more trouble, in fact he hadn't set eyes on her, but it was only a matter of time before their paths crossed and he had no idea how it would be. Ending relationships normally meant avoiding all contact until the danger was past – rule number one – but in a place as small as Hangburton there was no chance of that. Neither could he withdraw from the wall-hanging project, not without causing a rumpus. Besides, sewing the panels gave him pleasure, allowed him to forget everything else, even if it was only for a few hours at a time.

Perhaps he should have a word with Sidonie and put her in the picture, provided he could get her on her own. But that idea was promptly quashed when she swept past him in the high street one morning with barely a nod in his direction and a distinctly frosty expression. Great. So now he was about to ostracised by the whole of the village on top of everything else.

He was saved from the potential ordeal of the next embroidery group meeting by a well-timed invitation to Millie's house for supper and a 'chat'. She wouldn't say what about but her tone indicated she had news, and it was with a certain amount of trepidation that Gus lifted the fish-shaped door knocker on Friday evening.

He had always liked Star Street – a neat terrace of slate-roofed ex-railway workers' houses hugging the brow of the hill overlooking Park Station. If he had had to guess which house was Millie's he would have guessed correctly. The exterior walls were painted a light, summery blue and the little gravelled square of garden hosted several enormous terracotta pots spilling over with pink and white geraniums and something lime green and frothy that he couldn't instantly name. A gold-coloured sun fixed to the wall beside the door beamed a smile just as welcoming as the human version that greeted him, although behind the smile Millie seemed slightly on edge.

'It's only pasta,' she said, leading the way to a cosy room with buttery yellow walls and a vast red sofa banked with a multi-coloured mountain range of tapestry cushions.

'Perfect.' Gus smiled as the embrace of the sofa and the promise of comfort food brought his anxiety levels down to almost zero. Whatever Millie had or had not discovered, he felt sure he could handle it now, as long as he didn't have to wait too long.

He didn't. The bowl of pasta still steamed gently on the cushioned tray in front of him when Millie, beside him on the sofa, suddenly said:

'I found her. Cecelia, Catherine's sister, which makes her your natural aunt, of course. There aren't any more, only her.'

'Bloody hell.' Gus dropped his fork, smattering the tray with tomatoey sauce. 'I mean, I wasn't expecting…'

Millie smiled. 'Sorry if it's a bit of a shock but you knew I was looking.'

'It's just so fast.'

'I know. The records all matched up straight away. They don't always.'

'And you can get all that on the internet?'

'You can now. You have to join up to a site in order to view the actual records and make doubly sure you've got the right person, check birth dates, places, parents' names. I checked very carefully, lots of times, made sure it all tallied, and I searched the electoral registers for up-to-date information.'

Gus undid another button on his black polo shirt and tugged the collar away from his neck to let in air.

'Edwin James Harte and Hilda Mary Harte, formerly Redshaw.' He spoke the names almost to himself, seeing them in his mind's eye just as they were written on Catherine's birth certificate.

'Catherine's parents, yes.'

'And, what else?'

'Don't let your food go cold. I'll get you another beer in a minute.'

Obediently Gus took up his fork. 'Better not, thanks, as I'm driving.' Besides which, his liver would turn to sponge if he continued to attack it the way he had been doing.

Millie waited until they'd finished eating and she'd taken away the trays before she said, 'I know where she is. Cecelia.

At least I'm fairly sure. She was born in 1940, two years after Catherine, which makes her seventy now. She married a Josiah Punchard and they're still in the Newcastle area.'

'Blimey, you have been busy.'

Gus thought guiltily about Millie poring over the computer night after night, because that's what she must have done in order to have come with all this information so quickly.

'Do you mind?'

'What? No, not at all. I'm impressed, that's all.'

Gus tried to marshal his thoughts. He had an aunt, a real, live, blood-related one, and an uncle who sounded as if he'd come straight out of Dickens. Had he wanted to know? Could he really cope with all this new information now that it was here in front of him? Millie had a cardboard folder beside her; he had only just noticed. She opened it now, revealing the birth certificate he had lent her and a sheaf of printed pages.

'Print-outs, from the records. As proof, kind of,' Millie said, passing him the folder.

'Thank you.'

Gus sat looking down at the papers, allowing his eyes to do no more than skim them randomly, catching a name here, an address there. He snapped the folder shut and dropped it on the floor in front of him as if it was red-hot.

'I won't look now. Another time, maybe.'

'It's yours. Take it with you.'

'When you said you know where she is, this Cecelia, do you mean you know where she is *now*?'

'They're in the phone directory, the online one. Thank goodness they're not ex-directory, otherwise we wouldn't have stood a chance.'

Millie had done well; it was true, he was impressed. It was what he'd wanted – information about his birth mother, some sort of clue as to who she was, where she came from, her real circumstances rather than those he'd dreamed up for her, and then he might, he just might, achieve peace of mind. So why did he feel so ambivalent about it now? He looked at Millie sitting quietly beside him. He couldn't keep on expecting her to come up with ideas, tell him what to do, could he? He had to get a grip, take control. God knew how.

'I could just ring her then, my aunt, simple as that.'

'You could. The number's in the folder. Or you could write, if you'd find it easier.'

'Or,' Gus said, dropping his gaze to the carpet, 'I could do nothing, leave it alone and hope it'll all go away of its own accord.'

'You don't believe it will, though, do you?'

Gus looked at Millie. She was gazing intently at him, her blue eyes soft with kindness and concern. It made his throat constrict.

'No, I guess I'm stuck with it.'

'So, will you contact her?'

'I don't know, Millie. I really don't. She might not want to speak to me.'

'Well, you'll never know unless you try.'

'You think I should, don't you?'

Millie reached across and took Gus's hand in both of hers. 'Only you can decide what's best, Gus. No-one else.'

She let go of his hand. He hadn't wanted her to. Just for a split second, it felt unbearably lonely to be separated from her. And just for a split second, he was tempted to kiss her, a temptation so strong that before he knew what he was doing he had leaned towards her and his lips were on hers, so lightly, so swiftly that it hardly qualified as a kiss at all.

The second one definitely qualified.

Chapter Fifteen

What *had* he been thinking about, kissing Millie? She was his friend, a special one, despite not having known her long; he'd shared so much of his inner life with her, and she with him, that they'd almost become each other's therapist. That was how it was between them, how he wanted it to stay, and Millie, by her reaction to his crassness, obviously felt the same. Only now he'd gone and ruined it. It wasn't even as if he could blame it on alcohol, which tended to be his top favourite cause of such embarrassing aberrations.

Had Millie kissed him back? Despite his obsessive replays of the moment, he still couldn't be sure. The second time, when he'd kissed her properly, her head had made contact with the back of the sofa; a certain amount of lip movement in response to the pressure was inevitable and proved nothing. Whatever, Millie had seemed equally shocked. She'd muttered something about having left the cooker on then taken herself off to the kitchen for a good two minutes, leaving him perched anxiously on the edge of the sofa while the kiss buzzed about the room like a trapped wasp.

She'd seemed normal when finally she did return, if a little pink in the face. He had, he thought, acted with similar composure but it had not been long before he'd found himself in the car and heading home, having politely refused coffee with the weak excuse that it would keep him awake all night. The politeness had continued on both sides, almost to the extent of formality, until the time had come when Millie could decently, and clearly with some relief, show him out of the house.

So now what was he supposed to do? Manners dictated that

he should ring or send a note to thank her for her hospitality, but since he'd already proved he was no gentleman it seemed somewhat futile. In fact it was probably best that he distanced himself from her altogether, at least until he could stop flinching every time he thought about it.

'Do you not think you're a bit long in the tooth to be fooling around with women's affections? It's high time you knew better, in my opinion.'

Sidonie sniffed and crossed her arms, slotting them into the ravine between her stately bosom and the swell of her stomach.

Gus couldn't help but agree, and not only on Jessica's account, but he wasn't about to admit as much. He shuffled his feet on grass that looked as if it was mown every other day and finished off with a pair of nail scissors. He felt like a schoolboy being hauled up before the headmistress. He resented the feeling.

'So are you going to tell me what happened? My daughter seems to think it's none of my business.'

Well, it's not, is it? Gus raised his head and gave Sidonie the benefit of a full-on, challenging stare.

'There really is nothing to tell.'

Sidonie hurrumphed, then changed tack as Gus began to walk away. A placating hand landed on his arm.

'I thought you were good for her, that's all. You seemed to be getting along so well, the two of you. I was so disappointed when Jess told me you'd called it off,' Sidonie said, making it sound as if he'd dumped her a week before the wedding.

She leaned conspiratorially towards him and whispered somewhere close to his left shoulder, although there was no-one else in earshot. 'She's not had an easy time of it, romantically speaking.'

Ah, so that was why Sidonie felt the need to poke her oar in. She was desperate to offload her daughter. He would not have considered it so impossible a task; she only had to perform her Mrs Bennett act on one, not a shed-load of them.

It was Tuesday afternoon and all eight members of the wall-hanging group – Rosemary from Beauty Untold, Grace from the post office, Sophie, Nicole and Gemma, whom Gus had privately tagged the Yummy Mummies, as well as Sidonie, Jessica and Gus – had gathered at Rosemary's house, a wedding-cake white affair on the main road outside the village with green roof-tiles the colour of cheap peppermint creams and sod-off gates which, on closer inspection, weren't so grand as they seemed since you had to get out of the car and open them yourself. Gus had nipped outside for a breather while the women tinkled about with tea cups and cake forks in Rosemary's dazzling kitchen, having summarily dismissed his half-hearted offer to help.

Coming here today and facing Jessica had been daunting enough as it was without being hassled by her mother. Jessica herself, as it happened, was proving relatively easy. Quieter than normal, she was focussing all her attention on her sewing, directing what little conversation she did make to the group in general. Bent over his own work, Gus had felt the heat of her gaze upon him at times, but that was all.

'Well, I'm sorry about that but I didn't upset her on purpose,' Gus automatically whispered back, then raised his voice to normal. 'There's no going back, if that's what you were wondering,' he said, feeling suddenly defensive.

It was at moments like this that he wished he smoked. He thrust his hands into his pockets and willed Sidonie to go back inside and leave him alone. Instead, she continued to stand next to him, clearly digesting his words and looking somewhat deflated.

He sighed. 'Look, Sidonie, I wouldn't worry about Jess if I were you. She'll be all right. After all, it's not as if she's exactly fresh out of the nest.'

He could have bitten off his tongue. Sidonie now looked not only deflated but shocked and a little hurt. He must have touched a nerve, referring to Jessica's age in such an off-hand manner.

'I am well aware of that,' Sidonie said, rising up and thrusting the chest at him. 'But then, as I have already pointed out, neither are you.' She stalked away up the garden and disappeared into the house.

Oh God. Gus gave a rockery stone a vicious little kick, then sucked his lips in sharply as the pain radiated from his big toe. From within the depths of the house, someone called that tea was ready. They would have to wait; he needed a few more minutes. He crossed to the other side of the garden and stood, hands behind his back, pretending to admire a contemporary water feature comprising a slab of grey stone the size of a railway hoarding down which a silky curtain of water slid before disappearing into a pebble-lined gulley with an expensive hiss. This latest garden accoutrement had apparently been designed, but not of course built, by Rosemary's husband, known at the Dog and Trumpet as Nouveau Nigel.

Gus liked Rosemary and Nigel, though. They were good-hearted people. How they spent their cash should not be up to their neighbours to decide. Even so, he couldn't help smirking as, five minutes later, he glanced through the inch-thick slab of glass supporting his tea and cupcake to meet the blank-eyed stare of a pair of alabaster dolphins glued together in a distinctly copulatory fashion.

Jessica had somehow managed to oust Grace from the chair next to him and had positioned herself sideways on it with her knees pointing firmly in his direction, effectively providing a barrier between him and the Yummies. She didn't like the way they flirted with him – she'd made that clear on a number of occasions – and Gus's return banter, heavy on the eye movements, had earned him more than one frosty stare which had fallen on stony ground. She seemed to think there was something wrong in people having fun that didn't include her. At least she had on a decent length skirt, Gus thought, noticing that she did look slightly abashed as they made eye contact.

'Your panels are fantastic, Jess, especially the one of the gibbet at Hangman's Corner. You've really captured the darkness of the subject,' he said truthfully.

'Do you think so?' Jessica visibly relaxed. 'Thank you. They're nearly finished. I'm going to help Mum with the border when they're done. Yours are coming on nicely. I like the way you've represented the battle with the little shields and things.'

Gus smiled. 'They were easier than soldiers.'

He looked up and caught Sidonie regarding the pair of them with intense interest, as was everyone else. Any minute now someone would fetch a light and shine it into his eyes. He scowled down at the embroidery on his lap, picking up the needle and stabbing it randomly into the material. Eventually, sensing nothing more was to come of the exchange between him and Jessica, the others returned to their own work.

After a while, Jessica suddenly bundled her sewing into a bag and stood up. 'Must fly. Hair to do before my date tonight,' she announced, unsubtly emphasising the word 'date', raising her eyes theatrically to the ceiling and looking sideways at Gus to make sure he was listening.

A general 'Woohoooo!' emanated from the group.

'Do we sense a new romance brewing?' Sophie asked, a touch insensitively.

'Oh, it's only Dan,' Sidonie said scathingly, with one eye on Gus. 'He's going to a fortieth birthday bash and she's his plus-one. They've known one another all their lives. They're practically brother and sister.'

Jessica turned bright red, cast her mother a look of pure hatred and stomped out of the room, ponytail swinging angrily. Seconds later, the front door banged shut, a car engine roared then puttered, presumably while Jessica struggled with the gates, then another bang and a final roar that faded into the distance.

Looks were exchanged among the group but nobody spoke for a while, until Rosemary turned to Sidonie and, with a pursing of lips and a knowing incline of her head, said, 'Send her along to the salon and I'll give her an Indian head massage. For free.'

Nicole offered Sidonie a lift home, thus drawing attention to the fact that she'd been left stranded.

'Thank you. That would be very kind,' Sidonie responded, smiling stiffly.

The group then rose as one, thanking Rosemary for her hospitality and scurrying towards cars or, in Grace's case, setting out for the walk home. They were great walkers, Grace and her husband, Gordon. Gus had seen them striding past his house on Sunday mornings, booted and anoraked, and carrying enormous backpacks. Gus offered Grace a lift. She declined but came and stood by his car as if she had something to say.

'I hope I'm not poking my nose in where it's not wanted...'

'No, go on.' Gus fired the key and sprung the locks.

'I was only going to say you don't want to be worrying about Sidonie. Her bark's worse than her bite.'

'Somehow I doubt that,' he said, entertaining a fleeting vision of Sidonie's incisors sinking excruciatingly into his fleshier regions.

If he had learned one thing about Jessica's mother it was that she held a certain amount of sway among the Hangburton residents, despite Grace's attempt at reassurance. He quite expected at any moment to find himself branded as some sort of lothario and outcast from the community altogether.

'I don't envy her, having *that* little madam for a daughter, make no mistake.'

The way in which Grace leaned eagerly towards him indicated that there was more to come on this subject, should Gus be a willing listener. He wasn't; he had no intention of being drawn into tittle-tattle about Jessica. Grace, however, planted her walking boots more firmly into the gravel.

'Did you know my Aunt Augusta?' he asked, more for reasons of diversion than a desire to know the answer, and in any case it seemed rude just to drive away.

'Oh *yes*. Well, as much as anyone knew her. I was born in this village. What I don't know *isn't worth knowing*.' She tapped the side of her bluish nose and winked.

Gus could well believe it, having wasted precious minutes standing helplessly in the post office queue while the chit-chat continued up ahead. But perhaps he could turn this situation to his advantage. He had never asked anyone in the village about Augusta before, thinking there was nothing anyone could tell him that he didn't already know and believing, mistakenly as it turned out, that his business was entirely his own. But now...

'What was your impression of her?'

'Impression? Well, I'd say she was *aloof*. I don't mean in a nasty way – she was pleasant enough and people liked her and respected her, oh yes, but she never got too much *involved*. There was always a kind of *mystery* about her. Of course, the less someone says about themselves the more they get talked about. Stands to reason.'

Doesn't it just, Gus thought. He was very tempted to let this drop now on the basis that nothing he had found out about his aunt so far had helped him in any way whatsoever, but curiosity urged him to see this out – that, and a new-found tendency to stick pins into himself.

'What was mysterious about her?'

Grace didn't answer his question directly. Instead she gazed unseeingly over Gus's shoulder towards the trees at the side of the road. 'Yes, it's funny the things you remember...' She looked back at him. 'I could only have been about six but it's come back to me, clear as day. We were in the park, my mother and I. There was a bit of a *playground*, not much, not like they've got now, just a couple of wooden swings and a little slide. I got off the swing and ran over to my mother. Your aunt was there, sitting on the seat next to her, and she had a *pushchair* with a child in it. They were talking, her and my mother.'

'What about?'

'Oh, this and that, like mothers do. I got bored and ran off.'

'Is that all you remember?'

'It was *afterwards*, when we went home for tea. My mother was telling my dad about the baby – little boy it was – saying that although Augusta had moved to Hangburton some months before, no-one had seen any sign of a husband and wasn't it *funny*.'

'But my aunt wasn't married. She didn't have any children.'

'Oh, I know that now, but at the time it seemed everyone was talking about this *baby* and wondering where he'd come from, and then of course the rumours started. Somebody said he must be Augusta's secret love-child and off it went, round the village like a blaze in a cornfield.'

'Did nobody think to ask her whose child it was?'

Gus was incredulous. Were they really so desperate for a spot of salacious gossip that they'd rather believe their own made-up stories than try and get at the truth?

'Oh yes, somebody plucked up the courage, eventually.'

Grace drifted off again. Gus waited, feeling his heart hanging weightily behind his ribs like a carcass on a butcher's hook.

'And?'

'Oh, right, well, *apparently* – and I didn't hear this, I wasn't there – but *apparently* she said he was her brother's boy and she looked after him from time to time to give his poor mother a break. Oh!' Grace looked intently at Gus as light dawned. 'Was that *you*, then? It *was*, wasn't it! Well, I *never...*'

'Yes, I think it must have been.' Desperate to escape now, Gus opened the car door and stepped in. 'And now I really must be going.'

Seconds later, he drove the car out on to the road, raising a hand to Grace. As he glanced in the mirror he saw her gazing after him, an expression of distinct excitement on her face as she embraced her latest newsflash and polished it to perfection in preparation for public release.

Over the next few days, Gus carried out surveys of two properties in Brighton then, having fired off the reports, kicked aimlessly about the house, not wanting to stay in, not wanting to go out.

His overriding emotion was one of anger on behalf of Liesel. She'd been a lovely mother to him, the very best. She was good and strong and wise – proud, too, as Elspeth had pointed out. She was not in any way, shape or form his *poor mother*. So why had she relinquished her care of him to a sister-in-law she hated, even if only for the occasional day? He couldn't have been that difficult.

It took a while for him to realise that the scrappy bit of information imparted by Grace was simply the product of her, possibly faulty, memory and the subject of loose gossip at the time. Unreliable, then, and yet Grace had been so certain, and it wasn't something she'd be likely to make up.

He rang Elspeth. 'Did Robert ever tell you that my mother – Liesel. I mean – had difficulty accepting me because I was adopted?'

'No, never. Why would she have?'

'What I said. I wasn't her natural child and it was harder than she thought.'

A silence, then: 'Gus, you're over-thinking this. You're looking for answers, I understand that, but you mustn't start fabricating.'

'I know, but...' and Gus told Elspeth exactly what Grace had told him. He seemed to wait forever for her reaction, but knowing Elspeth, she was considering her words carefully. He loved her for that.

'Even if that were true and Liesel did feel a bit overwhelmed at times, she wasn't a saint, Gus. She was an ordinary woman, a mother, doing the best she could. You can't ask more than that of anyone,' Elspeth said.

'I know, and I don't. It's just that all these things seem to be adding up, making everyone seem different from how I thought they were.'

'Yes, I can see how disconcerting that must be, but Gus, there could be a very simple explanation. Supposing Liesel wasn't well and Augusta wanted to help? Robert was older and able to look after himself, but he wouldn't have been much use with a baby, and your father had the business to take care of. Under those circumstances, wouldn't you have put aside your feelings and taken Augusta up on her offer? She was a nurse, remember.'

Gus sighed and raked his hair back with his free hand. 'Yes, I suppose so.'

When he'd said goodbye to Elspeth, he sat and tried to shuffle his thoughts into some kind of logical order. He didn't have first hand information and he hadn't had children himself, so how would he know exactly how parents felt, how they acted in any given situation? As usual, Elspeth was right. There was a simple explanation and he should accept and believe it; that was all he needed to do. In any case, wasn't it a good thing that Augusta had looked after him sometimes? Was it not further evidence of her generous nature?

He looked around him at the ultimate manifestation of this generosity. It was a good house and he appreciated being its owner. Yet even while he was telling himself this, the spectre of Robert swam before him until he was tempted to have a nameplate made and nail it to the wall by the front door: 'The Millstone'.

Gus wanted to talk to Millie. Even more, he wanted to be in the little back room at the shop, drinking tea and putting the world to rights. Several times he made it as far as the phone, until he remembered.

Feeling as if he would burst out of his skin unless he did something positive, he phoned Cecelia. And he was sober at the time.

'I do not speak to cold callers,' a haughty voice informed him, after he had explained with some difficulty the reason for his call. 'Please go away.'

'No, please, you don't understand. We're related. I'm your nephew. I'm called Gus but my real name is Matthew, Matthew Harte, as was.'

A frozen silence, then: 'How *dare* you? Ringing up here, pretending to be a relative! I warn you, I don't fall for scams.'

Fearing she was about to put the phone down, Gus heard himself wittering on, pouring out his words and tripping over them in his haste to make himself understood since this was, in effect, his only opportunity. Eventually, he tailed off.

'So you're claiming to be my sister's son and, as such, my nephew? Is that it?' Cecelia's voice had climbed down a little.

Gus sank into the chair with relief. 'Yes, that's it,' he managed, breathlessly.

'And what proof do you have of this, this... *connection*?'

'The usual. Birth certificates, records. You can see them if you like.'

'That won't be necessary.'

'Actually, I should point out that when I said I was your nephew, strictly speaking I'm not, not legally anyway, because of my adoption out of the family.'

Gus felt this was a point worth making in case Cecelia thought he was after her money.

'I am well acquainted with the laws of adoption, thank you. I was a legal secretary for many years. Assuming all this is above board and you are who you say you are, what is it that you want from me?'

It was only now that Gus became aware of the Geordie accent struggling to make itself heard above Cecelia's cut-glass pronunciation of the Queen's English.

'I don't want anything. No, that's not strictly true, of course, otherwise I wouldn't be ringing but I'll come to that in a minute. Cecelia...'– he heard the sharp intake of her breath as he made free with her name – 'I'm very sorry for shocking you like this. I should have written first, I see that now, but there seemed no way to wrap it up.'

'There is no need for *wrapping up*, as you so succinctly put it,' cut in Cecelia. 'I'm not weak in the head.'

'I wasn't suggesting that you were,' Gus persisted, 'but all the same I'm sorry if I've offended you by calling out of the blue.' An impatient sigh emitted from the other end. Gus took a breath and continued. 'I've been having some difficulty in coming to terms with my past. What I'm hoping to find out is whether you knew anything about the circumstances of my birth and why my mother... did what she did.'

Gus's forehead broke out in a sweat. This could be the moment when he began to make some sense of it. He transferred the phone, sticky with the heat from his palm, to the other hand.

'Well, obviously she couldn't keep the child. It was unthinkable. And now if you don't mind I really do not want to talk about this any longer.'

'No, hang on, I didn't mean why did she give me up for adoption. I meant what she did afterwards. Cecelia, do you have any idea about that, because if you have then I really need to know. Please,' he added. 'Catherine was only twenty-two. She had her whole life ahead of her...'

'How *dare* you speak her name to me? That name was never spoken in our house again, *never*, and I'll not hear it now!

We were a God-fearing family and she brought disgrace upon us. She was wicked, *wicked*, the spawn of the Devil!'

Gus reared up out of his seat. His heart gave an almighty thump. 'Don't speak about my mother like that! What gives you the right to judge? Have you never heard of compassion or forgiveness?'

'*Forgiveness*? Only God can forgive.'

'Well, it looks like he abandoned her along with everyone else!' Gus yelled. 'You destroyed her, you and all the rest of them killed my mother with your bigotry and your cruelty, and if that's what religion does then I'm glad I've no part in it!'

'We did no such thing. Whatever fate was in store for that lass, she brought it all on herself and I only hope she's spent her life repenting her sins.'

'Wait… wait a minute.' Gus faltered as the truth hit home. 'You didn't know, did you?'

'What didn't I know?'

'Catherine drowned herself, soon after I was born.'

Gus flinched as his own words sent spasms of pain through his body. A wave of dizziness captured him. He could hear movement at the other end but Cecelia didn't speak.

'Are you still there?' he demanded.

Silence, then: 'That is entirely irrelevant. My sister was dead to me from the moment she walked out of the door and I refuse to discuss it any further. Goodbye.'

Gus stared at the phone as he realised she'd cut him off. He put it back in its cradle and slumped forward, clasping his shaking hands together. He had never felt so alone in his life.

Chapter Sixteen

Millie stood by the window and watched as the green and yellow butt of the train disappeared round the bend in the track. He wasn't there. He hadn't been there last Thursday either, nor the one before that, neither had he been on an earlier train, a later train, or the same train but on a different day. And he hadn't phoned.

Obviously, he didn't want to see her. Obviously, she had done or said something to annoy him, or he had grown tired of her droning on about Karen and Jack. Obviously.

She had, of course, considered the possibility that something had happened to him, he'd had an accident or been taken ill, in which case some friend she had turned out to be since she had not even bothered to find out. It wasn't a likely explanation, though. Gus, she felt certain, had not been struck down by a deadly disease nor crushed beneath the wheels of the proverbial bus. It was never going to be that straightforward.

She missed him; she missed their friendship. But friends did not share kisses, not like that. Fighting her ambivalent feelings only gave rise to a strong sense of déjà vu as she thought guiltily of Jet. He and Gus might be poles apart in most respects but the outcome was the same; Millie wasn't looking for romance or sex or, heaven forbid, love. Not with anyone. There simply wasn't enough left in her emotional store. All she wanted was for things with Gus to go back to the way they were, before.

Charmaine thought she was over-dramatising. She didn't say so outright but that was what she meant when she advised Millie to forget what happened – if she really must – and treat Gus exactly as normal. Phone him, ask how he was, say anything, but just speak to him, put an end to the silence, and then Millie would discover that there was a perfectly good reason why he hadn't been in touch. Men, Charmaine said, were notoriously bad at communicating. They didn't necessarily mean anything by it; most of the time they simply forgot.

All this came after Charmaine had become so over-excited about Millie's brief encounter with her train man that she'd almost had to be forcibly restrained until Millie could make her understand that the whole thing had been a colossal mistake.

She wandered through to the shop, leaned on the counter and flicked idly through a catalogue that had come this morning. A sudden movement caused her to look up, just in time to see Jet zoom past the window at breakneck speed. Seconds later he zoomed past in the opposite direction, arms flailing, a daft grin on his face, and then a clattering noise followed by a heavy thump propelled Millie to the shop door. Jet was sprawled half on the pavement and half in the gutter while the skateboard, relieved of its load, careered blithely ahead.

Millie burst out laughing. Jet sat up, rubbing his skinned elbow and gazing up at her with a mock-doleful expression which made Millie laugh all the more. He grinned and hoisted himself to a standing position, clearly with more difficulty than he was prepared to admit.

'That cheered you up, didn't it?'

'Did you think I needed cheering up?'

Jet shrugged. 'Not necessarily. Been a bit down lately, though, I thought.'

'Just a bit,' Millie said, tempering this admission with a smile.

'Fancy pictures tonight?'

'Yes, all right.'

Jet rocked back on his heels, clapping a hand to his forehead. 'Blimey, that was easy. How about a drink after?'

'Don't push it,' Millie warned, but there was a smile on her face as she went back inside the shop, leaving Jet to retrieve the errant skateboard from where it had lodged behind the wheel of a parked car.

Life went on, with or without Gus Albourne.

The money had arrived, all one hundred and fifty thousand pounds of it. Millie had dealt with the paperwork weeks ago but felt curiously unaffected, as if it was a mundane chore, like sending in a meter reading. Then today, when she had typed in the password to her special new account and stared for several minutes at the impossibly large balance, excitement had rippled through her and almost made her laugh out loud until she remembered how she had come by it.

The shop door tinkled. Millie twisted round in her seat and leaned sideways to see who it was. Violet Mabey came halfway into the shop then backed out again to double-check that Frosty's lead was firmly tied to the railings and the lead securely anchored to his collar. By the time the bell sounded for a second time, Millie was out in the shop, and smiling.

'Bring him in, Violet. It looks like it's coming on to rain.'

The creases on Violet's face deepened to canyons as she smiled back in surprise.

'Oh, are you *sure*?'

Millie simply smiled again, the smile of the lady of the manor bestowing her old clothes on the maid. The sign on the door distinctly said 'No dogs please'. This directive wasn't just for hygiene reasons but rather so that Millie could enjoy herself playing Lady Bountiful when the mood struck her. It was only a bit of fun, winding up the customers, pretending she was making a sacrifice in flouting her own rules. Couldn't do any harm, as long as she stuck to those who would never spot such subterfuge even if they were hit over the head with it. Or was that worse? Who cared if it was, Millie thought, imagining the figure on the screen she had left open in the back room.

As it happened, her little bit of fun paid off because Violet didn't take a quarter of her usual time choosing what she wanted and handed over her money without prevarication and with a stern eye on Frosty, presumably in case he lifted his little leg in the direction of the stock.

When they'd gone, Millie returned to the computer and

stared at the screen for a minute before resolutely switching it off. The money may be a reality now but her decision not to touch it until Karen was safely home held firm, despite Charmaine's appeal to Millie to 'go out and treat herself'. She didn't need treats and she wasn't, as a rule, materialistic – not that she viewed this as a virtue; it was just a fact, a part of her nature which Karen had inherited, along with stubbornness.

Gus didn't set much store by possessions either. Millie remembered thinking as she'd been shown round the cottage that he could have fitted most of his personal belongings into one large rucksack. When she'd said as much, he'd told her he'd done exactly that when he was twenty-one. He'd spent a year travelling – or 'dossing about' as he put it – around Thailand and India. The poverty he'd witnessed had made him feel ashamed to have so much and after that he'd kept only the things he really needed to have around him.

Gus. He kept doing this, dropping into her mind like the perfect apple from the top of the tree. She looked across at the counter holding the tea things. Two mugs stood next to the kettle. They looked companionable, an illusion easily shattered by the shiny dryness of one and the liquid brown residue inside the other. She looked away.

A train rumbled past, gathering speed as it pulled out of Park Station. Millie didn't get up. It wasn't his day, it wasn't his time, and since it had stopped at Park it wasn't even a semi-fast. Suddenly she longed to tell him she'd watched him on the train, share it with him, discover how he would react. The feeling was so overwhelming that the phone was in her hand, her thumb clicking through the list, before reason took over and stopped her. It might unnerve him to know that she watched, make him wary of her. Nothing to be gained. Everything to lose.

She stared out of the window towards the far side of the silent track where a wall rose like a cliff-face, so high that its top was invisible from where she was sitting. The weeds that grew from the cracks in the stonework had sidled quietly into flower, daubing the greyness with pink, yellow and mauve. Gus, behind his newspaper, would not have noticed. Millie felt sorry about that.

She continued staring across the track, letting her eyes drift out of focus until the flowers merged into a bright, blurry mass of colour. The emptiness of a railway line after a train had passed through was like none other: pure, absolute, and startlingly silent, as if the train had never been. It was one of the first things she had noticed when she was introduced to the railway as a small child. Anticipating the train's arrival then watching it thunder past, feeling the air flow, fast and cold across her face, was exhilarating but it was standing on the hushed platform afterwards, her hand tightly inside her mother's, that made her pulse race, and still did.

Rain began to patter on the window. Millie shifted her gaze from outside and looked at the phone. She was as much to blame as Gus was for the distance between them, she understood that now. The kiss had confused her, caused her to make assumptions she could no longer justify, but they were friends, they were equal; she had no need to wait. The realisation sent a stream of adrenalin through her veins. She knew also that she didn't want to talk to him on the phone. They should be together, in person, so that nothing could be misconstrued.

At four o'clock, an hour earlier than usual, Millie closed the shop, hurried home to pick up the car, and set off to Hangburton.

Leaving the boring stretch of motorway that offered the quickest route to the village, Millie cut her speed as she plunged into a shady green tunnel of overarching trees before emerging onto a winding lane bounded by open fields, and there, just ahead, was the squat Norman tower of Saint Saviour's. Having forced away the last vestiges of doubt as she left Brighton, a sense of fatalism had overtaken her. Either Gus would be in or he wouldn't. Either he would be pleased to see her or he wouldn't. Whichever it was, she would deal with it.

She missed the turning the first time and had to drive the length of the main street before she could put enough distance between her and the traffic, make a tight three-point-turn on the forecourt of the Dog and Trumpet, and drive back the way she had come. Approaching from the other side, she felt slightly disorientated and began to wonder whether she'd got it right, but yes, here was the little outcrop of shops she remembered and just beyond, Prosperity Terrace.

There was no obvious parking space but the sight of Gus's car caused a sweep of anxiety that sent her heart-rate soaring. Keeping her eyes on the road, she drove on a short distance and stopped in front of a pair of larger semi-detached houses. Checking that she wasn't blocking anyone's driveway, she switched off the engine, tweaked her fringe into place, and got out of the car.

Prosperity Terrace sat on a shallow rise with a gentle slope at either end connecting the path in front of the cottages with the main pavement. As Millie walked self-consciously up the slope, her fingers tracing the handrail, she realised she had no idea what she was going to say when he opened the door, but that didn't matter. She would take her cue from him and it would all pan out naturally from there. Even so, she wished the house was a little further away but already the slope was behind her and she was on the rickety brick path at the top.

A few yards ahead, someone, a woman, came out of one of the cottages and, waving jauntily behind her, turned along the path facing Millie. Millie counted rapidly along the row. It was. It was Gus's house. Her feet stalled but the message had been slow to reach them and she was almost outside number nine before she came to a standstill. The woman, fortyish and slender, with enviable cheekbones, a jolly-hockeysticks ponytail and a heavy-looking canvas bag slung over her shoulder, was smiling, looking in some way pleased with herself. The smile was clearly left over from her visit because it vanished as soon as she set eyes on Millie. The expression that replaced it was enquiring but not politely so; in fact, she looked almost affronted.

Millie doubled back a few steps, pretending to scan the numbers of the houses while her mind grappled with this unforeseen circumstance. The woman stepped off the brick path and onto the grass bank, skirting Millie as if she was contagious but not taking her eyes off her. She began to walk on, then suddenly she turned.

'Which number are you after?'

'Oh, number nine, but not this nine. I've got the wrong road. At least I think…'

'Yes, you must have,' the woman flung at Millie, as if daring her to contradict. Then, hopping back on to the path, she marched on, ponytail swinging, pausing only to glance back and deliver a wide-eyed stare.

Feeling slightly shaky from this strangely confrontational encounter as well as stupid for not having stood her ground, Millie walked the few steps to Gus's front door, stood there for a moment to gather herself, then pressed the bell, feeling slightly mollified by the protection offered by the brick porch. She stepped back and waited but the door remained closed. Thinking she detected the sound of movement within, she gave two more short rings and listened hard. This time she heard nothing. She waited and waited but still he didn't come.

Had he peeked out of the window, seen who it was, and decided he couldn't face her? Gus could never be that unkind, surely, but how well did she really know him? Or, perhaps – she remembered the satisfied smile on the face of Gus's recent visitor – it was one of those moments when he would not have answered the door to anybody.

Turning round, she hurried back along the path. There seemed to be no feeling in her feet while the rest of her was aflame with resentment and humiliation. There was no doubt in her mind now. Their friendship had meant no more to Gus than a pleasant interlude, a little hobby to fill the time, and now that time was being filled by someone else, someone younger, prettier, and obviously with a whole lot more to offer, he had dropped Millie like a hot brick. Right, if that was the way it was to be, it was fine by her.

She slammed the car door so hard it nearly took off the hinges.

Chapter Seventeen

Gus stood rigidly in the shadowy recess at the kitchen end of the hall, virtually holding his breath, for a good five minutes after the doorbell had rung for the second time. It would be just like Jessica to come back and surprise him, throw herself bodily at him when his defences were down. The conversation he'd just had with her had been so unexpectedly natural and lacking in any kind of undertone that the initial relief it had brought him had soon given way to suspicion.

Relaxing his stance a little, he leaned back against the cupboard door, forgetting for the moment why he was standing there until he heard the crack of the wood and something falling inside, the broom, probably. Standing up straight again but maintaining his position, he leaned his head to one side to gain an oblique view of the sitting room window but as far as he could see there was no-one peering through it. If she was still at the front door she'd have been ringing the bell again by now or peering through his letterbox. Of course, she would know he was still inside the house – there was no way out other than the front door or over the back wall into the stinging nettles – but it felt somehow safer to keep up the pretence of his sudden unavailability. And it was kinder, too, in the long run, because the sooner Jessica accepted it was over, the happier she would be.

His back was stiffening up. Peeling himself away from the cupboard door, he made a dash for the kitchen. She must have gone. In any case, what kind of a man hid in his own house, from a woman? He filled the kettle and made tea, making as much noise about it as possible while he belted out the first verse of *Jerusalem* for added effect. That was better. He felt much more cheerful now.

Jessica had been going round the streets dropping off leaflets about forthcoming events in the village hall. Her 'penance', she called it, giving him a pointed look. He hadn't asked what she meant but he'd guessed from the unspoken hint that her volunteer post-woman duties were something to do with her childish behaviour towards him. He had not expected an apology but perhaps this was one; the closest she could manage, anyway. Well, she needn't don a hair shirt on his account. Of course, if she was truly remorseful she would have put the leaflet through his letterbox without ringing the bell, but he'd done the decent thing by asking her in, they'd had a pleasant enough chat about this and that, and she hadn't come back. Gus sipped his tea and decided to let go of his suspicion.

It was time he let go of other things, too. He couldn't carry on tormenting himself, putting his life on standby while he stumbled around the margins of depression because of events he couldn't change; all this soul-searching was as unhealthy as it was futile. Elspeth was never going to change her mind about the money and it was insensitive of him to expect her to. He must respect her wishes and leave it at that. As for his birth mother, the sadness of her situation would haunt him for the rest of his days but it would not overtake his life, not any more. He would never know Catherine's true story and he wasn't meant to. The house had whispered its secrets. There was nothing else.

All the same, it wouldn't hurt to drop a line to Cecelia, a brief note apologising for ringing out of the blue and causing her upset. He didn't regret a single word he'd said but something – conscience, an inherent sense of duty, perhaps – was pulling him towards it. At least then she would have his address and phone number, just in case. He would do it this afternoon, get it over and done with, and then he'd be free to concentrate on other, less demanding, aspects of his life.

He had his surveying work to keep him occupied, his second embroidery panel to complete, his visits to the capital still beckoned, and in his spare time he would finish refurbishing Augusta's bedroom, then he could stop feeling guilty every time he passed the door. He might move his bed in there or keep it as a spare room and study, he hadn't decided yet, but he would make it as fresh and appealing as it deserved to be, a real enhancement to the house.

He would stock up the fridge and kitchen cupboards, too, and cook proper food. He'd rather let things slide lately, living off toast and oblong dinners, washed down by far too much alcohol. And he'd buy flowers. There had always been flowers in the house when he was growing up. His mother, his real mother, the one who had brought him up, used to say that if you smiled at a flower it would smile back and you'd forget all about being grumpy. She'd made him try it with a daisy when he'd been down in the mouth about going back to school after the long summer holidays; it had worked.

Millie would enjoy that little story. *Millie*. If he didn't get in touch with her soon he'd have lost her friendship forever, and all for the sake of one uncontrolled moment. She had been all in blue that evening; a long cotton skirt with tiny blue flowers and a plain lavender-blue top that matched her eyes, with a deep V-neck, more revealing, more enticing, than anything he had seen her wear before.

But it had not been just about that. When he was with her he felt new and alive, less self-absorbed. She made him smile, brought out the best in him, and that, ultimately, was why he had kissed her, not because of her sweet face and old-fashioned film-star shapeliness, but to express all those other things beyond mere physical attraction. He knew that now, whereas Millie, of course, did not. From her point of view, he had leapt on her with all the finesse of a mating tom-cat.

The knife-blade of memory struck out at him, pure and clean. *Oh God*. He put his tea down on the draining board and ran a hand through his hair. Talking to Millie again would not be easy but it was the difficult things that gave the most rewards; he had learned that in his life, if little else. It might be better to phone her, though, and assess the lie of the land rather than turning up at the shop unannounced. He could invite her out for a meal, Sunday lunch perhaps, as an ice-breaker – assuming there was ice to break – and a thank-you for all she had done for him, including finding Cecelia. Then if she agreed, it would be a starting point for getting their friendship back on track. Yes, that's what he would do. He smiled at the prospect.

He strolled down to the Dog and Trumpet that evening, a little earlier than usual because it was curry night and he had yet to stock up on his own supplies. The usual suspects were clustered around the bar, not all of whom Gus could yet name, although he knew two of them were called David, the one with the beard was Matt, and the older, snowy-haired one was George. One of the Davids was married to Sophie from embroidery.

'See you've given that Jessica the elbow then,' he heard as he sat down at a table by the window with his steaming plateful.

'We ended it, yes.' Gus smiled, amused to find the eyes of the group upon him as though a big, important announcement had been made.

'Can't say I'm surprised,' George muttered into his pint, whereupon the others murmured and nodded in agreement.

'She can be a bit of a handful, that one,' Sophie's David said. 'Many have tried but few have succeeded.'

They all laughed, including Gus, although he felt guilty for doing so.

'What went wrong then?' someone else asked, in a manner which suggested a lust for salacious detail rather than true concern.

'Nothing. She wasn't my type, that's all.'

More laughter. 'Must be more to it than that.' George appealed to his mates. 'Am I right or am I wrong?'

'Tuck in, I would,' David number two said, indicating Gus's plate. 'Expect you need building up.'

The others sniggered.

'She's very nice, as it happens,' Gus said, feeling aggrieved on Jessica's behalf more than on his own account. 'It just ran its course, that's all.'

Sophie's David brought his drink over and sat down at Gus's table. 'Sorry, mate. Nothing meant by it. Just joshing, you know?'

Gus nodded, looking round at them all. 'Drop it now,

though, shall we?'

Finishing his meal, he took his plate up and handed it over. A small mixed group stood round the other side of the bar. Glancing across, he vaguely recognised a few of them from around the village but he didn't think he knew the tall, blond-haired guy with the look of a young Robert Redford who stood in their midst. He had a presence about him; he'd have remembered if he'd met him. Suddenly the man looked up. Meeting Gus's gaze head on, he took a deliberate step towards him, as if he was about to come over and say something then changed his mind. Gus looked on, puzzled, as the man turned away and drained the rest of his pint. Moments later, he left by the side door.

'See you, Dan,' someone called after him.

Two days later, Gus was on his way to carry out a mortgage valuation on a barn conversion when he saw Jessica standing, glum-faced, at the bus stop at the end of Hangburton's main street, wearing a short black-and-white dress and carrying an enormous red tote bag. The whistled fragments of a half-remembered tune crumbled into dust as he automatically applied the brake.

The window descended, letting in a lungful of dry, summer heat. 'Hey. Can I give you a lift anywhere?'

'No thank you.' The tote bag described a forceful half circle and came to rest against Jessica's knees while her eyes searched the air above the car.

He was tempted to drive on but the Monet-blue skies combined with his still intact optimism and resolve had given him an air of bonhomie that he couldn't ignore. He glanced behind at the encroaching traffic.

'Are you getting in or not?' he called, forcing Jessica to acknowledge him properly.

What was the matter with her anyway? They'd parted on good terms when she'd called on him, but perhaps it wasn't about him and she was in a mood about something else. Well, he wouldn't ask again. The road behind was clear now. He folded his arms and waited. Out of the corner of his eye he could see her teetering from one high heel to the other as if she was making up her mind. Finally, she trotted over and got in beside him.

'Where's it to be then?'

Gus smiled beatifically, feeling, for once, in complete control of the situation.

'I'm getting the train to Brighton. Meeting a friend,' Jessica said brusquely, holding herself rigidly to one side so as to put as much distance between the two of them as possible, the tote bag crushed inelegantly between her shins.

'Haywards Heath station do you then?' Gus smiled again, refusing to let her ruffle him.

'Yes. Please.' This time a smile, thin and reluctant.

It wasn't too far out of his way. He wondered why she wasn't using her car; Jessica and public transport blended as happily as oil and water. She read his mind.

'Car's in dock. Brake shoes. Whatever.'

This economical offering was accompanied by a slow pump up and subsidence of her shoulders while her face remained static and expressionless.

'How's your mother?' Gus asked after a while, feeling he should at least make some attempt at sociability.

'Spring cleaning.'

'But it's...'

'I know.'

Engulfed in silence once more, Gus considered this monosyllabic version of his ex-lover and decided that beneath the facade another story was gathering force like an unspent volcano. His mouth tasted suddenly of the tomatoes he'd had for breakfast.

The village and its tagged-on string of development fell away and they were into open country where the fields on either side slumbered beneath whiskery blankets of heat-baked corn. A lean brown rabbit shot out of the hedgerow. Gus checked his mirror and braked, just in time to the see the animal clear the tarmac and spring into the grass verge on the other side.

'Close one.' He blew out air. 'I never like to kybosh the wildlife, not if I can help it.'

He glanced at Jessica. The sudden movement must have jolted her out of her torpor because she'd twisted round in her seat and her eyes were lasering into him while her chin quivered dangerously.

'Jess?'

'You lied. I asked you if there was anyone else and you swore blind there wasn't.'

Gus's summer-morning lightness evaporated completely. 'No, Jess, I didn't lie. There was, is, no-one else.' *Not that it matters now*, he was tempted to add, but didn't.

'And you're still doing it! Lying!'

Jessica began tugging at the clasp on her seatbelt. An elbow caught him sharply on the arm.

'Jess, leave that alone, for God's sake, and keep still. You'll have us off the road in a minute.'

Gus slowed down as much as he dare. What the hell was wrong with her?

'You said there was no-one else but there is, isn't there? You might as well admit it, Gus, because I've seen her.' *So there*, she might as well have added.

'Oh well, if you've seen her it must be true and I must be the one that's wrong because isn't that always the way?' Gus threw up his hands, leaving the steering wheel unguarded for a split second before clamping them down again. 'Oh yes, silly old me. I've just remembered I've had someone else all the time. Well, it's very good of you to bring that to my attention. I must look her up some time.'

A moment's quavering silence, then: 'So who is she, then?'

Gus clamped a hand to his forehead. 'Jess, for Christ's sake, it's no-one. I am not, and never was, going out with anyone else. Okay?'

'But I saw her going to your house, the other day when I brought the leaflet. Chin-length blond hair out of a bottle, much older than me, much fatter than me, skimping on the make-up, not from the village. Ring any bells yet?'

The words rattled out like ball bearings. Gus thought hard whilst trying to keep his attention on the road. Blond. Slightly older than Jessica. Not stick-thin. Not made up to the nines. Not local. *Millie*.

'Nope. No bells.'

Except the one on his front door that had rung three times straight after Jessica had left. Please, no…

Jessica was yanking at the belt again. 'Let me out.'

'Don't be daft. We're miles from anywhere.'

Gus increased speed, both to prevent Jessica from attempting escape and to propel himself faster towards the leafy embrace of the town's approach. Jessica seemed to settle down, at least bodily; every nerve in her face was mobile with accusation. The town centre forced a slower speed. Gus took the roundabout and was about to head for the road where the station was, when the lights changed to red.

'This'll do.'

Heaving the tote bag onto her lap, she flung the seatbelt aside and levered the door handle.

'Wait. I'll drop you closer,' Gus said.

'Stuff it, and stuff you.'

She was gone.

Gus waited until Sunday evening to ring Millie. The delay wasn't entirely due to nervousness – after his monumental faux-pas at their last meeting he had salvaged just about enough composure to see him through – but if Millie had been the visitor from whom he had secreted himself like a hunted fox, then swift action on his part might seem like too much of a coincidence.

Even so, the ritualistic preparations necessary for a call of such importance, one where the outcome might not be in his favour, began at least fifteen minutes before the handset was lifted. The chair was in exactly the right position to receive the last rays of a dying sun, the first drink of the evening was modestly poured, the tumbler stamping a dark circle on the review pages of the Sunday paper, and he had washed his hands and combed his hair – it was a battle of sorts – taking a little extra time to examine the parts of his crown each side of his widow's peak for further signs of retreat.

But after all that, it was a very short conversation and Gus soon found himself leaning back in his chair watching the shadows steal the golden haze from the walls and wondering if Millie had yet stepped into the bath that was purportedly running.

He had pressed the handset closer to his ear so that he might catch the innocent gush of tap water, as though the forward trajectory of his relationship with Millie depended solely on its detection, but had heard nothing. The falseness of his cheery tone could not have gone amiss at the other end of the line – it certainly grated with him – and yet at first Millie had sounded pleased to hear from him. Its undisguised truth was there in her voice but had swiftly departed and the lunch invitation had netted him a distant, almost chilly, response. She would think about it and let him know. That was the best she could do for now, she'd said, cutting short his attempt to seal the arrangement and leaving him in this almost unbearable state of suspense.

Two possibilities then. She was either still embarrassed or angry about the kiss, which seemed unlikely, or Jessica's description had been spot-on; Millie had been his caller that day and had taken it into her head that he didn't want to see her. Whichever it was, Gus felt slightly annoyed. Did she really see him as that untrustworthy? Naturally he hadn't mentioned either incident on the phone, nor asked her what was wrong – how could he without seeming like a complete idiot? – and Millie hadn't said anything either. It came to him now that this might be the end of the line and her prevarication over lunch was her way of sending him away for good.

He finished his drink and went resolutely to his computer to finish off a surveying report and submit it by email but immersing himself in the routineness of the terminology was not quite enough to dispel his latest round of gloomy thought.

Unsurprisingly, the cave dream visited him that night, but this time it ran on as far as his rescue. And when finally he was released from his rocky prison, Millie was there instead of his parents, the lowering sun outlining her with celestial brightness, and suddenly he wasn't a boy but a man, and she was kissing him.

It was only a slight setback, Gus told himself as he purposefully got up early the next morning and set off for the little supermarket in the village before he'd had breakfast. As usual, he was making something out of nothing. If Millie didn't call him there was no reason why he shouldn't call her, he reasoned, nipping smartly round the end aisle and slipping into the checkout queue in order to avoid Sidonie, whom he'd spotted in fruit and veg.

The message he found on his answerphone on his return was his reward for such positive thinking. He couldn't help but put this spin on it; he deserved some luck, didn't he? The bright tone of Millie's voice seemed to have cost her a little effort, but no matter, she had rung and accepted his invitation. All he had to do was call her back at the shop and the prize was his. He did so immediately.

'Millie, we are all right, aren't we?' he asked carefully, once he'd arranged to pick her up on Sunday.

A miniscule silence, then: 'Of course. Why?'

'Oh, no reason. I'm sorry it's been a while since I got in touch. I've had a lot on, workwise…'

'Has it?' Millie cut in. 'I hadn't noticed. I've been busy myself, with the shop and everything.'

The quick response, and again the forced brightness in her tone, unnerved him slightly, making him want to ask her again if everything was all right between them. But she'd said yes to his invitation. What more did he want? Instead, he asked if she'd made any progress in her search for Karen. She told him, with a measure of excitement, that she had made a small discovery and she would tell him all about it over lunch. Gus breathed a sigh of relief at this outwardly normal end to the conversation and threw three eggs into the pan instead of his usual two.

The weather obliged on Sunday, sunny and warm but not too hot and no wind, Gus thought with satisfaction as he stood outside the back door to test it out. He had booked a table at a pub with a garden, hoping they'd be able to eat outside. If lunch was a success – there was no reason why it shouldn't be – he could take her for a drive around the country lanes and bring her back here afterwards, show her the progress he'd made with Augusta's room and seek her advice on curtains and whatnot.

The phone rang just after eleven, as he stood in the bedroom in his boxers and a red and blue checked shirt which was destined to go with either the clean charcoal grey chinos with the slightly too-tight waistband or the comfortable black cords with a small crusty deposit on the knee that might scrub off. He bolted downstairs to answer it.

'It's Jenny, there's been an accident. Can you come?' Elspeth wheezed.

Above the sound of his sister-in-law's laboured breathing, Gus heard a clattering noise and then, more distant, the sound of sirens.

'Yes, of course. Where?'

'They were in the minibus. There was a crash, with a lorry. She's not... she's all right, but can you come?'

'Where, Elspeth?'

More gasping, then: 'Princess Royal.'

Gus dashed back upstairs and struggled into the chinos. Down again, he scrabbled through his address book for Millie's home number and rang it. *Come on, come on...* No reply. No answerphone. Grabbing keys, wallet and mobile, he dashed out of the house.

Having caught the minimal set of directions aimed at him with good intent by the harassed woman on the desk and vaguely digested them, Gus hit the swarming corridors, shoes squeaking on the rubber floor, nostrils tightening against the soupy air that smelled of warm flesh, stale linen and cleaning fluid. He seemed always to be heading in the opposite direction from everyone else. He pressed on, his mouth suddenly drying as he passed the open doors of the cavernous lift. Then, after a fruitless scan of the few occupants in the short-stay ward, he heard a wailing sound that froze his feet for seconds until, following the sound, he alighted upon a side room.

Jenny sat on the bed, fully dressed, propped up by pillows,

Elspeth on the chair beside her, stroking Jenny's hand. She stood up as she noticed Gus. As she came towards him, he saw tautness and high colour in her face, eyes swimming behind tightly held-back tears.

'Thank you, thank you,' she said huskily into his shoulder as he held her.

'Hey, hey, what's all this?'

Gently he held Elspeth away from him, his hands on her shoulders. Jenny wasn't injured in any obvious way; his more immediate concern was Elspeth's distress.

Jenny's wails grew louder. A nurse appeared in the doorway and gave a knowing little nod. 'I'll pop back later and do her obs once she's calmed down a bit.'

Jenny's lanky, jean-clad legs began to agitate against the white waffle blanket.

'No! I want to go home!'

'Jenny, darling, it's all right. There's nothing to be scared of.' Elspeth went to the bed and held a hand over her daughter's forehead, lightly pressing and lifting away in a gesture that spoke of years of necessary soothing. 'That's it, my love, that's it,' she crooned, as the noise began to climb steadily down.

Gus stayed within the periphery of the stuffy little room, feeling almost intrusive at this glimpse of how life must have been for the two of them; three when Robert was around. It was the unfamiliar that caused his niece the most anguish – strange rooms, strange noises, strange smells, strange people, strange textures; all were demonised by the ever-watchful mind of a young woman whose life would have taken a very different turn but for one random moment of compression, the covert eviction of oxygen. It was so, so unfair.

He and Clair had talked about having children but it was always in terms of 'one day'. They were still young enough to have the luxury of delay, at least for a year or two. Still young enough not to be pressurised into taking the next big step in life. And still young enough not to take into account any threat of potential danger lurking around the corner.

And then Clair had fallen ill, and after she died Gus had struggled not only with the grief of losing his beloved wife but with the loss of a child, or children, unknown.

Life was a lottery. Never had Gus been more aware of that than at the time of Clair's death, because playing on his mind was the thought that if there had been a child, who was to say that child would not have been like Jenny? He wasn't Robert, he wasn't even like Robert since they weren't blood-related. He didn't have it in him to bring up a child like Jenny. He'd known it then; he knew it now.

The girl's eyes alighted on Gus. She gave a little surprised gasp as if she had only just registered his presence. He gave himself a mental shake and went to her, touching her arm to place himself into context.

'Hey there, matey. How are you feeling?'

'I want Kieran. Where's Kieran?'

Jenny's worried eyes searched the room. She scrabbled at the blanket, her nails clicking on the threads.

Gus looked at Elspeth. 'Sorry.'

'It's not you, it's her friend, Kieran, she's fretting about. He was the only one who was hurt,' Elspeth said softly, turning her face away from Jenny. 'She doesn't know that but I suppose she senses it. She keeps asking for him.'

Elspeth told Gus what had happened. The minibus had been taking a group from the day centre to a zoo park when a lorry had lost control on the bend and swung into a ditch, clipping the minibus coming in the opposite direction and sending it off the road. It had toppled to one side as it came to a stop on the verge, causing the six strapped-in passengers more fright than anything else. The woman driver was fine, too, apparently, but shaken, as was the other carer, a young man who had been sitting at the back. Kieran had been travelling in the front seat next to the driver as a special treat. His belt had been a bit loose and he'd been knocked unconscious as the vehicle slumped sideways. Elspeth didn't know how he was but was anxious to find out.

'Why don't you go and see?' Gus said. 'I'll look after things here, no worries.'

Elspeth indicated Jenny's dancing legs. 'No, I'd better stay.'

She sat down again. In the absence of a second chair, Gus went across to the window and perched on the sill, and then, with a sickening rush of heat, he remembered his date with Millie. Checking first with Elspeth, he left the room and walked along the corridor until he found a door that opened to the outside. Standing by it, he took out his phone but even as he scrolled through he had already realised his mistake – he hadn't put Millie's home number into his phone, had never bothered to commit it to memory, and didn't know her mobile number. The only number on his contacts list was the one for the shop.

Idiot! Gus swung round on his heel as the truth slammed home. No, hang on. If he rang the shop number wasn't there an answerphone message that gave her other numbers? He scrolled again, pressed and waited. He heard the ring, three times, before it died. Gus stared at the screen incredulously. No battery.

'Fuck it!'

A female white-coated medic swung past him with only a slightly raised eyebrow. He was absolutely priceless! Couldn't he even manage a simple thing like charging up his phone? Well, Millie was well rid of him, assuming he'd managed to cock up again, this time irretrievably. But Jenny and Elspeth were his priority now. He trundled back to the ward, the phone a useless dead weight in his pocket.

Jenny was released an hour and a half later, during which time Elspeth had endured her daughter's sobbing fight with the nurse who took her temperature and blood pressure and the same tearful rage against the doctor who came to re-inspect her burgeoning bruises. The process was made even more difficult by Jenny's refusal to let anyone remove anything apart from her shoes. Gus had endured it, too, of course, but from a different perspective as he had Elspeth's welfare at heart as well as that of his niece, whilst he felt numb with guilt at his selfishness over his spoilt day.

It was clear as soon as they reached Elspeth's house that his continued presence was needed but that was fine by him. Having made the journey back in their respective cars, Jenny was already ensconced on the sofa under a rug and the kettle was on by the time he arrived. Jenny was calm enough to be left with a sandwich, a carton of juice, and the television on, while he and Elspeth sat in the kitchen.

'I saw some of the other parents as we left,' she said tiredly, 'and I spoke to Kieran's mum and dad. He's okay, a bit concussed and his arm's in a sling because of the impact but it isn't broken. He'll probably stay in overnight. Jenny seems to have forgotten about him for the moment. I keep thinking how much worse it could have been. If the lorry had done its thing a second later it would have ploughed right into the bus instead of just tipping it off the road and... Oh Gus...'

Tears streamed silently down Elspeth's cheeks. Gus was round the table and stooping to hold her.

'Don't. Don't think of what could have happened. Jenny's fine. They're all fine, aren't they? Elspeth, look at me.'

Elspeth looked up. 'The bloody minibus'll be a write-off.' She gave a strangled half-laugh, half-sob.

Gus felt her start to tremble. He held her closer, feeling his knees complain as he continued to stoop. Carefully he let go of her, pulling himself up. He drew the other chair closer to Elspeth and sat down, taking her chilly hand in his.

'You're shaking. It's the shock. Look, drink your tea.'

'It was just like before. There was a knock on the door and there were two policemen, and when I saw them I knew it all over again, I knew what they were going to say, I heard it, the exact words...'

Gus waited. He had half an idea what was coming. But he was here and he was going nowhere.

'They told me Robert had been in an accident. His car had gone under a lorry, only yards from the school. Nothing could be done. He'd been taken to hospital but he was dead before he got there.'

A loud sob came from Elspeth's mouth, from her whole body. She glanced fearfully towards the door to the room where Jenny was. Gus got up and looked. Jenny had fallen asleep with the juice carton in her hand. Red beads of liquid were easing slowly from the straw, dripping like blood onto her sleeve, but it didn't matter. He crept back.

'She's asleep. Elspeth, I'm so sorry. I didn't even think about that, not in the heat of it all.'

'I did. I thought of Rob every second I was in the car and at the hospital. I should have been concentrating on Jenny, but it was as if the last two years had been wiped away and I thought, any moment now, they're going to ask me to leave Jenny and they'll take me to another room and he'll be there, my Robert, and they'll want to know if it's him. And it will be. It will be.'

Elspeth broke into fresh, heartbreaking sobs. Gus bit his lip to fight back his own tears. He fetched the kitchen roll, tearing a sheet off and putting it in Elspeth's hand.

Jenny's accident had occurred at the same time of day, at the same time of year, as her father's, on a blue-and-gold summer's morning such as this. Robert, his big brother, who sat by his bed reading Gus's favourite stories on a loop while he recovered from measles. Robert, who abhorred lying but took the blame when Gus broke Liesel's heirloom Meissen vase. Robert, whose steadying hand on his shoulder gave him the strength to deliver the eulogy at their father's funeral. Robert, to whom he owed so much and to whom nothing more could be given, apart from support of the little family he had left behind.

Chapter Eighteen

Millie couldn't be angry with Gus. She wished in one way that she could but it wasn't happening. Whether this was because she didn't care enough or cared too much, she didn't know.

All day yesterday, once it had become crystal clear she'd been stood up and the sting of disbelief had passed, she'd felt no more than a vague sense of disappointment that rolled steadily along in front of her, refusing to gather enough impetus to raise it to a level which demanded some kind of action. So she'd made no attempt to contact him. Neither had he contacted her.

This morning the shop had welcomed her in with a subdued, apologetic air, as if it had been tipped off in advance. The disappointment she'd felt on Sunday had drained away to be replaced by a weary sadness that filled her limbs with sand and kept her movements slow and precise. As she counted out cloud-soft balls of pink baby-wool and bagged them up ready for a customer to collect, she saw in her mind's eye the dark-haired woman she'd encountered in Prosperity Terrace. Perhaps he had been seeing her all along but had seen fit not to bring her into the conversation, but then why would he? Despite the apparent closeness between herself and Gus, the intimacy of their communions in the back room of the shop, she had no right to expect to be given all the details of his personal life. And yet, stupidly, that was exactly what she had expected.

Letting her thoughts wander dangerously, she wondered if the woman – Gus's girlfriend, if that was who she was – ever thought of him as the kind of man who could happily go about kissing other women at random. That kiss, that moment of sheer joy and surprise and panic. She could still feel the pressure of his lips, taste him on her tongue...

No! Taking her finger from her lips, Millie closed her eyes, squeezed them tight, and refused to open them again until the wasted, tainted recollection had gone completely.

A little later, Millie collected a square of fourteen thread-count fabric, needle, scissors and a rainbow of silks, laid them out on the table in the back room and set to work with scrupulous concentration. All other thoughts shut out, she drew the needle deftly through the tiny holes, sighing with satisfaction as the creamy, perforated fabric began to disappear beneath an appeasing haze of colour. She worked quickly – cross-stitch, feather-stitch, silk-stitch, loop after glorious loop of lazy-daisy – snipping threads, pulling apart another skein picked at random to begin again with a new colour, left to right, across and downwards and circling, until her fingers scorched with uncompromising effort.

It was only then that she sat back, surveyed the results of her labours and noticed the colours she had chosen: yellows, greens, a bright, singing blue as well as a darker one, and a red as yet untouched. The design she'd created, too, held a resonance that stalled her heart for a second. It was the design on the bag, the bag containing Gus's things from his mother. The pattern and stitching weren't exactly the same – that would be impossible without the original to copy from – but the essence of it was there, the circular arrangement of flowers and leaves and little birds, as if her fingers remembered even if her brain was unsure. Drawn now to the blue like the one in which the initial *M* for Matthew had been chain-stitched, she reached for it, then stopped. The embroidery already completed had been a stream of consciousness affair. It would brook no spoiling by false attempts at realism.

Catherine's needlework bore the hallmarks of a natural talent that Millie, imbued as she was with a certain amount of artistic expertise, could never hope to emulate. But Gus... Yes, Gus had surely inherited his mother's flair. His adoptive father may well have encouraged and enhanced his son's skills with his tailoring lessons, but the secret of Gus's success with a fine needle came from a much deeper source. Had Gus realised this for himself, and if so, did it bring him any comfort? Millie so hoped that it did.

Setting aside her own embroidery, overlaying it with a piece of clean cloth to keep it safe, she thought about the contents of the drawstring bag, the random yet somehow complete choice of objects. She thought of chilly Sunday mornings floating on autumnal mists and small, strong hands slipping into shabby gloves before picking up the bible, the modern brashness of a poodle brooch defiantly adorning the lapel of a sensible coat. She thought of a childish wrist cheerfully imprisoned inside a coil of silver dented by anxious twisting, and of a simple button on a cotton fragment; an afterthought, hastily and fearfully sought from a garment that might have been a blouse, or a night-dress.

It would be easy for a nineteen-year-old to think only of material possessions in her fervent wish to give something of herself to her child, but Catherine Harte had more about her than that, a maturity of understanding, a generosity of spirit and an innate sense of right and wrong that owed nothing to a religious upbringing. They were more than just everyday objects in that bag; they were the essence of Catherine herself. Millie felt it instinctively, had done so from the moment of discovery. The idea was, and never had been, simply a figment of her imagination, but perhaps that was because she wanted there to be more to it, for Gus's sake.

He would never give up searching, no more than she would give up searching for Karen. The actions themselves might stop, the questions trail away unasked, but below the surface the quest would go on, for whatever had been lost, or whatever there was to be found. It was always so.

Cautiously examining her feelings after this spell of dreamy introspection, Millie realised that she wasn't sad. Instead it was as if a kind of rounding off had taken place, which might have been the end of something or it could have been the beginning; there was no compulsion to work out which.

She made herself some tea before going through to the

shop and passing a pleasant fifteen minutes chatting to Julie, her customer for the baby wool. Then she rang Charmaine to check which night they were booked for the theatre, which led to more chat, but before long, her pensive mood crept back and there seemed no choice but to give in to it.

Perhaps she needed this, a cool, quiet breathing space to counter the heated over-activity her brain had been subjected to lately. She sat down on the stool behind the counter and picked up the mushroom-shaped darning block that she kept by the till for luck, turning in it in her hand, feeling the worn smoothness of the wood. It had belonged to her mother and was as much a part of Millie's memories of her as the silver thimble on her finger and the flowered apron around her waist.

There had always been something that needed making or mending: cardigans to be knitted, cotton dresses to be smocked and hemmed, sheets turned sides-to-middle, woollen socks to be darned, the latter practices that most women had long ago abandoned, but this progression had quietly passed her mother by. Sometimes in the afternoons she would listen to Woman's Hour on the wireless while she worked, or she'd put on the Val Doonican LP, which wasn't allowed when Millie's father was in the house. Other times – Millie's favourite times – she would tell stories about fairy families who lived in toadstools and tree stumps, sagas that could go on all week, and all made up in her head, while Millie sat on the stool that was the old coal-box and drew the zip on the long tartan knitting bag back and forth, back and forth, until she was mesmerised by the hum of the zip, the click-clack of knitting needles, and the cosy words that spilled so easily from her mother's lips.

Gradually Millie learned that her mother was not much like those of other children and that she stood out from them for more intrinsic reasons than the mere separation of years. She had never expected to have children, had grown used to the idea of being without them, and then Millie pitched up when her mother was forty-two and her father almost fifty and gave them the shock of their lives.

It was almost five. Time to shut up shop, not that she'd done a hand's turn all afternoon, but that was the beauty of being your own boss. Rising slowly from the stool, her head still muzzy with memories, she turned the door sign round and was about to fetch her bag from the back when she heard a rap on the glass. The sudden intrusive noise had her spinning round, only to see Gus frantically gesticulating on the other side. It was with some confusion and a rapid mental regrouping that she let him in.

'I'm so sorry, Millie. This is the first chance I've had. I wanted to come rather than phone,' Gus squeezed out between desperate inhalations.

She was neither surprised nor unsurprised to see him. His face fell in response to this lack of reaction, the curt nod that allowed him entry, as if he'd been fully prepared to receive recrimination, a hero's welcome, or something in between, and didn't know how to deal with nothing at all. But it simply wasn't there to give, as if yesterday's debacle and the deliberations of the day had emptied her emotional store.

Once Gus had told his story – standing in the middle of the shop since she hadn't invited him through – and Millie had spoken words of genuine sympathy, for he'd obviously been through a traumatic time, his sister-in-law and niece even more so, she felt at a loss as to what came next. Clearly Gus did, too. He stood with his weight to one side, hands in pockets, effecting a casualness that he probably didn't feel, while Millie stood slightly apart from him, arms loosely folded, while the clock on the wall ticked into the silence and the two of them breathed the same parcel of tense air.

'I know I probably shouldn't ask,' Gus began eventually, 'but shall we try again, to make an arrangement, for lunch or something?' He grinned ruefully. 'I'm not usually this unreliable.'

Millie's resistance began to fold in on itself. 'I'm sure you're not, but I think it'd be best to leave it a while, see how we go.'

Go back to the way they were before, she meant, hoping Gus was astute and sensitive enough to understand. His barely perceptible nod, the studiously platonic peck on her cheek before he said goodbye, told her that she was.

He could hardly expect more. First he had introduced an ambiguity to their friendship by kissing her out of the blue and sending her into a tailspin from which she had barely recovered, then he'd removed himself from her radar altogether, and when she'd attempted reconciliation he'd left her standing on the doorstep like an unwanted double-glazing salesperson.

She didn't doubt his story about not having her phone number with him yesterday, and his concern for his sister-in-law was a big point in his favour but, even if he had stayed there overnight, surely he could have stolen a moment to ring her here at the shop this morning instead of leaving her to stew all day? None of this augured well.

Even so, as she closed the door behind him, intending to wait five minutes before she left to give him a head start, she began seriously to doubt her own sanity.

Chapter Nineteen

Ralph rang late one evening, just as Millie had stepped out of the bath. Feeling pleasantly relaxed and a bit woozy from her long, hot soak, she padded downstairs to answer it, tucking the phone under her chin while she tied the belt of her towelling robe.

Ralph was touchingly profuse in his apology for not having rung before but, having failed to locate anyone at the company reunion who knew a holiday rep named Karen, he had taken the liberty of giving out the details to 'a few likely candidates' and had thought it worth hanging on in case of any further developments.

He sounded more downcast than Millie herself; as she hadn't heard from him before she had already assumed there was nothing to report. She thanked him for his kindness and told him not to worry, there were other avenues to explore and she hadn't been relying on him entirely. The lie was justifiable – she didn't want Ralph to feel any worse than he already did – but the message was crystal. Millie was never going to track down her daughter through the Travelbugs connection.

On Saturday morning, she traipsed blearily to answer the door, thinking it must be the postman. Instead, two girls about Karen's age stood hesitantly on the step. Bible brigade, probably, despite the skinny jeans and studded shoulder bags too tiny to contain leaflets or copies of *The Watchtower*. Intending to make her apologies and shut them out, she started to pull the door to. There had been a party at Charmaine's last night to celebrate their wedding anniversary and Millie had been the all too willing recipient of John's generosity with the glass-filling. A doorstep debate, theological or otherwise, was definitely not on today's agenda.

'Are you Mrs Hope?' one of them said.

'I am, yes.'

'You know Mr Hitchin, don't you?'

'Mr Hitchin? I know a Ralph Hitchin. Is that who you mean?'

Millie tightened her grip on the door handle.

'Yes, that's him. He was one of the managers at Travelbugs,' the second girl said. 'Not that we had much to do with him. He was quite high up. Is it all right if we talk to you for a minute?'

'Yes, yes, of course.'

Millie opened the door fully and showed them through to the sitting room. Her head felt muzzy as if she might be about to faint. This must be about Karen. Why else were they here? She dropped into the armchair before her legs gave way.

'Please…'

She waved a hand in the direction of the sofa. The girls perched delicately on its edge with barely a wafer of space between them. The one with long blond hair had a look of Karen about her. Millie's heart gave a tug.

'I'm Sarah and this is Tierney,' she said, indicating her friend who had red hair like Charmaine's but short and tousled.

'I'm Millie. Was it Ralph who sent you?'

'Sort of,' Sarah said. 'It was more this mate of ours, Lewis. The three of us were reps together in Crete, the summer before last. Mr Hitchin – Ralph – spoke to Lewis at the reunion do and told him you were trying to get in touch with your daughter.'

'Karen, yes. Do you have any news? Oh, do tell me…'

'We aren't here to tell tales on anyone,' Tierney said, looking anxious. 'We thought we were doing the right thing coming here, didn't we?'

Sarah nodded. 'I became a travel rep to get away from home. They were giving me too much grief, at least, I thought so at the time.' Sarah lifted her eyes. 'My mum and dad were dead upset because I didn't get in touch for ages. I didn't realise how they felt, not until after I made it up with them, so I thought if you were as upset as my mum was, that wasn't right.

162

That's why we came, after Lewis told us what Mr Hitchin said.'

Millie felt a rush of warmth towards Sarah, towards both of them. Such kindness from strangers.

'Whatever you tell me, I promise I won't let on it was you, if that's what you're worried about.'

Oh please, just get on with it!

'Okay,' Sarah said. 'Well, Lewis asked us if we remembered this girl, this other rep, who came to Crete while we were there, but she didn't get on too well so they moved her to another resort or she left Travelbugs altogether, one or the other, we never found out. Lewis thought the girl Mr Hitchin described sounded a bit like her, except her name wasn't Karen, it was Katya. That's why Lewis didn't say anything to Mr Hitchin at the time, but he did get your address from him. He was giving it out left, right and centre, apparently.'

Millie inwardly blessed Ralph for his diligence but at the same time she felt a pinch of disappointment. This wasn't going to come to anything, was it? These girls out of the goodness of their hearts were trying to help, but they had the wrong person. And yet, and yet... The name Katya switched on a tiny light in her mind; she had no idea why. Besides, these two must have thought there was a possibility to have taken all this trouble.

'So, if we could see a photo of Karen?' Tierney was saying.

'Oh, of course, yes.' Millie got up, went to the windowsill and picked up a framed photo of Karen on the beach, her hair flying in the wind. She was laughing, so happy...

Millie swallowed. 'She was younger in this but she hasn't really changed.'

She handed it to the girls then raced upstairs to fetch the photo she carried in her handbag.

'This is more recent.'

Sarah and Tierney studied each of the photos, taking so long that Millie could hardly breathe. Eventually, they nodded at one another.

'I think it might be her,' Sarah said.

'So do I,' Tierney added. 'But I can't be a hundred per cent.'

'How much per cent?' Millie's voice was husky, hardly

there.

'About eighty?' Tierney looked doubtfully at Sarah.

'About that,' Sarah agreed. 'There was one other thing – Lewis said he thought Katya came from Brighton.'

'Was there anything else? Did she say anything about her background, boyfriends?'

'No, not really, sorry,' Tierney said. 'As we said, she wasn't around for long. None of us got to spend much time with her.'

Eighty per cent! Millie clung to the figure, plucked out of thin air under pressure from her, it was true, but it was enough to set her heart pumping madly. But *Katya*? She searched her mind, trying to reignite the miniscule spark the name had conjured earlier, but it had vanished. It seemed a bit drastic for Karen to be using a different name. Millie had once thought it was possible but she hadn't really believed it. Could Karen really hate her that much? Millie felt suddenly close to tears. The girls must have noticed; they sat forward on the sofa, their faces soft with concern.

'Are you okay?' Sarah asked, glancing at Tierney.

Millie swallowed, gave herself a mental shake. 'I'm fine. Just a bit tired, that's all. I was at a party last night.' She smiled.

Sarah brightened. 'We're going to one tonight. That's why we came down to Brighton this morning, from London.'

Millie felt relieved. At least they hadn't made the journey especially to see her.

'It was so thoughtful of you to come. I know you said Karen – Katya – might have left the company but I could try phoning again, couldn't I, now we think she might have been in Crete? They must know her real name because of her passport.'

The girls exchanged looks.

'No good,' Tierney said. 'Travelbugs went into liquidation a month ago.'

Millie sat on Karen's bed in Karen's bedroom and hugged Karen's pillow as fiercely and protectively and lovingly as if it was Karen herself. Since her surprise visitors had left around two hours ago, she had been afloat with optimism and sunk with hopelessness in alternate, more or less equal, measures. At least she had two more names and phone numbers in the red-spotted notebook, and she'd given the girls her email address and all her numbers including the one at the shop. She would ring Ralph later to thank him.

Sarah and Tierney had promised to Facebook anyone and everyone who might know where Karen/Katya was, leading Millie's overstretched mind to ponder the grammatical merits of the verb *to Facebook*. The girls had already sensibly checked the online presence of Katya/Karen themselves and had drawn a blank, but they would have lots of friends on there they could contact, unlike Millie. In any case, her own Facebook account had probably lapsed through lack of use by now.

A seagull screamed overhead, waking Millie from her daydream. Propping the pillow against the wall – Karen had ditched the headboard when she was fifteen; very uncool, apparently – she opened the top drawer of the small white cabinet that stood beside the bed. The contents were exactly as they had been the last time she'd looked. Why that should be a surprise was absurd and incomprehensible, and yet surprise was precisely what Millie felt.

A paperback with the tongue of a bookmark poking out, an empty Ventolin inhaler, a squashed pack of paracetamol, a flyer from a music festival – all still there – and beneath them, a sad flotsam of lip salves, biros, tampons, scratched-off bus passes and a miniature Paddington Bear on a defunct key ring. Millie touched none of these things. She simply looked at them for a long moment before closing the drawer.

The second drawer contained a few forgotten items of underwear and a neatly-folded pair of red pyjamas that Karen had worn when she was twelve. The pyjamas were a poignant reminder of her daughter's tendency to hang onto items from her past, for reasons that Millie felt echoed her own in her penchant for routine. Again, she looked but didn't touch.

The bottom drawer was jammed so full of old notebooks, diaries and school exercise books that it had to be waggled vigorously from side to side in order to open it. Leaning down from the bed, Millie grabbed the handle and performed the necessary action so effectively that the drawer surrendered with a crack, came away from the cabinet altogether and thudded onto the carpet. Sliding off the bed, she sat down and began picking out items at random.

Diaries from previous decades, the days crammed with tiny writing until the third week in January before trailing off into emptiness; notebooks of similar vintage with lists of pop stars, Christmas presents, and scribbled sums; a junior school library project for which she'd won a prize – all well-trodden territory. None received more than a cursory glance before going back in the drawer. When Karen came home, Millie would suggest a clear out.

When Karen came home.

'She'll be back when she's ready,' Charmaine had said last night, catching Millie stealing a quiet five minutes alone in her kitchen. 'Perhaps...' – Charmaine had not looked at Millie as she said this – '...you should stop looking and just wait.'

Millie understood precisely her friend's reasoning behind this sudden turnabout. It was born out of kindness, concern for Millie's welfare, but... 'No,' Millie had replied. 'I can't. Can't stop. Not until I find her.'

Charmaine had given her a hug, perilously tilting both their wine glasses, and gone back to the party, leaving Millie to grapple with a sudden jolt of jealousy towards Charmaine, whose own children had never done anything as inconvenient as disappearing. Her son and his family were three miles away in Hove, her daughter in Toronto. Charmaine had once bemoaned the distance. What Millie wouldn't give to have that same distance between herself and Karen; geography was a mere snap of the fingers compared with the icy tundra separating hearts and minds.

This morning, on the doorstep, as Millie had shown the girls out, Sarah had turned to her and said: 'She must be all right, your daughter, otherwise you'd have heard by now.'

Alive. That was what *all right* meant, in that context. Sarah had intended her words to be reassuring, but instead they'd caused a flutter of doubt that seemed to be growing rather than subsiding. For Sarah to have said that, she must have considered, if only for a moment, that something terrible could have happened to Karen. But it hadn't. Despite the fact she hadn't been in contact, despite Jack O'Brien – Millie shivered as she met again that dark-eyed stare – Karen was out there somewhere, living her own life by her own rules. Millie had to believe that. If she didn't, she was lost. She gazed around the room that was so empty of Karen yet so full of her. Like Millie herself.

Edging both hands under the drawer, she manoeuvred it back into place with a long exhalation. One item had escaped the pile – a fat school exercise book with a tatty cover and inky writing on the label. *Rough Book. Karen Hope. Form II Alpha.* Hoisting herself back onto the bed, Millie flicked through the pages, finding homework instructions, rough plans of essays, heavy with crossings-out, a slapdash diagram of a bunsen burner, probably copied from the blackboard, and then a page in a neater hand that Millie at first did not recognise as Karen's until she realised that the names written down the centre of the page like the cast of a play were trial signatures. Millie and her classmates had gone through a similar phase, writing their names as if they were autographs for adoring fans, trying out different surnames, mostly those of the currently favoured pop stars. How little life changed.

Karen Louise Hope the list began, then *Karen Hope* several times in varying writing styles and sizes. Then, the surname abandoned, *Aisha, Anastasia, Natalia, Larisa, Katya.*

Katya. The scene came flooding back: the kitchen clock racing towards eight-thirty, Millie throwing together a packed lunch for an only just mentioned geography field trip, Karen unconcernedly eating toast at the table and between mouthfuls berating her mother, only half seriously, for saddling her with such a boring first name.

'Why couldn't you have called me something less ordinary, like... Katya?'

Chapter Twenty

The assistant manager of the Croydon supermarket had either never heard of the Data Protection Act or was having no truck with it, because it had taken only a swift phone call to discover that Jack O'Brien had left and gone to work as a night attendant at a petrol service station. Much encouraged by this lackadaisical approach, Millie had asked which petrol station it was and where she might find it, and if – she had crossed her fingers at this point – he could possibly give her Jack's home address. The petrol station, she was told, was 'not a million miles' from the supermarket, definitely within the South Croydon area but he didn't know where exactly. As for Jack's address, that seemed to change quite often but he could give her the most recent one they had on record.

Marvelling at how easy this part of her quest had been, Millie had begun to wonder whether the assistant manager had his own personal axe to grind with his erstwhile employee. She shouldn't be surprised. What was a surprise was that Jack had managed to get himself a job in the first place, let alone two, considering his criminal record, unless the social worker who had spoken for him over the drug thing also had a hand in his employment.

Swinging into the supermarket car park, which seemed as good a starting point as any, she turned off the engine and studied the downloaded map of South Croydon and surrounding area. Aware that she had no idea whether Jack worked every night, she had plumped for a Wednesday, for no other reason than it sat neatly in the middle of the week, and things were likely to be quieter on a weekday than at the weekend.

The clock on the dashboard said twenty past eight. What

time did night shifts begin? It seemed reasonable to assume that they finished around seven or eight in the morning, so unless the shift lasted twelve hours she'd arrived far too early. She hadn't thought this through, had she? She'd been too concerned with the trickier aspects of the mission to have considered the obvious.

On the second map, a more detailed one showing the streets in the immediate area, she had circled the rough location of where Jack supposedly lived. She really didn't want to go there, not if it could be avoided. She had only taken the address as a kind of insurance, but it would pass the time even if she didn't have the courage to knock on the door.

She glanced at the empty passenger seat, imagining it filled by Charmaine, Jet, or even Gus, but she had not wanted the distraction of another person's presence. Karen, by her disappearance, had issued her biggest challenge yet and any attempt to water it down would feel as if she, Millie, was in some way doing her daughter a disservice. No, this was something she had to face, and face alone, foolhardy or not.

She refastened her seat belt, started the engine and drove out into the street.

Millie's heart leapt as she spotted the name-plate of Jack's road. The traffic behind meant she could not slow down sufficiently to turn into it at once, but a mini-roundabout and couple of left-hand turns delivered her, more by luck than judgement, to the other end of the road. The houses here were not dissimilar to the lanky Victorian terraces in Albany Road and she wondered as she crawled by whether she was in the right place because the address she had was a flat in a block. But as she neared the end of the road, the terraces abruptly gave way to a row of local authority houses, at the end of which stood Craveney Lodge – a single, three-storey building with shared balconies spanning the upper floors.

She pulled the car into the kerb and stopped. The lower end of the road had been fairly quiet but here there were little knots of people leaning against walls, chatting or smoking, while rock music bled into the street from open windows. Several pairs of eyes swivelled in Millie's direction. Without thinking too much about it, she got out of the car, locked it, and followed the cracked concrete walkway to the block's entrance, praying that the interest she was attracting did not extend as far as her wing-mirrors and hubcaps.

Not until she had traipsed up several disinfectant-smelling flights of stairs and emerged on to the topmost balcony did it occur to her that she might just find someone else behind the door of number thirty-one other than Jack. Could Karen be here, too? *Could she?* Millie's remaining breath drained away. Why had she not thought of that before? She stood still, holding onto the peeling iron railing of the balcony. Of course she had thought of it; at least the idea had been there, right at the back of her mind, only she had not allowed it to surface... until now.

The evening air rushed coolly into her lungs as she forced herself to breathe, then, turning away from the unremarkable panorama of South London, walked quickly along the balcony before she could change her mind and rapped on the frosted glass of number thirty-one. Silence. She rattled the letterbox flap. Nothing. Sensing movement on the balcony, Millie turned and saw a woman standing by an open door, wearing a white stetson and white cowboy boots with a great deal of fringing in between. She stared uncompromisingly at Millie.

'Waddya want?'

Millie produced a smile. It bounced off the mask of the woman's face, leaving no impression.

'I'm looking for... Mister O'Brien. There doesn't seem to be anyone in.'

'O'Brien? That 'is name, him that works nights? You're wasting your time, love. Crawls out of his pit around three and buggers off out. Christ knows where to. Bag o' tricks if you ask me.'

The woman edged closer in a manner which suggested a lifetime of suspicion. Millie caught a whiff of Thierry Mugler's *Angel* with a back-note of Rothman's.

'What did you want 'im for?'

'It doesn't matter. Look...' – she undid the buckle of her shoulder bag, reached inside and pulled out Karen's photo –

'Have you seen this girl, here, anywhere, please? Her name's Karen, or she might be calling herself Katya.'

The woman stared at the photo for what seemed like a long time, long enough for Millie to hear a whisper of hope, but eventually she shook her head.

'Nope. Never seen 'er, and that's God's honest.'

'Well, thank you anyway,' Millie said, believing her.

'Who shall I say it was, if I see your *Mister* O'Brien?'

'Oh, no, there's no message, thank you.'

The woman backed away towards her own door and, pausing only to spit carefully over the side of the balcony, disappeared inside.

Millie flung a chocolate bar into the glove compartment where it joined a tube of wine gums, a packet of chewing gum, a cellophane-wrapped sausage roll, a carton of blackcurrant juice and a book of second-class stamps. How many petrol stations did they need in South Croydon, anyway? Enough to tank up the Grand Prix several times over, by the look of it. With no sign of Jack at any of them, there had been no choice but to pose her question directly to the staff on duty. The responses she had received so far – all negative – ranged from the blatantly disinterested to the downright hostile, but she'd come this far and she couldn't give up now.

Starting the engine again, she drove off yet another forecourt and headed in what she thought was a different direction from any she had taken before, although she couldn't be certain. She had definitely seen signs for some of these places already – Selhurst, Broad Green, Fairfield... Sutton – that was a new one. Millie cracked on, taking turn-offs at random. There seemed little point in trying to follow the map; even if she was revisiting old ground, she might have missed something.

It was dark now, not just dusky but properly dark. She had hardly noticed the change. Ahead was another roundabout, and beyond it an arced green roof and a petrol sign. This was one she hadn't tried; she would have remembered the row of rocketing leylandii at the back. Achieving the correct exit with only a little dithering, she pulled up on the forecourt but already she could see inside where only a female assistant stood behind the counter. It wasn't a job Millie would have wanted, that was for sure, not at this time of night anyway.

A car and a lorry were heading for the exit but all the pumps were free. She pulled into the service area, topped up, and went inside, purse at the ready. The assistant, whose lopsided name-badge announced her as Joanne, gave Millie a friendly smile as she dealt briskly with the petrol sale.

'Anything else?'

'Actually, yes. Does a Jack O'Brien work here?'

'Jack? Yes, why?'

This was it. *This was it!* Millie's hand flew to her mouth. She felt wrong-footed and almost panicky. All evening she'd been waiting for this and now she hadn't a clue what came next. She glanced anxiously over her shoulder, half expecting to see Jack looming over her, but there was no-one.

'It's just that I know him, that's all,' she said, trying to sound casual. 'I couldn't remember if this was the place. I would quite like a word with him, if he's about.'

What was she saying? Supposing Jack was lurking somewhere at the back of the shop and Joanne called him out? She hadn't planned to do this in front of an audience; in fact she hadn't planned very much at all, had she?

Joanne yawned widely, covering her mouth after the event. 'He comes on after me. Half ten, if I'm lucky. Wait around if you like.'

'No, it's all right. It doesn't matter.' That was the second time tonight she'd said it didn't matter. Once more and she would start to believe it herself. 'I'll catch him another time, I expect. Anyway, I've left the car...'

Waving vaguely towards the fuel pumps, Millie hurried out of the shop, anxious to remove herself from centre-stage in case Jack happened to be early, although this seemed unlikely, given Joanne's comment.

It was past ten now. Roaming the highways and byways of Croydon had at least had the advantage of eating up time. Millie drove away from the petrol station, continuing along the same road; if she kept in a straight line she should have no trouble finding it again. The vast shadowy plains of a deserted recreation ground came into view. Millie pulled in, stopping on the path that ran alongside it and subsided into her seat in an effort to relax but in her wound-up state it was impossible. She took the sausage roll from the glove compartment, unwrapped it, and took a bite. It tasted of fat and artificial meatiness. She put it back and ate several squares of the chocolate instead, washed down with a draw from the blackcurrant juice carton.

The rapid injection of carbohydrate worked, perhaps too well. As the desired calming effect took hold, Millie felt the intensity of her mission begin to drain away, leaving its likely futility hanging around in her mind like an unironed sheet until she began seriously to wonder whether she shouldn't just go home and forget the whole thing. The vaguely-rehearsed words she would deliver should she encounter Jack had already evaporated into nothingness anyway. Likely as not, she would only stand there with her mouth open if she did manage to confront him.

She took out her mobile phone. The friendly face of the lit screen confirmed the time on the dashboard: ten thirty-five. She checked for messages. There were none. Aware that she was prevaricating, she switched off the phone with a decisive thumb-press, refastened her seat belt and headed back to the petrol station.

He was there. She felt his presence before she saw him, his long-limbed movements languid as he served the driver of the parcel delivery van that waited, engine trembling, just past the pumps. Millie slid the car round the edge of the forecourt, keeping close to the boundary fence, stopped in the least-lit spot and waited until the van driver reclaimed his vehicle and drove off into the night. Then she got out of the car and walked firmly towards the shop.

Adrenalin shot through her veins and attacked her feet like a bucketful of scorpions as she realised that Jack had already spotted her. The distance from the shop door to the counter seemed to have stretched three-fold since she was last here, giving those deep, dark eyes ample time to bore their way into her skull before she arrived. Jack took a step back and folded his arms, exposing bony white wrists sprinkled with black hair as the cuffs of his uniform shirt receded. His face settled into a sarcastic grimace.

'Well, well, well. Look who it isn't.'

'We'll do away with the pleasantries and cut to the chase if it's all the same to you.' Millie looked Jack directly in the eye, pushing herself through the discomfort until it felt almost easy. 'I need to see Karen, or at least speak to her. Do you know where she is, or have a number, anything, that would help me do that?'

Jack unfolded his arms and stepped forward. It took all Millie's resolve not to step backwards in response.

'And why should I tell you if I have?'

'No reason why you should, I realise that – I'm not stupid – but if you care about my daughter at all, if you've ever had the tiniest bit of feeling for her, then perhaps you might find it in your… in you, to tell me, because what I need to say to her is important and she would want to hear it, believe me.'

Jack threw up his large hands. Greasy curls waggled above gleaming, narrowed eyes as he shook his head incredulously.

'Believe *you*? What is this, some kind of *joke*?'

Millie hauled breath into her non-functioning lungs. She'd walked into that one, hadn't she? Jack was, of course, referring to the time – that glorious time – when Karen had left him, all too briefly as it happened, and Jack had come to Star Street looking for her.

'Well, you won't find her here,' Millie had declared. 'She's gone travelling with a friend, hiking round Europe. Last I heard they were picking grapes in Italy. There's no address, nothing, and she won't be back for months, perhaps not at all. She said something about Thailand. Just accept it, Jack. She's gone, you've lost her, and that's that.'

After Millie had shut the door in Jack's face, her legs had all but given way as she'd hidden behind the curtains in the living room and watched him lope away down the street and out of their lives, hopefully for ever. Karen had phoned that evening. Could she come over and collect the spare duvet from the airing cupboard? The window in her room didn't fit properly and let in a draught. Of course she could have it, Millie had said. No need for her to come; she would drop it over for her after work tomorrow.

And she had, taking just twenty minutes to cross Brighton, to Karen's flat. That was when they were still friends, of course. Before Karen knew what Millie had done.

Jack gave a contemptuous hoot of laughter. Clearly he was remembering Millie's lie, too. And what came after.

'You must be pretty desperate if you've come all this way to find me,' Jack was saying now, his brow creasing as he attempted to work this one out.

'Yes, I'm desperate. I'll make no bones about that. Look, if Karen's with you, then I'll say nothing about that, I'll not cause any trouble – she's old enough to make her own decisions and live by them. All I want is a number, an address, or even for you to pass on the message that I need to speak to her on an urgent family matter.'

'You want to speak to Karen on a *family* matter, eh? Now, there's a first,' Jack said, staring levelly at Millie. 'You wanna know why she left? Well, it wasn't anything to do with me. You wonder why she never came back? Look at your own pathetic little life. Look in the fucking mirror.'

Millie frowned. What was all that about? They both knew why Karen had left. It was because Millie had interfered in her daughter's life once too often, as Karen saw it. She'd gone off in a major strop and pride had prevented her from coming back. A tragic situation, but a simple one. Why was Jack raking that up, making it sound like something it wasn't?

'I don't know why you're saying that...'

Jack gave a sneering half-laugh. 'No, you really don't, do you?'

Whatever this was about, Millie had no intention of being dragged into it. It probably meant nothing at all. He was spouting nonsense for the sake of it, trying to wind her up. Well, it wouldn't work.

'Jack, do you know where Karen is?'

Millie spoke slowly, emphasising every word.

175

'No, I sodding well don't! Not that it's any of your business.'

'You're not still seeing each other then?'

Jack did not reply. Instead, he turned round and picked a red disposable lighter out of the display box. His eyes unwaveringly on Millie, he tossed the lighter from one hand to the other and back again, then snapped it into life with his thumb, thrusting it forward so that the flame was inches from Millie's face. This time she did recoil, out of shock rather than fear. The fear was there, though. She could feel it rising from the core of her being, spreading like fire through her limbs and down her spine. Remembered fear. So very much like the real thing.

Jack flicked his thumb away and the flame vanished as fast as it had come. He threw the lighter back in the box. Millie stayed where she was, a few steps back from the counter. Without taking her eyes entirely away from Jack, she glanced through the window at the deserted forecourt, the harsh, steady glow from the various lighting points pooling on the concrete and throwing the unlit areas into near-blackness. The only sign of life came from the occasional car swishing along the road that now seemed impossibly distant.

But she wouldn't run away. Not this time.

She took a deep breath and looked Jack in the eye. 'When did you last see Karen, or speak to her? How long ago?'

Jack shrugged. 'Dunno. Can't remember.'

Millie sighed. 'Couldn't you at least try? Was it in the last six months, the last year? Look, Jack, do you have a mobile number for her, a newer one?'

For a moment she thought he wasn't going to answer, that once again she was going away empty-handed. His voice, when he spoke at last, was quiet, different. He seemed to be struggling to form the words.

'We were all right, we were, and then she decides... Anyway, it's been ages since... since I last talked to her. Then she must have got rid of it, her phone.'

He lowered his eyes, staring down at the counter. When he lifted them again there was no trace of challenge or attitude.

Instead Millie saw something softer, younger, and startlingly vulnerable.

And then she knew. Karen had not only abandoned her; she had abandoned Jack, too. And she had broken his heart.

Millie looked at him now and saw the boy he had been, a confused, poorly-raised boy, the youngest sibling scrambling through life at the tag end of a bunch of hellraising brothers with no decent role model to look up to. Remove the rose-tinted glasses and no doubt an evil streak would reveal itself – Millie wasn't that naive – but what she wanted now was to give something to Jack. She had come here for the sole purpose of taking what she could from him to help her search; she had not considered his feelings in all of this, although to be fair, she wasn't aware he had any until now.

Jack stared levelly back at Millie. It was a hard, accusatory stare, full of the antagonism she had come to expect from him, yet behind the expression in those darkest of eyes, a hint of the vulnerability she had seen only minutes ago still remained, a sign of the inner struggle that was Jack's cross to bear.

'I did have some news of Karen,' she said.

Jack jerked his chin up, his face alert, yet wary.

'She got a job as a holiday rep. Crete, I heard, but then she appears to have left and no-one I spoke to knows what happened to her after that.'

'Crete, eh? Could be another one of your lies then, couldn't it? How do I know you're not making it up?'

Jack stepped back and propped himself against the display unit, arms loosely folded, ankles nonchalantly crossed. Jack in repose seemed far more threatening than in confrontational stance.

'Yes, well, I'm sorry about that,' Millie said, feeling the nerves in her stomach begin to twitch as the untruthful apology slipped out. 'I'm not lying now, though, not about the travel rep job.'

'You sure?' Jack's eyes narrowed to gleaming slits.

'There'd be no point, would there? As I said, she left, and anyway the company went bust so the trail's gone cold.'

Jack gave a firm little nod and lapsed into pensive, lip-biting silence. Matters here were clearly at an end and Millie had to make her escape. He made it easy for her.

'You can clear off now.'

Millie turned and walked between the aisles of crisps and bottles and newspapers. As she reached the door, she heard:

'That's it! Fucking clear off and don't come back! *Bitch*!'

Chapter Twenty-One

Perched on the top rung of the step-ladder he used for decorating, the tallest one he had although it wasn't really up to the task in hand, Gus snipped away at the long, stiff branches of forsythia that had shed its ochre flowers months ago and was in serious need of a trim. At least it had begun as a trim but was now more like wholesale decimation. It would be all the better for that, he thought, adding to the thick twiggy bunch in his hand before dropping the lot onto the ground and starting again.

Forsythia, apparently, was virtually impossible to destroy; he could hack it back with impunity. This information he had acquired with practised ease, having casually brought his shrubby problem to the attention of Rosemary and the Yummy Mummies. In fact they'd jostled verbally with one another to be the first up with words of guidance. Quite sweet, really. Gus chuckled to himself. He must remember to ask them about the white-blossomed giant in the opposite corner that also threatened to block out a fair chunk of light. He couldn't even put a name to that one, let alone know if this was the right time of the year to cut it.

He stretched his body to its fullest extent, the toes of his trainers gripping the wooden step as he worked the secateurs amongst the topmost branches. There, all done. Returning to ground level, he looked up with satisfaction at the patch of new blue-white sky uncovered by his efforts, then surveyed the huge ragged nest of twigs and greenery at his feet and decided to leave it right where it was. It was near enough to the end of the garden not to offend the eye of anyone looking out of the neighbouring houses or his own.

Not that anyone other than him was likely to be looking.

He doubted Millie would be paying a visit any time soon, especially after her last experience. She had been remarkably forgiving about his failure to make their lunch date, as was her nature, of course. He had, however, detected a soupcon of chastisement that he chose not to dwell on and he'd been denied the haven of the back room, which could have been a kind of statement or – and Gus decided this was the most likely – it was simply a matter of timing.

The slightly strained atmosphere had made him wary at the time of saying the wrong thing. Nevertheless, he'd left the shop under the impression they had reached some kind of mutual understanding about the way in which their future friendship was to be conducted, but the more he thought about it later, the more Millie's intentions diminished in his mind, both in clarity and purpose, until he was no longer sure what they'd agreed or what either of them wanted.

Deep in thought, Gus stood for a while in the same spot, the cold weight of the secateurs in his hand. He liked Millie, more than liked her; that much was becoming increasingly clear, but the idea of getting closer to her – supposing he ever had the chance – frightened him, and it wasn't solely because of Clair. It seemed more to do with the way he'd changed, how his relatively carefree, forward-looking side had gone and got itself buried beneath his new anxieties, so much so that he hardly recognised himself these days. That was no basis for a new relationship, was it?

Giving himself a metaphorical shake, Gus returned to more practical matters. He took the secateurs back to the shed and gave them a wipe with a bit of cloth before putting them in the trug with the other hand tools, more in belated deference to Augusta than his own concern for such trivialities. Then he fetched the step-ladder, folded it up, and stowed that in the shed as well.

It was still only half past ten. The rest of Saturday stretched promisingly before him and yet, unusually, he had no idea how he wanted to fill it. Again, as he walked back indoors, Millie came into his mind – not that she was ever far from it. The shop would be closed but perhaps he could risk giving her a call at

180

home to see how she was and ask if he might pop in next week. Having something to look forward to might spur him on to do something useful with his day.

The phone rang before he had time to pick it up.

'Great minds,' he said, smiling as he heard Millie's voice. He flinched as his lip cracked; his first smile of the day.

'What?'

'Doesn't matter.' Why had he been so worried about talking to her? It seemed stupid now.

Millie was telling him about an exhibition of artwork using textiles that was on at Brighton Museum. She was going anyway and she was wondering, if Gus wasn't doing anything else, although she expected he was, whether he'd like to meet her there. But the Saturday traffic... it'd take him ages to find a place to park...

'What time?'

'I saw Jack O'Brien. This Wednesday just gone.'

Ah. This, then, was why they were here. Millie wanted to confide in someone, and she had chosen him. Realistically, he might not have been her first choice but he decided not to run with that. He'd got lucky; that was all that mattered. In the gallery, he had been slightly perplexed at Millie's obvious distraction as she stood in front of each exhibit, half-seeing, moving onto the next as if she was on a duty tour of inspection. Now they were at one of the glass tables in the museum café on the balcony with the soft echo of voices around them and a ragged stream of visitors drifting through the hall below.

'Saw him? You mean you went looking for him?'

'I wasn't sure if I was going to tell you, until now.' Millie buttered her scone, smoothing the knife across with steady concentration, not looking at him properly.

'Because of what I'd say.'

'Precisely.'

'Does it matter to you, what I say?'

Millie put the knife down and looked at Gus, her eyes showing faint amusement. 'Surprised you have to ask. Let's get it over with, then.'

'Get what over?'

'The big telling-off.'

Gus's turn to be amused. 'Not much point after the event. You know what I think anyway.'

'That I shouldn't have gone on my own. Not at night.'

'At *night*?' Gus banged down his cup. Heads turned. 'For heaven's sake, Millie, whatever were you thinking? Why didn't you ask me... someone, to go with you?'

'Because I needed to do it on my own. For Karen. That was the point. At least it felt that way at the time. He was like this huge weight round my neck, dragging me down, stopping me getting on with things, with finding her. Anyway, here I am, perfectly safe and all in one piece.' She laughed.

Gus didn't see anything to laugh about. He would never underestimate Millie; he knew enough about her to know how brave and independent she was, capable of anything she put her mind to. But going after that Jack character after all she'd said about him, which actually, now he came to think about it, wasn't very much.

'So what happened? Did you talk to him?'

Millie nodded, then described in detail the events of Wednesday night. Her words had a guarded feel about them, a hint of incredulity, as if she was telling the story for her own benefit as much as his. He let her finish, restraining himself with some difficulty from interrupting, but at the end all he could say was: 'Oh, Millie,' as he visualised a lone figure walking away across the petrol station forecourt, her head held high, her mind in turmoil.

'You've never quite explained about Jack,' Gus said, after a moment. 'You've told me what he was like but not really what he did, what led up to all this. If you don't want to talk about it, though, I do understand,' he added, as Millie looked doubtful.

'No, it's all right, I want to tell you. I just don't want it to sound...' Gus waited. 'As if I'm completely neurotic.'

'You shouldn't be so hard on yourself,' he said, thinking he was a fine one to talk.

Millie gave a resigned smile. 'I did all I could to stop Karen seeing Jack, and then when she dumped him I was so proud of her, but he came looking for her and I told him she'd gone travelling, said it on the spur of the moment. A complete lie, of course, but amazingly he believed me.'

'Yes, I remember you saying.'

'Did I? Oh yes. Well, I knew it wasn't enough. Since Karen was still living in Brighton, there was every chance they'd bump into one another and we'd be back where we started. It was as if he had some kind of hold over her. She seemed fascinated by him, I don't know... Anyway, I'd been to a craft exhibition in London with Julie – she's one of my regulars. We got off the train at Park – it was quite late – and as we went over the bridge we saw a little gang hanging about in the dark. They were smoking and it was obvious from the smell what it was. Julie said it wasn't the first time she'd seen them there. I only got a glimpse as we went past but I was sure I saw Jack and I don't know if it was my imagination but I swear he looked right back at me. Couldn't get it out of my mind afterwards, and I couldn't help thinking that if Jack was using cannabis, or worse, then how long would it be before Karen was, too, if she wasn't already? So I wrote to the police tipping them off anonymously – I'm not proud of it but I'm not sorry either. Shortly after that, the little gang got busted and Jack got a fine and community service, not just for using but supplying, too. He only got off so lightly because it was a first offence and his social worker spoke up for him.'

'Good for you,' Gus said, then aware that he might have sounded patronising: 'It was a brave thing to do, as it goes. Not sure I would have had the guts.'

Millie smiled. 'No guts involved, just anger for the way he treated Karen, which was quite shameful at times.' She thought for a moment. 'Funnily enough it didn't make me feel better although it might have opened her eyes a little. Perhaps revenge isn't as sweet as people make out.'

'Hardly revenge. You were just looking out for your daughter.'

'I was, but that wasn't the end of it because then it was Jack's turn to get his own back. When Karen took him back and let him move into the house in Croydon, he obviously knew then that I'd lied about her going travelling and maybe he had seen me that night and realised it must have been me who'd told the police.'

'He couldn't have been certain it was you.'

'I know, that's what I kept telling myself, but what he threatened me with was... well, it was heavy stuff. Didn't really line up with getting me back over a simple fib.'

'He *threatened* you?'

'One of his brothers was into arson – delightful soul – and Jack said that if I contacted him or Karen again or tried to split them up, his brother would burn my house down at night with me inside it.'

Gus was appalled. Millie, on the other hand, seemed calm, almost matter-of-fact.

'I've spent so many nights not sleeping, jumping at the slightest sound, prowling round the house... you wouldn't believe.' She laughed. 'And I've smelled smoke just about everywhere since.'

'I'm not surprised,' Gus said, marvelling yet again at the bravery of this woman. He waved at the waitress for the bill, waiting until she brought it before he spoke again. 'So, how do you feel about Jack now?'

'That's just it. I'm not sure how I feel. I'm not afraid of what he could do to me any more. At least, I wasn't. There was a moment there, in the petrol station, when it all came rushing back – the lighter, the flame... and then when everything changed and I saw the real Jack, I thought, this is all over. But now it seems it's not that easy. Oh dear, I'm not explaining this very well, am I?'

'You're doing fine.'

'Gus...'

'Yes?'

'Do you think you can ever stop being afraid, once you've started?'

'Can fear be unlearned, you mean?'

Millie nodded. The way she looked at him, appealing to him, trusting his response, made him feel like an imposter.

'Yes,' he said. 'I'm certain it can.'

184

Chapter Twenty-Two

Gus looked at the pair of size ten brown shoes on Elspeth's kitchen table – she never was one for superstition. The sight of them when he arrived had given him quite a start. The laces were frayed, the desiccated leather beneath their dangling ends scored across with hairline cracks. Sturdy of sole, and of purpose, the shoes bore the imprint of their wearer as surely as if he had just stepped out of them. Gus fought the constriction in his throat.

'I felt like that, too,' Elspeth said.

'But you don't now?

'No.'

Elspeth picked up the shoes and burrowed them briskly into a carrier bag. The scrunch of papery plastic caused the Dalmatian to turn full circle in his bed before settling down again with one gauzy eye open.

'Everything else went at the time, his clothes, his other shoes, but these were his favourites, the ones he wore every day and did all his headmasterly things in. I couldn't turf them out before. They seemed too much like *him*. They can go now though.'

So what had changed? Gus enquired, suspecting he knew the answer. He was right. The fresh flood of pent-up grief that Jenny's accident had released, difficult though it was both for Elspeth to endure and Gus to witness, had brought a new acceptance, a different kind of perspective to life without Robert. The memory-shape of him no longer depended on props to keep it constant; in fact, they somehow hampered it, Elspeth said, raising quizzical eyebrows to check if Gus understood.

He steepled his fingers, gave a slow, pensive nod. This was, he supposed, the next stage on for Elspeth – a natural progression, a reminder, too, that people must deal with life's dramas in their own way, without pressure or outside influence.

'Right then.' He smiled brightly, snapping the mood. Picking up the bag containing the shoes, he gathered up the top, giving it a twist as if it contained no more than potato peelings. 'Where do you want this?'

'In the wheelie bin by the front door, if you would.'

'Sure?'

'Yes,' Elspeth said, the brightness of her smile matching his own.

When Gus returned, the table held another object, a large, battered box made of stout tan leather. On the top, among a multitude of scratches and a patchy film of dirt, lay the ghosts of ancient, haphazardly-applied luggage labels. Elspeth opened the lid, allowing the outer leather casing to flap down, revealing a second box of tooled leather with a brass handle and lock.

'It belonged originally to your...   no, I mean Rob's grandfather...'

For the first time Elspeth looked flustered.

'It's okay.' Gus waved away her embarrassment. 'What's inside?'

'This is the last of his things and now it has to go, too.' She nodded at the box, not answering Gus's question. 'I have photos, our wedding rings and Rob's watch. The look in his eye, the sound of his voice, the way he was, that's all in here.' A light finger touched her temple. 'Nothing's lost, you see. Nothing ever is. Even if you can't see it or remember, it still exists.'

Gus gazed out of the window, finding it hard to meet Elspeth's eye. When he did, she was smiling, a quiet, encouraging smile, as if what she was really telling him lay beneath the words, or beyond them. After a moment, she produced a tiny key, unlocked the inner box and lifted the lid. A faint musky smell escaped, the smell of past lives.

'It was Robert's treasure box. That's what he called it. He brought it with him when we got married and we used it to keep birth certificates and important stuff in until... well, all that's been taken out now but there are other things I wanted you to see, Gus. That's why I waited till you came.'

'I've never seen this before. I didn't know he had it,' Gus said, aware that he was prevaricating as he felt a swoop of anxiety.

'Well, you know what children are,' Elspeth said. 'I expect it was his secret. You must have had them too, secrets, when you were young?'

'No, not really,' Gus replied, wondering if he was the only person in the world who didn't have secrets, unless his Thursday escapes to the capital counted. But that wasn't really a secret; it was just that nobody knew because he had never told anyone.

'Well, anyway, sit down and I'll show you what's in here.'

Gus sat. Elspeth lifted out a clutch of school exercise books, some crayoned pictures, their edges curled with age, a number of matchboxes with foreign labels, an unused pencil with Robert's name in gold lettering, a handful of badges, and a shrivelled conker on a string. These she set to one side with a little shrug and a smile, then delving in again she brought out a pocket diary, then another. Boy Scout diaries, 1959 and 1960. She pushed them across the table towards Gus.

He looked up at Elspeth. He wasn't sure he wanted this.

'It's all right,' she said, waving a placating hand. 'Don't start worrying. When you look, though, you'll see why I had to show them to you, give them to you, if you like. You can take them home. You don't have to look now.'

'No, no.'

That would be worse. Whatever he would find, he needed to get it over and done with.

'Did you know about these?' he asked.

'I knew they were there, yes, but I'd never read them. They weren't mine to read.'

'Have you read them now?'

'I've read enough, yes. You do need to see.'

Elspeth looked at Gus. In her long, direct gaze he read concern, encouragement, a kind of excitement. It was then that

187

he understood that what he was about to read was, in some way, of immense importance. He drew in a long breath, let it out again slowly, turning the first diary over in his hand but not opening it. It smelt of Robert, felt like him.

'Were you a Boy Scout, too?' Elspeth asked, trying, perhaps, to balance the moment with lightheartedness.

'Me? No, I didn't like being organised.'

Elspeth gave a knowing little laugh. Gus widened his eyes at her, then, realising he couldn't delay any further, opened the diary. On the first page was inscribed in his brother's small, precise writing his full name, address, blood group and next of kin, whom he'd put down as his mother. Gus turned to January. There were three days to a page, leaving the writer no option but to pare down the size of his script even further. Not all the days were filled in. Several were blank or housed the overflow from the previous day.

It seemed 1959 had begun with a spell of hard weather. Skipping over epic snowball fights and longest slide competitions, Gus flicked on through the months. A birthday outing, scout camp, a wristwatch acquired, an English prize won, a goal scored, the arrival of the grammar school acceptance letter, then a Sahara of unrecorded summer days, apart from a brief mention of the annual holiday in Dorset, centring on the number of crabs caught in a bucket.

Gus looked up at Elspeth.

'No, there's not much in that one, not in the early part,' she acknowledged.

He read on.

Wednesday 2nd September: I keep having a dream that I'm drowning in school uniform because everything I've got is about a hundred sizes too big! I asked Dad to turn the sleeves on the blazer up but he said I've got to grow into it.

Monday 7th September: If Rogers and his gang call me a swot once more I will not be responsible. No good walking the long way round as they will only follow me. As if I care.

Wednesday 16th September: Mam was funny with Dad for getting home late from shop. I made out I had loads of homework so I could stay up here. All gone quiet now.

Thursday 17th September: Geoff says his mam goes funny sometimes because of how old she is. Expect that's the matter with Mam but it might not be because Geoff's mam is really old. Scouts was boring tonight. I've got to carry the banner on Sunday again!

A scattering of entries over the next few weeks dwelt on the trivia of school and friends, but Gus sensed a subtle difference between these and the entries that had gone before. The writing was bigger, less careful, spilling across the dividing lines as if deliberately so. There were crossings-out, too, impatient to-and-fro pencilled scrubbings. Gus peered closer, trying to see what lay beneath, yet with the feeling that the unfilled sections of the diary had more to hide.

A cup of tea appeared at his elbow. He smiled his thanks. The first taste scalded his mouth but he kept going, sipping and reading, feeling the alternate burn of liquid and words.

Monday 5th October: Big blow up tonight when Dad got in. They shut the kitchen door but I could still hear it upstairs. Dinner had burnt bits in it. Dad came up later to say sorry, so did Mam, but she'd been crying I could tell.

Tuesday 13th October: Mam is still really odd, keeps giving me great big hugs as if I was a baby or something. I get my homework done at break and go round Geoff's house after school as much as his mam lets me.

Sunday 15th November: Church parade and ceremony at the memorial. I forgot my poppy so I pinched one off the wreath before we set off but it fell off halfway. Went to Geoff's house afterwards so late home for dinner. When I got home Dad had gone.

Gus stared at the final phrase, letting the implications wash over him until they found a borehole and rushed in, drowning out his latent hopes that none of it was true after all, that it had all been one big misunderstanding. He turned the page, hardly daring to read more but unable to stop.

Monday 16th November: Mam will not say how long Dad will be away. I went up in the attic and the big suitcase has gone. She wouldn't say where he was when I asked her but then she threw the photo of Aunt Augusta right across the room. It smashed and a bit of glass got in her thumb and she cried. It was awful. Then she told me where Dad had gone.

Saturday 28th November: Dad is still not back and we had tickets for the Magpies. He has done something really bad. No-one has said what but I think it's got something to do with <u>ANOTHER WOMAN</u>. I hate him and I hate AA, I truly do. I don't ever want to see her again because she upsets Mam too much and someone has to be on her side. It is strange about Dad seeing someone though as he is quite old-fashioned and nearly starting to go bald.

Gus didn't know whether to laugh or cry. He settled for a rueful smile instead.

'It's all here, isn't it?' he said. 'Just as you said. Poor Robert.'

Elspeth raised her eyebrows in reply.

'Is there much more of this?' Gus flicked through the remaining pages, most of which seemed empty.

'Not in that one, no,' Elspeth said, glancing at the second diary. 'Funnily enough, Robert doesn't mention his father coming back but perhaps he didn't feel like writing about it any more. There's a bit about school exams and then an entry just after Christmas. That's about it.'

The writing of the final entry was small and neat again.

Tuesday 29th December: I got all the usual stuff for Christmas plus a new watch as the last one got lost. The turkey and everything was scrumptious. Dad was a bit quiet and did a lot more washing up than he normally would do, then we all played this game I got which turned out to be a bit stupid. Mam and Dad seem all right though. Which is good. AA did not come Boxing Day, first time ever. Good thing as I agree with Mam she is EVIL.

Gus closed the diary and turned to the one from 1960, the year of his birth, his heart fluttering high up in his chest. There was very little written in the first few months, apart from a sentence or two about school and scouts, a good film seen at the pictures, more exams, and in the middle of all this, a sad little entry:

Saturday 19th March: Everything here feels a bit strange.

190

When they talk it's like it's in code. No-one says the proper words for things like they've got a complete new language just for the two of them. Mam does not say AA's name at all, ever. She calls her die Zicke which is German for bitch. Dad doesn't like it as AA is his sister but he only has himself to blame.

Gus flicked on through a reef of blank pages until he came to another entry, the writing small and intense.

Thursday 21ˢᵗ April: AA was here when I got home from school and Dad was home too. I didn't know she was coming but I think Mam must have done as she was a bit funny at breakfast. They were talking for ages with the door shut then Mam came out and rushed upstairs and banged her bedroom door. I didn't know if I should go in there or not but I didn't, then later something happened which is TOTALLY INCREDIBLE. We are getting a baby! It is a boy who hasn't got a proper mam and dad so we are taking him and he is to be my brother except he won't be my real one.

Monday 23ʳᵈ May: The baby is coming at the weekend. His name is Matthew and he will be Albourne like us. I asked where we would get him from and Dad said AA and some other woman she knows would bring him here. Mam and Dad are being extra nice to me all the time and EXTRA EXTRA nice to each other but sometimes I think they don't mean it, at least Mam doesn't. I don't know what it will be like to have this baby. They are a bit old for it I think. I told Geoff's mam and she went all red in the face.

Gus swallowed, closing the diary. He couldn't read any more. Elspeth took it from him.

'I'm sorry, Gus.'

He nodded. 'It's fine. You did right to show me. Is there… anything else?'

'Not much. I think life must have taken over from the diary-writing.'

'Or I did.' Gus smiled.

'Yes.' Elspeth slid a thumb between the pages. 'You'll like this bit he wrote in June. Listen. *I only just passed the Geography test because the baby yelled all night. I don't know why he can't do it in the daytime but he's usually asleep then.*'

Gus laughed. 'I always was awkward.'

He wondered why Robert had not recorded the actual day of his arrival. It felt almost like an affront, but of course it would have been as Elspeth said; there were more important things to think about than the writing of schoolboy diaries. His heart went out to Robert. His world must have turned upside down. He hadn't considered the impact on his brother before.

'Who do you think the other woman was who brought me to the house?'

'I thought about that,' Elspeth said. 'I think she must have been from the home, a friend of Augusta's probably. It was quite common for babies to be placed by private arrangement, as long as they went to a good home. There was always another poor little mite to take its place not far behind... oh, sorry. That sounds awful.'

'No, no, I know what you mean.'

Gus was thoughtful for a moment. The second diary was still in Elspeth's hands. She seemed to be deep in thought, too.

'I was so lucky, wasn't I? I could have been sent anywhere, to anyone.'

'You could, but I'm glad you weren't.' Elspeth smiled and turned back to the diary. 'There's just one more little thing. *Mam cried a lot this morning and was cross with Dad. He said it was because she was tired and he got AA to come and take the baby so she could have a rest. They argued about it a bit but it must have worked because she was better later. I am on Mam's side though. I don't want AA to look after our baby either.*' She looked at Gus. 'Robert never held grudges, not usually, but he certainly held onto that one.'

'He must have had his reasons,' Gus said.

He stared out of the window at the swaying branches of the trees. Something was beginning to stir within him, a memory, or the shadow of one. It was more the memory of a feeling than a tangible incident. Tension, at home, when he was small. Strong, unbreakable threads criss-crossing between Liesel and Henry, stringing through the air in the house like a cat's cradle of invisible cotton, sometimes woven from the echo of a careless word, sometimes from nothing at all. He remembered the worry scratching away at his skin without realising at the time what it was that he found disturbing.

The word 'cheese' came hurrying towards him like a bouncing ball. He reached out, caught it just in time. He must have been about seven or eight – old enough, at any rate, to take notice – when there was a sudden, furious argument over some cheese. His father, he thought, struggling to remember, had thrown some away, thinking it to be stale, only to be met with harsh accusations from his mother, who held frugality in higher esteem than any religion. The cheese was eventually fished out of the bin, wiped off and put back in the fridge. Gus had refused to eat any cheese until he could be sure a new block had been purchased but his father had no such choice.

Then there was the hanging of the picture, an unremarkable piece of art, at least to a child; it was all hills and sky. 'Higher.' 'Lower.' 'No, no, not there!' Then, from his father: 'Do it your bloody self then.' The picture had been allowed to drop heavily to the carpet as his father's even heavier steps took him off to the shed. The sharp ache in Gus's stomach had lasted the rest of the day.

No family life was perfect, no childhood immune, except in his imagination, he knew that now. Memories were made to order, to fill a need; they were not necessarily based on truth. In a strange way he found this comforting.

'Thank you, Elspeth,' he said, smiling.

Elspeth smiled quizzically back. 'What for?'

'Well, you know...' Gus shrugged, momentarily embarrassed. For one awful moment he thought he might be going to cry. He bit his bottom lip hard.

They gazed at one another, a long, warm moment of mutual understanding, then a clamour broke out: a diesel roar, the toot of a horn, a long, hard push on the doorbell. The dog rose from his bed and lumbered to the door, Elspeth following, Gus close behind.

'Hi Mum!' Jenny said, turning to wave at the driver of the special taxi, who toot-tooted again and sped off. 'Uncle Gus!'

She cavorted undaintily into the hall, holding up her palm to high-five him. 'Have you come for lunch, Uncle Gus?'

'Nope.'

Jenny and Elspeth both opened their mouths to speak. Gus silenced them with a hand.

'You're coming back with me, have lunch at mine. Then we'll drive over to the farm and look at the alpacas.'

Jenny made as if to throw her arms around Gus. Her mother beat her to it.

Chapter Twenty-Three

The house wasn't hard to find, despite the absence of a number, because of the clowns. Just as described by his mate Tom from the agency, they covered every inch of the front door, disguising the panels, the letter-flap and the skylight with multicoloured magnificence in a hectic tangle of vertical hair, spaced-out faces, striped and spotted bodies and strangely disembodied limbs.

Standing in the shaded porch, Gus felt in his pocket for his glasses and, in fumbling to put them on, managed to drop his little recording machine. An oily-looking doormat broke its fall. Retrieving the machine, switching it on and pushing his glasses into place, he felt about in his other pocket for the set of keys, but as he probed gingerly around the place where the lock ought to be, his fingers encountered a square section of rough wood and a small hole. No lock then. The buggers must have sawn it off. He gave the door a shove. It gave way and he stepped inside, averting his eyes from the leering red mouths. Clowns, in his opinion, were sinister in the extreme.

The odour of elderly chip-fat that greeted him did nothing to dispel his crotchety mood. The housing market was experiencing a mini-boom and he'd worked solidly over the last ten days, managing only to sidestep Thursday by working on Saturday morning. He'd planned a nice long lie-in this morning followed by a leisurely breakfast before going over to Elspeth's to help her move a wardrobe, but he couldn't let Tom down. As he'd gazed up at the roof and chimney from the other side of the road, which was in a quiet, residential area to the north of Brighton, he'd cursed out loud the surveyor who had so thoughtlessly snapped an Achilles tendon doing a charity fun run, leaving Gus the only other professional available at such short notice on a Monday morning. He shouldn't complain, though; at least being busy kept his mind off other things.

Murmuring to the tape about the crumbling wainscot in the hall, Gus continued his journey through the high-ceilinged rooms. The place had been turned into a squat and its owner, having returned from somewhere African and far-flung, had moved heaven and earth to evict his unwanted tenants and was now anxious to shift it, by auction if necessary. Actually, Gus thought, peeling off posters to examine walls and crawling on all fours around abandoned bean bags and piles of newspapers with his damp meter, it wasn't in too bad a condition and should be easy to mortgage.

The kitchen offered up several unsavoury delights. A vat of yellowing cooking oil, presumably the source of the smell, crouched on the stained hob. There were dirty plates in the sink and a worm-cast of spaghetti over the plug hole, while the putrid collection of grey-furred fruit inexplicably lined up on the windowsill would have no problem in stirring the creative juices of Tracey Emin and her cronies.

Gus's own juices were decidedly unstirred as he glanced out of the window at the narrow yard that formed the return and the dingy scrap of garden beyond it. Sighing, he rattled the handle of the back door, made a quick inspection of the rear façade – a couple of minor cracks and a leaky downpipe – before returning inside and trudging upstairs. Arriving at the first floor landing, he pushed open doors at random. The quicker he could get round, the sooner he'd be back home with the rest of the day at his disposal. The bathroom was surprisingly clean and bright with no sign of damage or mould. A faint soapy scent that hung in the air seemed almost recent. Giving the contents of the shelves a closer look, he noticed that the toiletries seemed fresh, and some, like the almost full shampoo bottle, hardly used. There were even a couple of decent-looking towels draped over the side of the bath. He wondered if the occupants had left in such a hurry that they'd not been able to take any of this stuff with them, but that wasn't usual. Usually there would be time, far too much time in his opinion, for possessions to be gathered and packed; he'd seen some of these so-called evictions.

Slightly puzzled now, Gus pressed on, prodding and peering, muttering his findings into the machine as he went. The three bedrooms he entered were empty, apart from a sagging futon and a mish-mash of discarded clothing in a corner. The fourth bedroom, he understood, was on the floor above. The narrow staircase emitted mouse-like squeaks as he mounted it. He hoped there were no actual mice; he couldn't abide the things. Reaching the top, he squinted into the gloom, his palm smoothing the wall in search of a light switch. He found it, clicked it on. Nothing. No light bulb, but in any case the electricity probably wasn't connected.

The landing area looked and smelt pretty much okay, though. He had a torch but decided to give it no closer inspection – time was getting on – and he definitely wasn't venturing into the confinement of the loft-space, the trap-door to which he could just make out above his head, even if there was a ladder, which he doubted. It would be all right up there, he was sure, sure enough to write it up as being sound anyway.

He pushed on the door of the front bedroom. It gave way grudgingly, the reason for which was apparent when he stepped inside; someone had attempted to add colour and comfort to the floorboards by loose-laying a patchwork of free carpet samples. Stepping over the squares dislodged by his entry, he looked around. The curtains were closed. They were thick, brocade ones, effective at shutting out the light. There was more stuff in here than there had been in the other rooms, including a full clothes rail, a chair draped with more clothes and a stand-up mirror with beads and chains looped across it. A double bed stood against the chimney breast, with a high, old-fashioned wooden headboard and a mountain of bedding.

Again, Gus wondered why all this was still here when presumably it had been useful to its owners at some point. Stepping across to reach the window, his foot encountered something solid. Cursing the obstacle, he looked down and saw a rucksack, the straps straining to contain the bulging contents. Frowning, he tweaked one of the curtains aside and as he did so, he heard a whisper of a sigh and a faint twang of springs. Inhaling sharply, his gaze snapped to the bed which, cast into the full light of day, revealed itself to contain not only a toppling bank of pillows and a slurry of quilts but a sleeping girl.

'Shit!' The expletive left Gus's lips unbidden.

The quilts bounced and the girl sat up, opened her eyes wide and gave a little scream.

Gus held up a hand. 'It's all right! Sorry, sorry…' He edged towards the door. 'I didn't know there was anyone here, honestly.'

'Who the *fuck* are you?'

The occupant of the bed shook her hair off her face and yanked the top quilt towards her, wrapping it protectively round her upper half, although Gus had already noticed she was wearing some kind of t-shirt or pyjama top.

'I *said*…'

'Gus Albourne, chartered surveyor. Come to survey the house,' Gus said hurriedly, holding aloft the damp meter.

Despite her show of bravado, the girl shrunk back and hiked the quilt up to chin level. She looked young, possibly still a teenager. There was vulnerability as well as suspicion in those blue eyes, which the cheap stylised flower print enveloping her only served to enhance.

'It's okay, I'm going,' Gus said, his hand on the door.

'No! I mean go downstairs and I'll be down in a minute.'

The bedclothes were flung back and bare legs appeared over the side of the bed. Gus averted his eyes.

'But I really think I ought'

'No, I said wait! You think I was born yesterday? You get out of here now and the next thing I know the police'll be round… You're not the police, are you?'

'No.'

'Or the council?'

'*No*, look…'

'Then there's no need to rush off is there?'

'I suppose not,' Gus said, wishing he was anywhere but here. 'I'll be downstairs then.'

198

On his way down, Gus considered phoning the agency but he'd left his phone in the car, and in any case he really ought to find out what was going on here first. He didn't have long to wait before the girl appeared in the kitchen wearing jeans with thick socks and a baggy grey jumper. Now he had a proper look at her, she was older than he'd first thought, early twenties perhaps.

'Look, I don't have anywhere else to go, right, so you'll leave me alone, pretend you haven't seen me.'

It was an order rather than a request, delivered with an upright, folded-arm stance and a very direct gaze. Gus decided to ignore it for the time being.

'Why are you still here? I was told everyone had been moved on.'

'We were but some of us came back. They didn't secure it that well. Stupid fools never do. The others have gone, though, so it's only me now.'

'But you really shouldn't be here, should you? It isn't your house. It belongs to someone else, the person I'm acting for today, as it happens.'

She tossed back her long fair hair, fastened him with a withering look.

'His own bloody fault then for leaving it unoccupied for so long, wouldn't you say?'

Gus was about to argue the point but thought better of it. He had better things to do with his time than waste it faffing about here.

'When will you be leaving? I'll come back and finish the job then.'

'I'm not. Didn't you hear what I said?'

'I don't see that you've got any choice.'

'You're going to dob me in. I knew it!'

She covered her face briefly with her hands. Gus felt almost ashamed, as if it was his fault she had to leave.

'It's not a case of dobbing anyone in,' he began, tempering his voice, 'but I need to know what to tell the agents that sent me. The place is going up for sale and they can hardly do that with you in it now, can they? So what's it to be? There must be somewhere you can go, surely?'

'I could stay with friends pro tem. Rather not, though. I don't like being beholden, and anyway I like it here.'

'What about your family?'

'Who said I had one?'

'Well, haven't you? Where are your parents?'

'We're not in contact. Not that it's any of your business.'

Gus ran a hand through his hair. He wasn't getting anywhere here.

'You shouldn't be doing this. There must be something better out there. I take it you don't have a job, but there is a benefits system.'

'Damn cheek!' She flew at him, eyes blazing. 'I don't need their pitiful bloody system! I don't need anything or anyone and for your information, *Mister* whatever-your-name-is, I have a perfectly good job and this is my day off, thank you very much.'

Gus held up a hand. 'Sorry, I just assumed... well, I shouldn't have, and I'm sorry too that I gave you the fright of your life turning up in your bedroom like that.'

She shrugged. 'I've had worse. I'm not scared that easily.'

'Even so...' Gus sighed. He waved a hand vaguely around. 'How do you manage here anyway? Not exactly the Hilton, is it?'

The girl bristled visibly, following Gus's line of sight and gazing at the mess as if it was the first time she'd noticed it. 'I've not had time to clear up yet. I wasn't expecting visitors.'

'No.' Gus shook his head then waited a little before he said: 'When you do get round to it I'd get rid of that for a start.' He indicated the pan of oil. 'It's stinking the place out.'

'Yes, well, I would have done but I didn't think I should pour it down the sink in case it blocked it up.'

'Fair point.'

The girl padded over to the sink and filled the kettle. 'I'm making tea. Want one, since you're still here?'

She switched the kettle on. It hummed into life.

'How come you have electricity?'

She shook her head bemusedly, as if he'd asked the most

200

stupid question in the world. 'Howard reconnected it, no problem.'

'Is Howard a friend?'

'Sort of.'

The throwaway answer came with a frown and a sardonic half-smile, as if she couldn't understand why on earth Gus was interested. He was beginning to wonder that himself.

'And where's this Howard now?'

The girl raised her eyes. 'Gone, like the others. Expect I'll run into him again at some point.'

In another squat, probably, Gus thought.

'It's not that bad here, you know,' she continued, watching his expression. 'The boiler's not working so you have to heat kettles all the time but that's luxury for some people.'

She cast him a look that defied him to disagree, then continued with the tea preparations, taking milk out of a surprisingly clean, well-stocked fridge before putting a mug down on the counter against which Gus was standing, there being nowhere to sit. She leaned against the opposite counter, wrapping her hands around her mug of tea as if she was desperate for the warmth. It struck him for the first time how chilly it was in here although it was a lovely summer's day outside. He remembered the layers of quilts on the bed. She was too thin, of course.

'Where do you work?' he asked kindly.

'A shop. We sell vintage clothes and stuff. Actually I more than work there, I'm a partner. There are two of us, me and a friend.'

Gus smiled. 'Sounds good. Brighton's just the place for that sort of thing, isn't it? I imagine you do quite well.'

She eyed him cautiously, aware of the potential trap. 'There are good and bad days.'

'But you could pay rent if it wasn't too high.'

She sighed. 'Yes, I suppose so.'

Gus thought for a long moment, aware that he might very well live to regret his next move, but he'd meant what he said. Whatever her circumstances – he shivered to think what those might be – she shouldn't be living like this, all alone in this big

201

house with no lock on the door and about to be evicted again once word got back, which it would do eventually even if he didn't, as she put it, dob her in. Who knew what kind of traumas she'd been through? Something must have happened for her to have no family to call on – or so she said. He looked at her standing there, hair unbrushed, stretching the sleeves of her oversized jumper and bunching the ends of them tightly in her hands. Against his bidding, his heart gave a little tug.

'I might be able to help you find you somewhere to live, if you're agreeable to that?'

She gave a scathing little laugh. 'Yeah, right.'

'No, no, it's nothing dodgy. I could say *trust me, I'm an estate agent,* but that wouldn't be funny and not entirely true, but I am a surveyor and I do have contacts in the business. I could look out for a studio apartment for you.'

'Would that be before you hand me over to the authorities or after?'

'I didn't say I'd do that, did I?'

'You didn't say you wouldn't either,' she snapped, giving him an accusing, wide-eyed stare.

'No, so now you really will have to trust me,' Gus countered, giving her a direct look back.

'Okay, okay, you're trying to help. I suppose you are, anyway.' Doubt crept back in, creasing her brow, painting a brushful of shadow around her eyes.

'I am. Look…'

'Why would you do that for someone you don't even know?'

Why indeed. She wasn't convinced – he couldn't blame her for that.

'Because I want to, and if that's not good enough it'll have to be.'

She gave him a long look, as if she was considering this, then she smiled, the first proper one he'd seen. It lit up her face, brought with it a taste of something almost like recognition that sent a tingle down his spine. Aware that he was staring, he glanced out of the window before looking back at her. He swallowed to moisten his mouth.

'Don't expect anything to happen straight away. There might be a bit of wait. I can't summon up a flat out of the blue.'

'All right,' she said. 'Thanks.'

'So how do I get hold of you, other than here, that is?'

She went over to a small cork board where a fan of take-away menus and scraps of paper was secured by a single drawing pin. On top was a small white business card with purple and silver writing. Detaching it, she handed it to him.

'How was it for you?' she said.

'Sorry?'

She raised her eyes. 'That's the name of the shop. *How Was It For You?*'

'Oh, right.' He gave the card a cursory glance then slid it into his pocket. 'I'll be off now, but I'll be in touch as soon as I've made some enquiries. And you take care of yourself.'

'I always do.'

Gus walked along the hall, opened the front door then stopped, turned round. She was leaning in the kitchen doorway, arms folded, watching him. He took the card she'd given him out of his pocket and looked at it, tilting it towards the light and holding it slightly away from him the better to read the small print. Below the name and address of the shop, in purple letters, it said: *Proprietors, Maxine West and Katya Hope.*

Gus held up the card. 'And you would be?'

'Katya.'

'Hope?'

'Says so, doesn't it?' She turned and went into the kitchen, closing the door behind her.

Chapter Twenty-Four

'But what if she hasn't got references? She won't be able to rent without those, will she?'

Millie couldn't say she was surprised at Gus's kindness and the way the girl he'd found in the squat had got under his skin but, even so, the plan sounded mighty risky considering his professional status. If he did manage to find her somewhere to live, she might renege on the rent or let in some of her dodgy squatting friends to trash the place. He wouldn't be so popular then with his mates at the agency.

'Then I'll just have to write them myself,' he declared, lifting his chin.

Millie laughed, unsure if he was being serious. 'You said she was working, though – that'll go in her favour.'

'Yes, a shop, one of those that sells vintage stuff. Not only working, she more or less said she owned the place. How was it for you?'

'How was what for me?' Confusion swept heat to Millie's face.

'No, the shop's called *How Was It For You*?' Gus seemed equally embarrassed. 'She gave me a card…' He went to reach into his top pocket but stopped himself. 'Not got it with me.'

'What's she like?'

'Like?' He seemed to be having difficulty understanding the question. 'Well, you know…' He gave a dismissive little wave. 'Too thin.'

'They're all too thin,' Millie said.

Gus's mobile sang out. 'Sorry.' He seemed almost relieved as he leapt up from the table and took out his phone.

He went and stood in the doorway leading through to the

shop, facing away from Millie, his muttered conversation just low enough to prevent her from hearing the actual words. Denying her curiosity, Millie got up and put the kettle on again. As she waited for it to boil, two trains sped past in quick succession, one coming in, one going out. The familiar sight reassured her. This was good; this was how it should be. Gus had arrived unexpectedly, adding a nice frisson of surprise to an otherwise ordinary Wednesday afternoon. This would be the third lot of tea she'd made; clearly he was in no hurry to leave and yet he seemed tense, as if he might at any moment spring up and rush out of the door.

The kettle puffed steam and switched itself off. Millie poured and took two mugfuls back to the table. Perhaps Gus was thinking about his birth mother again and the aunt who had left him the house; that could be why he was so jumpy. Neither was ever far from his mind and she did so wish she could help, but mentioning it now might be unwise. He knew he could talk to her if he wanted to.

'That was Tom,' he said at last, pocketing his phone and sitting down again. 'There's a new property just come on. It's in town, just off London Road, by the fire station. Two one-bed flats on the ground floor and four studio apartments above, all newly renovated. Keys should be available next week.'

'And you're thinking one of the studios could be right for Goldilocks?'

'I didn't say anything about her hair.'

Millie laughed. 'No, Goldilocks, the girl who broke into the three bears' house and fell asleep in one of the beds.'

Gus gave a fleeting smile. 'Oh, I see. She might have changed her mind by now, of course. I mean, would you let a strange man virtually set you up in a place?'

'And they don't come much stranger than you,' Millie said, grinning as Gus faked a pained expression. 'No, I don't suppose I would, but I'm of a different generation.'

Gus rose abruptly to his feet and stood by the window, his back to the room, shifting his weight from one foot to the other, as if he was trying to strike a balance. Watching him, Millie clasped her hands tightly around her mug of tea as if she needed to steady herself for whatever was to come. After a minute he swung round, a smooth, decisive movement.

'Millie, would you do me a favour? Would you come with me to see her? She'll need to get a shift on if she's going to get one of the studios. They'll be snapped up in no time.'

'Oh.' Surprised, Millie put her tea down and looked up at him. She felt a little disappointed.

'Ah, you're hesitating,' he said, raising a forefinger. 'No matter. I only thought it would look better from her point of view if I had female company, but it's taking too much for granted, I know that.'

Millie stayed silent, taking this in. It made some kind of sense, she supposed. Gus's earnest expression, however, made no sense at all. Why was this so important to him?

'Well...'

'No, no, it's fine. Forget I asked. Stupid idea. Don't know what I was thinking.'

'Couldn't you just give her a ring? Her number will be on the card, won't it?'

Gus's face showed a flush of colour; it went away so fast that Millie thought she might have imagined it. 'Only the shop one. It might be difficult for her to talk at work. It'll be better in person.'

'In that case, of course I'll come,' Millie assured him, still slightly puzzled but anxious not to disappoint. She was tempted to add: 'Unless there's someone else you'd rather take,' as she pictured the dark-haired woman tripping along Prosperity Terrace, but she didn't. Had he only chosen Millie for this mission because of the two of them she looked the most motherly? She decided she didn't care.

Gus was smiling now. 'That's great,' he said. 'Thank you.'

Millie had to laugh at the clowns, though she doubted the neighbours did. This was a desirable, normally expensive, road, popular with middle-class families because of its position firmly in the middle of the catchment area of a high-performing primary school. It was also firmly outside the net curtain catchment area, and the occupants of the nearby houses had no option but to make their interest all too clear as Gus put a firm foot to the bottom of the camouflaged front door and nudged it open with the proficiency of a seasoned house-breaker.

Millie followed him in, slip-sliding across junk mail and free newspapers. 'What's that awful pong?'

'Chip fat.'

Gus stood at the bottom of the stairs and called out: 'Anyone home?'

Silence. He looked at Millie, biting his bottom lip, as if he needed reassurance from her, then gave his shoulders a little shake and stalked purposefully along the passage as if he owned the place.

'Kitchen looks tidy,' he said, turning back before she had a chance to see for herself. 'Doesn't look as if anyone's used it lately.'

'Why did you think she'd be here, anyway? Wouldn't she be at work?'

'It's her day off. The shop's definitely closed on Mondays. I checked.'

As is mine, thought Millie. Charmaine was minding her grand-daughter and she hadn't liked to ask Jet. Not only would he have his own business to attend to, she was still feeling guilty at having refused his invitation for a drive into the country and a drink on Saturday evening.

'Should we check upstairs? Would you like me to?' she offered.

'No, I'll go. I know which room.'

Gus was already sprinting up the stairs with light, proprietary steps that made Millie feel, very slightly, as if she was on the outside of something and that her own vicarious sympathy for the girl was superfluous.

Moments later he came bounding down again.

'She's gone.' He rubbed his head, disappointment showing in his eyes.

'Completely gone?'

'Yup. No clothes, nothing.'

'Well, there's gratitude for you,' Millie said, pulling the front door open.

'She doesn't owe me anything,' Gus said flatly, causing Millie to regret her flippancy.

The short journey back to Preston Knits was completed mostly in silence. This girl, Millie thought, both hands clutching the edge of her seat, this girl who without a grain of conscience had set up home in a stranger's house without permission and had not even had the courtesy to let Gus know she was moving on, had changed something in him. Watching him surreptitiously as he drove, she could sense it, could almost see the Newton's cradle of thought set up behind his eyes.

She sat for a moment in the car after it stopped, giving him the chance to say what was on his mind, but he merely leaned across and opened the door for her and she had no choice but to climb out.

In defiance of the city's seaside location, the night was uncommonly sultry. The pubs nearest the Theatre Royal were elbow-to-elbow with drinkers while the smokers and general overspill had claimed all the outside tables, the more jubilant among them peppering the pedestrianised concourse with Saturday night joviality.

Charmaine took Millie's arm. 'A different watering hole for us, I think. Let's try the Foundryman up the hill.'

The Foundryman would be heaving, too – it always was – but Millie kept quiet. A walk would be lovely. Despite the warmth and lack of breeze, the night air felt refreshing after the plush-seated stuffiness of the theatre.

They took a zig-zag route through the narrow streets, Millie content to follow Charmaine's lead. Small, quirky shops, shuttered antique markets and reclamation yards petered out the further up the hill they went, giving way to snug rows of tall terraced houses, their basement windows half concealed beneath litter-stuffed grills in the pavement. Turning the corner into such a street, Millie could see a couple of shops at the far end of the otherwise residential stronghold. One had a flag sign protruding at fascia level, purplish, with curly silver writing that glinted in the steady fall of light from the street lamp. The actual words, indecipherable from this distance, were shaped with a resonance that stalled her feet. She let go of Charmaine's arm, then had to patter after her in order to catch up.

'Non-functioning footwear, I see,' Charmaine said, glancing down at Millie's wedge-heeled sandals.

'Yes, well I wasn't expecting to be walking over cobbles.'

Millie took her friend's arm again as the shop sign sailed closer within her line of vision. *How Was It For You?* she read. Why did it sound familiar? She hadn't been along here in months and it didn't look to be her kind of shop anyway.

'Hey, see that dress?' Charmaine pointed at a bell-sleeved mini-dress on a sinister headless mannequin as they drew level with the back-lit window display. 'My mother used to have one just like it.'

'I think you'll find that was you,' Millie said, her mind busy elsewhere.

Yes, now she remembered! *How Was It for You?* was the name of the shop where the girl worked, the one Gus had turned into some kind of personal project. Behind the window display she could make out a row of handbags hunched along a shelf like boulders, a rocket launch of lava lamps, necklaces slung from hooks, and baskets on stands overflowing with sundry items, like the ones she had in the shop.

Charmaine was tugging at Millie's arm.

'Come on. There's a big cold glass of wine with my name on just around this corner.'

'No, wait…'

Below the posters on the glass door, in the bottom left hand corner, was a purple-and-silver themed notice giving the opening hours, and underneath, two names. *Maxine West. Katya Hope*.

'Mill, what is it?'

Millie shook her head, slowly, unable to believe what her eyes were telling her.

'Karen. I think it might be Karen. *Katya Hope*, look.'

Charmaine looked. 'Oh. Oh my God…'

It was almost midnight when Millie rang Gus. No, he hadn't been asleep, he assured her. She chose to believe him. Not that it mattered; waiting until morning was an impossibility.

'I know,' was all he said when she'd finished speaking. *I know*. Then: 'I'll come tomorrow, early. We'll talk then.'

And with that, Millie had to be content.

In her heightened state of alertness, she had the front door open almost before the car reached the top of the hill and swished into the street's Sunday-morning quiet.

'I'm so sorry,' he said, rushing inside. Unshaven, pale as parchment, he looked as bad as Millie felt after her sleepless night. 'I've handled this all wrong, messed up completely. I can't believe I did that.'

'Sorry? What do you mean?'

'Show me her photo, Karen's photo. Please.'

Millie fetched the picture of Karen from the windowsill and handed it to Gus.

'Yes,' he said, after a long moment. 'It's her, the girl from the squat. I couldn't be sure because of the name – Katya, she said – but I just had a feeling. There was something about the way she looked, her smile…'

Millie stood in the middle of the room, back straight, hands clasped together as if in prayer, while Gus launched into a rambling explanation. If he'd told Millie straight away that he suspected the girl he'd stumbled upon was Karen, he said, and it transpired he was wrong, he'd only have been piling more distress on her. That was what he'd thought at the time but now he could see that the scheme he'd dreamed up could have had an even worse outcome. If Millie and Karen had come face-to-face at the squat, with no warning, how would either of them have coped? No, he'd made a bad decision, the worst ever, and he wouldn't blame Millie if she threw him neck and crop into the street.

'All I can do is apologise for being such an insensitive idiot,' he ended.

Millie stayed silent, while Gus stood helplessly on the rug in front of the fireplace, distractedly rubbing the top of his head. She caught his gaze, held it there. And then she smiled, a long, slow smile.

'You found her. You found my Karen.'

Chapter Twenty-Five

Gus clicked off his phone and gazed bemusedly through the windscreen at the hedgerow with its backdrop of plump, green hills and the dismal stew of cardboard containers and plastic bottles littering the lay-by in which he was parked. He would never, if he lived to be a hundred and fifty, understand the contrariness of women.

All that time searching, the constant disappointment, the utter weariness of living a life diminished by loss, and now she had found her daughter – or rather he had, a minor technicality – and she wanted nothing to do with her.

That wasn't strictly true, of course, not in the simplistic way his brain expressed it, but what was he supposed to think? What was he supposed to say? Nothing, apparently, except to describe in impossible detail to the point of distraction the girl herself, to which, from Millie's point of view, there had been a satisfactory outcome. Karen, or Katya, whatever she called herself, was alive and well, back in Brighton, and she had a job.

There must be more to it than that, more that Millie wanted, Gus had suggested, taking care to choose his words carefully. But back came the response that she was frightened of wanting more. Yes, he could see that, or pretended he could; he didn't want her thinking he was a crass, blinkered oaf who could only see what was right under his nose.

And yet it had seemed to him – and, so, he had thought, to Millie – the most straightforward of situations. Millie searched and had found. But now she was doing the opposite of what Gus expected. The whole thing was bizarre, frustrating almost to the point of anger. When he'd left her yesterday, her mood had been buoyant, joyous even. Dismissing his angst over the clumsy way he'd handled the situation – there was absolutely nothing for him to apologise for, she'd insisted – she'd given him the distinct impression that first thing on Monday morning she would ring *How Was It For You?* and make her first contact with her daughter in two years. She wasn't overly confident of a good result, naturally, and the prospect of confrontation scared her silly, but nevertheless, that was what she was going to do. No other option had even been hinted at.

And now this. Gus had tried not to sound too dismayed when she'd rung him just now – it was, after all, her personal affair and not really any of his business – but still he felt he had earned the right to try and dissuade her from this stagnant acceptance, this... *non-event*, if only to make sense of the hours they'd spent mulling it all over in the stock-room confessional.

Although immoveable on the subject, Millie hadn't sounded entirely happy with her own decision. How could she be? Deep down, she must want to see Karen, have a good long talk with her and, hopefully, bury the history that had prised them apart. Yes, it would be traumatic but not in an insurmountable way, surely. He would have to go and see her again, talk it through face-to-face, that was obvious; phone conversations had the power to disguise and mislead.

He supposed there was no immediate hurry, though. Karen-aka-Katya, towards whom he now had increasingly ambivalent feelings, was going nowhere, apart from shifting her slender carcass from wherever she was currently dossing down to an as yet unpurchased lonely bed in a spanking new studio flat. Which was another thing; he could hardly get involved in that now, could he? He'd get Tom onto it, get him to phone her and arrange a viewing.

Meanwhile, Gus had other fish to fry. Work was still steadily increasing and he couldn't turn it down; the property market might suddenly dip, leaving him with no income apart from his rentals. Besides, although he might complain at times, especially when he fancied a lie-in, buildings fascinated him, always had. No two were the same, and probing to the very heart of their construction, ferreting out their idiosyncrasies, gave him a good deal of pleasure.

Having his free time curtailed meant, of course, that the refurb on Augusta's bedroom was far from complete. The wardrobe doors and bits of the bed stood about the hallway, his vague plan for piece-by-piece disposal having ground to a halt. The blancmange-flowered wallpaper turned out to be three layers deep, leaving him with more crevices and craters than actual wall after he'd attacked it with the scraper, and the plasterer he found through the agency lived by promises alone, none of which he had so far fulfilled.

Then there was the wall-hanging project. Dragged along one evening to Sidonie and Jessica's house to agree the finer points of the finishing off, he had found himself with yet another task to complete, the sewing together of a quarter of the completed panels. Not only were his protests of being too busy ignored, he was expected to carry out this tedious exercise under the watchful eye of Sidonie – and, by default, Jessica – in their house on subsequent evenings until the job was done. It wasn't that he'd lost interest; having seen all the panels set out on Sidonie's dining room table, he couldn't help but feel proud to have been part of the group's achievement. The wall-hanging, it had to be said, was a masterpiece of colour, stitchery and story-telling.

Jessica caused him no problems at these meetings. To her credit, she was keeping as low a profile as was possible, given her role as joint hostess of the present proceedings. She seemed to Gus to have grown smaller and paler in her attempt to blend into the background while she was in his presence, and he took this silent, colourless version of her as an apology for her latest outburst. Although he decided it was sincerely meant, it would have meant more if she could just come out with a simple 'Sorry'.

He bumped off the lay-by and continued his journey towards Haywards Heath, where boring but necessary chores awaited: a hair-trim, a visit to the bank, a big supermarket shop. He might, if he had time, call in at the curtain exchange and see if they had anything suitable for Augusta's old bedroom, premature though this might be.

Back home by lunchtime, Gus stood on a chair and carefully draped across the top of his wardrobe a pair of almost-new Dupion curtains in buttercup yellow, ensuring they were well covered by the plastic sheeting. They were probably miles too long but he could let them puddle on the stripped floor if he didn't get around to shortening them; he'd seen it done that way in magazines. Pale grey walls would do them justice, if ever he got to that stage. Millie would approve, he thought.

Millie. He felt guilty about her every time he remembered what lay ahead this evening – the first public viewing of the wall-hanging. She had said she'd like to see it, and Gus had for one rash moment considered inviting her but the thought of Millie and Jessica coming face-to-face, especially as they may unwittingly have already done so, made him decide that the potential for large-scale embarrassment made it not worth the risk. Millie would see the wall-hanging, he would make sure of that, but he would also make sure his pony-tailed ex was nowhere near at the time.

At half past six, Gus wandered along to the village hall and accepted a glass of cheap but not too disgusting fizzy wine. The wall-hanging was certainly impressive and again he felt a rush of pleasure and pride as he gazed at it. Now it was properly in place, taking centre stage on the far wall from which other, less prepossessing, works of art had been removed in deference, it seemed twice the size it had in Sidonie's dining room. She and Jessica had made a wonderful job of the border; an intricate garland of briar roses, hawthorn and sprays of blackberries, entwined together with cheerful disregard for the seasons. Sidonie, of course, had been right all along, as her dissenters now happily conceded. The border, with Hangburton's coat of arms at the top, was an integral part of the work, pulling together the individual panels into a logical, lasting piece of craftsmanship that would, over time, hold its own place in the history of the village.

Glass in hand, Gus drifted about the hall, keeping one eye on Jessica but otherwise mingling contentedly with the vicar, members of the parish council, and his village neighbours, who had turned out in satisfyingly large numbers. All the members of the group were there, of course, Rosemary and the Yummies flirting outrageously with him as if they'd been at the wine all afternoon – perhaps they had – while Grace from the post office abandoned her husband and clung, red-faced and stalwart, to Gus's side as if she felt it her duty to protect him.

An elbow dug him sharply in ribs. 'Look,' Grace said. 'A reporter! Isn't it exciting?'

A young man stood before the wall-hanging, struggling to hold onto a notebook and pen while he fiddled with the camera slung round his neck and talked at the same time to the chairman of the parish council. He was probably only from the local rag but Gus was surprised their effort had raised so much interest. Perhaps he shouldn't have been. All kinds of things got into the papers, the dailies in particular. Private things, of no consequence or interest to anyone but the people concerned. Things that in no shape or form could be described as remarkable.

At eight years of age, he had been mortified when his mother showed him the picture in the Daily Express, even more so when he read, with one finger tracing the text, the fulsome opinion of the journalist who had labelled him *a tremendously brave youngster.* Liesel had been puzzled by his tears; he didn't have the words to explain how he felt, that being hailed as something he was not was a disgrace rather than an honour. He was a fraud. He had not been at all brave inside the cave, not once the rest of the rocks and sand had fallen, leaving him a quaking, weeping mess of terror while his friend Arthur, two years younger, remained calm and dry-eyed. And he had not been brave since, not in confined spaces, places where he couldn't see out and no-one could see in and where he might so easily be held captive through mechanical or electrical or human failure.

His childish mind had not at the time made the connection between the write-up in the paper and the balding man who had come to the Dorset holiday house and snapped him and his mother and father in a stiff, unlikely row. Notebook in hand, the man addressed his parents in loud, jolly tones as if they hadn't a brain cell between them before, horror of horrors, bending forward and patting Gus – or rather Matthew, as his mother had insisted – on the head. Gus had decided there and then never to have anything more to do with reporters.

Families, Gus thought later as he stood to one side, his mingling duties done. Look at them all. Children of all ages raced noisily about the hall, the younger ones returning briefly to their respective parental groups every few minutes as if taken there by a gravitational force. As he continued to watch, he felt a sudden, sharp tug, not of loneliness exactly but of longing, longing to be somewhere, as if there were an empty space waiting for him to fill it.

Home. The word suggested itself, lodged firmly in his mind. What did it mean, *home*? Home wasn't about buildings or places or things. Home meant a person, or people, and, yes, of course he still missed Clair, always would. He missed his mother and father in a low-key kind of way, and Robert, of course. Catherine, too, still held a candle to his heart, the flame licking painfully close at times, as it always would, but he wasn't feeling that right now. It suddenly occurred to him that what he wanted was to see Millie, very much, and not just because of the Karen saga.

Laughing to himself, Gus raised his glass to the light and gazed at the pale dregs within it. What on earth were they putting in this stuff? He'd lost count of the refills that had been pressed upon him; he'd better stop now before he got even more maudlin. He felt a presence by his side, a light touch on his arm.

'Hello,' Jessica said. 'Great isn't it?' She indicated the wall-hanging.

'Certainly is.'

'Look at Mum. She's in her element.'

Sidonie trotted excitedly from one welcoming group to another, her heels click-clacking on the wooden floor, her colour high, her tinkly laugh, so like her daughter's, rising and dipping on a sea of voices.

'She looks happy,' Gus agreed. 'I'm glad. She deserves it. She worked so hard on this, knocking us all into shape.'

'Didn't she just.'

Jess still watched her mother but her eyes were glazed, as if she wasn't really seeing. Suddenly she turned to Gus. 'I don't suppose you fancy going for a meal after this?'

'Better not,' he said, smiling gently.

She smiled back. It was a warm smile, friendly, open, different. Only a swift lowering of her eyes gave away faint disappointment, and then it was gone.

'That's fine,' she said lightly. 'See you around, though?'

'Yes, see you around.' Gus's lips brushed her cheek.

As he left the hall a little later, he felt a corner had been turned.

Chapter Twenty-Six

In the interests of economy and the conservation of energy –
his, as well as that of the national grid – Gus polished off the
solidified remains of yesterday's lasagne, unheated and straight
out of the dish, before setting off for the Dog and Trumpet
around nine o'clock. All that fizzy wine had given him a
tremendous thirst.

David, Sophie's husband, beckoned Gus over as he went
in. Matt was there, too, and some mates of Matt's who Gus
knew vaguely by sight. He had wandered into a conversation
that seemed to be mainly about women. In mock-disparaging
tones they railed and complained and empathised, and Gus
wondered how long it would be before someone mentioned
Jessica. Thankfully no-one did, and the talk shifted to golf, a
sport Gus had never seen the point of.

Round the other side of the bar, a man sat alone, hunched
over an empty glass. Dan, Jessica's friend. Setting aside the
remembrance of their last silent encounter, Gus strolled round
and indicated the empty seat at the table.

'Sure.' Dan waved at the seat, smiling uncertainly.

'Pint?' Gus offered.

'I was just going… oh, go on then. Thanks.'

'I don't see you around the village much,' Gus said, after
they'd chatted generally.

'I'm away a lot, London mostly. I've got a little place by
the Barbican I use overnight when I need to.'

'Oh? What do you do then?'

'I'm a TV producer for the Beeb.'

'That so? I'd say that qualifies you for the man with the
most interesting job in the village award. From what I've seen

218

so far, anyway.'

Dan smiled. 'Don't know about that.'

'You know when I saw you in here the other time, were you..?' Gus ventured, after a little silence.

'Was I going to say something? Yeah, well, I was but...' Dan shrugged. 'Doesn't matter. I'd had a few pints. Feel a bit of a prat now, as it happens.'

'No need.' Gus waved a hand. 'What was it, though? You may as well tell me.'

Dan took a swig of beer and wiped the froth from his lips with the back of his hand. 'Okay, this is going to sound totally stupid, but I think I was going to ask you to go easy on Jessica. Or something in that line.' He laughed, gave his head a little shake. 'Told you it was stupid, didn't I? None of my business, for one thing.'

Gus was brought up short for a moment. He wasn't expecting that.

'You know I don't go out with her any more?'

'So I heard,' Dan said.

'So what's the story then, with you and her? I gather there is one.'

'Just a bit,' Dan said, widening his eyes. 'We go way back, our first day at senior school. I was dumb enough to let some fourth year lout relieve me of my cash at break. I hadn't a clue how I was going to get home but Jess found me hanging about at the bus stop and offered to lend me the fare...'

'Sweet,' Gus said.

'...only when she looked in her purse she only had enough money for herself, so what does she do? She doesn't get on the bus. She walks all the way home with me. It's bloody miles, and it was raining. She never stopped nattering from start to finish.'

They both laughed.

'So you've known her all that time, since you were, what, eleven, twelve?'

'Yeah. We hung out together on and off through school and college, went our separate ways, like you do, then when we both pitched up in Hangburton again we started going out

219

properly. The thing was,' Dan said, colouring up a bit, 'I'd been sort-of in love with her the whole damn time, since the bus thing, and when she agreed to go out with me I thought that's it, this is us, for life. First love and all that, you know how it is?'

Gus nodded.

'Well, after we'd been living together for four-and-a-half years she dumped me for some jerk of a cardiologist. Fancied herself as a consultant's wife, I imagine. She didn't get to be one. You know that, of course.'

This was all very interesting, Gus thought, as Dan went to the bar for more drinks, but it was all so long ago. It was hardly relevant now, surely?

'Anyway,' Dan said, sitting down again, 'Jess had other boyfriends, as I had girlfriends, but we stayed mates and saw quite a lot of one another – it's a small village, you can hardly avoid bumping into people – and it was all quite civilised, nothing messy. Then, out of the blue Jess announces that she's always loved me, always knew I was the one, blah-de-blah, and she wants to give it another go.'

'When was this?' Gus asked.

'End of last year, after a Christmas party. It wasn't a pleasant experience.' Dan raised his eyes, gave a rueful little laugh. 'It was too late, of course. By miles. I was well and truly over her. Well, I would be, after eight years. I guess I'd done a bit of growing up in between and I just didn't think of her that way any more. Besides, I'd met Anna by then.'

'Anna?'

'Yep. We're getting married next summer. You wouldn't have seen her,' Dan said in response to Gus's unanswered question. 'She's working in New York, in television like me, but her contract finishes in January, then she'll be back.'

'Blimey. So what does Jessica think of all this? I take it she knows?'

'She does. We had a good long talk. I owed her that, at least. The thing is, I'm not even sure she was really in love with me. She just thought she might like to be. Jess and I still see one another occasionally, as friends. Anna knows and she's cool about it. I admit I was relieved, though, when Jess started going out with you.'

Gus laughed. 'I bet.'

They sat in thoughtful silence for a while, then Gus said, 'It's funny, she never mentioned you, but then we never talked much about our pasts. We were never serious, Jess and I, at least, I wasn't. I think she hoped for more – God, that sounds arrogant! – and that was one reason I stopped seeing her.'

Dan nodded. 'She's a great girl, in her way. I'd like to see her settled down and happy.'

'Me, too,' Gus said.

Chapter Twenty-Seven

Millie had never seen Gus so earnest, so persuasive, so focussed on winning. This was another side to him and she felt privileged to be made aware of it. She sat in the back room of the shop, her hand cupped beneath his, hearing his emotional yet reasoned argument while she thought how lucky she was that he cared enough to want to stop her making the greatest mistake of her life.

Family, he said, was crucial. It bound us one to another, whether we liked it or not. Catherine had taught him that. Her legacy may have been small in material terms but the genetic bond was beyond price. It was there inside him, helping to make him who he was, and so it was for Millie and Karen. Why else would Millie have spent so much time searching? He understood now how frightened Millie must be of the consequences. Rejection was a possibility, that was true, but how would she know unless she tried? She mustn't be satisfied with so little, because sooner or later, it wouldn't be enough. Miss this opportunity now and it might never come her way again.

Listening to all this, as the trains journeyed endlessly back and forth along oily tracks and the shop phone rang unheeded, Millie couldn't help thinking Gus was being a touch melodramatic, but she realised it was because he was still fighting his own battles with the past, no matter how hard he tried to dismiss them. He was telling her that he couldn't let go, and neither would she, until some kind of resolution had been reached.

And so it was that Millie took out the red spotted notebook she kept for the purpose and, with slight tremor in her fingers, copied down Karen's mobile number and the number of the vintage shop, then entered them into her phone for good measure. Satisfied, Gus kissed her swiftly and triumphantly on the mouth, and left.

'He's a trier, I'll say that for him.' Charmaine gave up her attempt to rekindle the candle-flame inside the metal storm-lantern that swung above their heads, threw aside the matches and plonked down in her deckchair.

'Meaning what, exactly?'

'Only that his heart's in the right place, your friend Gus. No need to get a cob on.'

Millie sighed. 'I'm not, I just...'

She stared ahead of her. White nicotiana flowers spangled the twilit garden, scenting the air with nostalgic sweetness. *Going back.* Did she want that, a return to the taut high-wire that had constituted the relationship between her and Karen, and along which they seemed always to be moving in opposite directions? Because that, surely, was where they were heading, or would be. Better, then, to let Karen go on living her life the way she wanted to, the way that made her happiest, even if it meant that she, Millie, had no part to play in it. We don't have children in order to glue them to our sides with demands. Yet the only demand Millie had ever made on Karen was to be allowed to love her and encourage her but, at the same time, keep her safe. Was that so unreasonable? Perhaps it was. Perhaps that, the expectation of parenthood, was the greatest demand of all.

Millie shivered, pulled her cardigan round herself.

'Want to go in?'

'No, I'm all right. It's nice out here. Charmaine...'

'Mm?'

'You do understand, don't you, why I haven't done anything about it yet?'

Charmaine didn't reply at once; even through the gloom of evening, Millie could see the doubt in her friend's eyes. It had been the same with Jet. He'd pretended to go along with whatever Millie felt best, but that was Jet's way and she could tell that really he was thinking the same as Charmaine, and Gus.

But what was Millie expecting? Wholehearted endorsement from everyone – everyone who knew, that was – that she was right to prevaricate? No, however much she valued the opinions of the three people closest to her, the responsibility was hers alone. It was a big thing, after all, the biggest. Whatever she decided would bring an irrevocable turning point in her life. She had to be sure, whatever anyone else said or thought.

'What I do understand,' Charmaine said at last, 'is that you're afraid of what might happen if you take the next step – better the devil you know, and all that – but I think you're underestimating yourself.'

'Am I?' Millie's turn to look doubtful.

'*Yes*. Look how you went and winkled out that Jack character and stood up to him, and now you're starting to be less afraid of him, aren't you?'

Millie thought for a moment. It was true, her fear of Jack had abated – not entirely, but she was getting there. She remembered what Gus had said, that fear could be unlearned. She had been afraid of finding Karen, it was true, almost as much as of losing her forever. But Jack was Jack, and Karen, well, that was different.

'What if I never see her again?'

Charmaine's deckchair creaked. 'But you will, of course you will. Why wouldn't you?'

'If I don't get in touch with her now, there's no reason to suppose she'll get in touch with me either. She won't stay in Brighton, not for ever. Guarantee it.'

'Then,' Charmaine said quietly, after a moment's silence, 'you know what you have to do.'

Chapter Twenty-Eight

Millie sat on the edge of her seat, her eyes glued to the door of the café, the smell from the steaming coffee machines turning her stomach. What if she wasn't coming? What if she'd only agreed to this to get her mother off her back and had no intention of... Here she was! Millie's heart swelled with love as if it would burst out of her chest as Karen scanned the Saturday morning crowd, then, with a curt little nod towards her mother, stood casually at the counter. Her purse in her hand, Millie tried to stand but emotion overpowered her and she could only sit and wait as Karen bought her drink and came towards her.

Forcing back tears, Millie smiled. 'Karen. Oh, love.' She tried not to mind the lack of a smile in return.

'Is he your bloke then?' were Karen's first words, as if it was two weeks since she'd seen her mother, not two years. The chair squawked against the tiled floor as she pulled it out and sat down.

Millie quickly reorganised her thoughts. 'Gus?'

'Who else?'

'No, of course he isn't. What gave you that idea?'

'Oh, only that you mentioned him about a million times on the phone. Cool guy, though. For someone his age.'

Millie looked across the pink-clothed table at her daughter, drank her in, tried to inhale her scent. She wanted so much to throw her arms around her, kiss her, but there was a definite look-but-don't-touch air about Karen that must not be ignored. Neither must Millie rush this nor seem needy, although if this situation did not excuse a bit of neediness then she didn't know what did.

They were in the pink café, just off the North Laine where

Karen's vintage shop was. That wasn't really its name but she and Karen had always called it that because of its bright pink exterior and pink decor. As a place for reunion it came a close second to Star Street; it was one of 'their' places, or used to be. Millie was touched that Karen remembered; a small but poignant victory.

One of Karen's conditions for this meeting – arranged during a stilted phone conversation which had left Millie shaken and tearful but ecstatic – was that she would not come to the house. *The house*, she said. She didn't call it home. What did it matter, though? The only thing that mattered was that her daughter had been found and was here, which was all down to Gus. Millie couldn't help but smile at Karen's reference to him.

'He's just a friend,' Millie said. 'A very good one, as it happens. To you as well as me, wouldn't you say?'

Karen shrugged. Her shoulders looked thin, thinner than before. She was thinner all over by the look of it, although she seemed healthy enough. Her hair, too, had changed slightly. Still long, poker straight and glossy, it had lost its blond brightness and was darkened to the colour of expensive honey. It suited her.

'Did you go and see the studio flat? He didn't have to do that, you know, put your name forward,' Millie said, wondering how she dared to challenge her daughter so early on.

'Yeah, yeah, it's cool.'

Karen sank into her hot chocolate as if she wanted it gone as quickly as possible, along with her mother, perhaps. Millie's nerve-ends skittered at the prospect of being run out on before anything had been said or achieved. Another of Karen's conditions was that she wasn't to be cross-examined, but Millie was prepared only to meet her halfway on this.

'Where have you *been* all this time? What have you been doing? I don't expect chapter and verse, just some idea…'

Karen sighed and adopted a look of weary acceptance. 'Yes, all right, but I can't leave Maxine in the shop on her own for too long.'

The rattled-off potted account of the missing slice of her life was disappointingly unrevealing. As Millie listened and

226

digested, in the background her mind ran over the only rehearsed part of this meeting, to be delivered at an opportune moment.

The travel rep job had not worked out, Millie heard, confirming her information from Sarah and Tierney. Karen had quickly become disillusioned when they wouldn't let her loose on the kids' clubs because she didn't have the right kind of experience. Besides, with her fair skin she'd found the Mediterranean heat a bit tricky when you had to be on the go all the time. Millie smiled inwardly at this and wondered how she would have coped in Australia, had her wish to be sent there been granted. After that, apparently, she'd lived in Croydon for a while, but not in Albany Road, then North London, including a spell on a barge on Regent's Canal. *Just with friends*, came as standard every time Millie asked who'd she'd actually lived with. Nameless, faceless friends. She'd worked in bars and pubs mostly, and at the children's corner at the zoo, and selling jewellery in Camden market.

And was... *he* still on the scene, Millie tentatively enquired, meaning Jack, and received a quick 'No' in response, as sharp as a slap.

'So who dumped who?' Dangerous ground, Millie knew, but she couldn't resist.

Karen raised her eyes. 'Do we have to?'

'Yes, I think we do.'

'If you must know, it was me. He wanted other people around all the time. It was never just me and him.'

'Oh? And why do you think that was?'

'I guess,' Karen said, after a moment, 'he wanted things from them that he couldn't get from me.'

Millie didn't dare ask what things these might be – it was best she didn't know. Not that Karen was likely to tell her. Jack's expression, however, came back to her, the softer one she'd witnessed momentarily in the petrol station.

'Was he upset that you left him?'

Karen had been tracing invisible patterns on the table-top. She looked up, surprised. 'Yeah, just a bit. I had to get rid of my phone and everything. Look, can we drop it now?'

'Yes, sorry, love. I just needed to know that nothing awful happened...' Millie stopped. Whatever had gone on between Karen and Jack, Karen wasn't about to part with the details. Anyway, it was over now.

They fell silent for a while, Karen resuming her pattern-tracing. The time had come; Millie couldn't put it off any longer.

'I wanted to see you ever so much and I've missed you like crazy – I thought *I'd* go crazy myself at times – but that's not the only reason we're here. I've got some important news, something sad.'

She reached out, but Karen ducked her hands beneath the table and pressed back in her seat.

'If you mean about Dad dying, then I already know.'

The words flew at Millie and landed like a well-aimed punch. *Karen knew*?

'How? How did you know?'

Another shrug. 'The grapevine. I heard you were looking for me. It got mentioned along the way, by a friend.'

Confused, utterly overwhelmed by the burden of this new knowledge and all it implied, Millie was so overcome by sudden exhaustion she could easily have laid her head down on the table and wept. How had they grown so far apart, mother and daughter? And where was this... *coldness* coming from?

'But if you knew, why stay away? Weren't you upset? Didn't you care at all?'

She searched for Karen's gaze, tried to hold it with her own, and failed. Karen flicked her hair back.

'Maybe I care. Maybe I don't. I don't even know any more.'

'I don't understand, Karen. How can you not care?' Millie breathed.

'You mean you don't *know*?' Karen's blue eyes widened, advancing towards Millie as if they were on stalks.

Millie felt sick. 'Know what?'

'Look,' Karen said, sitting forwards, 'I might as well tell you. It wasn't because you ballsed up my love-life that I went away.'

'I'm sorry about that. I shouldn't have meddled, I realise that now. You probably won't believe me but I did what I did to protect you but I didn't take proper account of your feelings for…' – again Jack's name died on her lips – '…one another.'

Karen's eyes flashed a warning. 'I *said* it wasn't that. Aren't you listening?'

The snappy response drew looks from nearby tables.

'It's what I'm here for, to listen as well as to talk. Karen, please don't…'

'You want to know why I didn't get in touch when I found out that Dad… that he'd died? Oh, I knew you'd want me there with you, putting up appearances, doing whatever mothers and daughters do at a time like that, but I couldn't do it. Not the normal things other families do. Can't you see?'

Karen flung the end of this speech across the table as the salt pot hit the floor, banished there by her sweeping arm. People at the neighbouring tables had given up trying to pretend they weren't listening and were agog.

Millie's jaw dropped. She sat back in her chair as if she'd been physically winded. So, it was all about Mark. All this time and she hadn't realised how much his defection had affected Karen, how deeply she'd been traumatised. She had failed her daughter completely. She'd swanned along in the mistaken belief that her carefully worded motherly chats, her love and support throughout that difficult, long ago time and her resolute upkeep of daily routine had been enough to see the pair of them through. Karen had for a while been confused and unhappy, but gradually the natural resilience of childhood had worked its magic and given her back her bright, feisty, daughter, or so Millie had thought. But she'd been wrong, so wrong, and for the life of her she couldn't see how she could possibly put this right.

'Oh,' she said. It was all that would come. 'Oh, Karen, darling…'

But Karen hadn't finished.

'You *can't* see, can you? You haven't got the foggiest about how much I was hurt when I found out.'

Millie reached for Karen's hand, and this time caught it.

She gave it a squeeze, hung on tight.

'Of *course* you were hurting. You were only twelve when he left, thirteen when we divorced. I tried to help you. I should have done better, I realise that now, but I was hurting, too. I was in pieces, Karen, when he left me for that other woman. That's my only defence.' Millie raised her hands, a gesture of despair. 'Mark was my husband as well as your father…'

'But that's just it!' Karen yelled, scraping back her chair, leaping to her feet. 'He wasn't, was he? Mark was not my father!'

Millie felt a rush of heat so strong it threatened to drown her. Adrenalin lifted her to her feet. She grabbed Karen's arm.

'Sit down!'

Amazingly, after a moment's hesitation, Karen sat. Millie swallowed, fanned her face with her hand.

'What's this all about? What do you mean, he wasn't your father? And don't even think about running out on me now. Don't even think about it!'

The strong words seem to have an effect. Karen looked momentarily wrong-footed, as if she had expected to maintain the upper hand. She lowered her eyes and sealed her mouth into a straight line reminiscent of the sullen teenager she used to be. Millie's heart puckered but she had to stay strong, stay in control.

The eyes came back to meet Millie's. 'He said so himself. You were there, Mum, remember?'

Ah. 'You mean when things got a bit heated between me and your dad.' Millie took a deep breath. 'Look, Karen, people say all kinds of things in anger, stupid things, and I'm sorry if you overheard and took it all to heart. You never said… anyway that's not the point. What is the point is that it isn't true. Of *course* it isn't. Do you really think I'd have let you grow up not knowing who your father was? For God's sake, girl, what do you take me for?'

Millie's voice rose dangerously at the end of this speech. She glanced around the café. Fortunately it had emptied out a bit, although she wasn't in the mood to care what people thought.

She lowered her voice. 'There's no other reason you should have got the wrong idea, is there? Dad didn't say anything to you while I wasn't around, did he?'

'Might have done.' Karen shrugged, the stroppy child still in residence.

'Karen, don't play games. This is serious. All this time I've been blaming myself for driving you away and now I find out... oh, never mind.'

Millie felt shattered. She closed her eyes, feeling the pink walls of the café closing in, swaying nauseatingly around her.

'Mum, are you okay?'

She opened her eyes, gave a kind of snort. This, from the daughter who just now accused her of... But this *was* her fault, wasn't it? If she hadn't given Mark reason to doubt her right at the start of their marriage, they would not be in this situation now. She and Mark would still have parted – their problems ran deeper and he would still have fallen for the woman who ran the tea stall at London Bridge station, a woman who, in Mark's laughably clichéd words, *understood him* – but their daughter would not have lived her life plagued by doubts born of childish misunderstanding.

'So did he? Did Dad say anything directly to you? I have to know, Karen. Please.'

'Not exactly.'

'What does that mean?' Millie was starting to lose patience.

'It was the cards he sent me after he went, birthday cards and that. He always put "love from Mark", not "Dad".'

Millie's shoulders slumped. Why had she never noticed that herself? She tried to think back but her memory remained stubbornly misty, probably because, if she had noticed, she hadn't read anything sinister into it. Unlike Karen.

'I can't believe he meant anything by that, but even if he did, he is – was – your father, in every sense of the word. You have to know that, because it's the truth, and whatever you heard, or thought you heard, they were just words thrown out for effect, to cause pain. That's all it ever was.'

This was so unpredictable; whatever she'd expected today,

it wasn't this. She looked pleadingly at Karen. 'Can you see that now?'

'It's not that simple, is it? You say he said things in the heat of the moment but I don't buy that. There must have been a reason.'

'A grudge, certainly, but that's not a reason. Mark held a grudge about something that happened before we were married – it was that long ago, and deep down he knew it wasn't justified but he couldn't let go of it. I never blamed him for that and you shouldn't either. He was human, made the same mistakes as anyone else. And before you ask, no, I'm not going to tell you what it was all about because it's private, a part of our marriage that doesn't concern you. I'm truly sorry you got caught up in the fall-out, but there's really nothing more I can say, except to repeat that Mark was your dad, and that's an end to it.'

Karen fell silent. Her expression was so complex that Millie couldn't read it precisely, but she saw a smattering of hope there and clung wildly to it.

'You believe me, don't you?'

Karen shrugged in response, her gaze somewhere above Millie's head.

'Karen, please…'

'Don't push it, Mum,' Karen warned, getting to her feet again.

Millie heeded. 'I'll see you again soon, though?'

'I don't know. I'll think about it.'

Millie threaded her way along the crowded pavement in a fog of disbelief. How could it have gone so badly wrong? After the café door had swung closed, removing her precious daughter from her line of sight and leaving a stunned silence in her place, Millie had sat on for a while, immobilised by shock, unable to think or reason, unable, even, to feel. The numbness had barely passed as she blindly made her way through the web of streets towards the seafront. Perhaps she intended to throw herself off the end of the pier, or under the next bus that hurtled into Old Steine? Who knew? Who even cared? Millie didn't, that was for sure.

The glare of the water bludgeoned her skull as she turned a corner, brought her up short for a second, before she crossed the road and stood on the esplanade by the peeling green balustrade, her eyes squeezed against the light. Karen still didn't know about the money Mark had left them. By rights Millie should have told her but if she had, it might have seemed like a bribe. She hardly thought about it herself any more. It all seemed so long ago – Irene's letter, the funeral, Ralph – as if a lifetime had passed in between.

Breathe the ozone. Her mother's voice spoke inside her head. She always said that when they were by the sea. Millie breathed. After a while she began to feel better, clearer-headed. Perhaps her first instincts had been right and she shouldn't have got in touch with Karen. Perhaps, knowing her daughter was back in Brighton, she should simply have waited for whatever came. Perhaps.

But Gus wouldn't have it, not at any price, and she trusted his instincts more than she did her own. She should go to him, tell him what a disaster the reunion had been, making certain he knew she didn't blame him for talking her into it. But not today. Today she didn't want to talk to anyone. She just wanted to settle herself and not think too much. It would come right in the end. It had to.

Chapter Twenty-Nine

'Mark and I were in love. That's why we got married.'

'The best reason, I would have thought.' Gus slid a protective arm along the back of the sofa and was rewarded by Millie immediately leaning her head back against it.

He still felt confused about Millie. He wanted her in his life, certainly, but as a friend, a lover, a life partner? The first he already had, as long as he didn't go spoiling it again; the second, well it would be arrogant of him ever to suppose she was as attracted to him as he was to her. As for the third, that was the most confusing of all. But it was all academic anyway; Millie had given no indication that she was looking for a relationship, and even if she was, there was no guarantee she'd see him as a contender. She might prefer someone easier, like that Jet character, and who could blame her?

Gus became aware that he was scowling and that Millie had turned her head and was regarding him with a mixture of amusement and perplexity.

'Did anyone ever tell you that you look like the devil?'

'No, but I can see that I do.

He tried to adjust his expression, release the tension in his shoulders.

'It's mostly when you frown. When you smile your face opens out like the light's been let in. You should do it more often. Smile, I mean.'

Gus smiled, then pulled a funny face to cover a sudden twinge of awkwardness.

'That's better,' Millie said, settling herself back.

Saturday afternoon. A week to the day that the girl Karen had picked up Millie's life and wrenched it so painfully out of shape for the second time. Gus made an unwilling mental comparison: Jenny and Karen. Both had brought heartache and devastation to their parents' lives, the one in complete innocence, the other... well, that remained to be seen. He'd be inclined towards intense dislike of Karen if she hadn't got in first and softened him up with her fearless brand of charm.

'Would it help if you told me about it, why Karen got the idea that Mark wasn't her natural father?'

There wasn't a great deal to tell, Millie said. Paul had been a friend of Mark's, not a particularly close friend but one of a crowd of workmates from the railway. They used to go to dances and discos together, Mark and Millie, Mark's mates and their girlfriends. Paul was the only one who never seemed to have a girl with him. One night, before they headed home, Millie was in the queue for the cloakroom when Paul came over and told her he'd fallen for her, just came out and said it, without warning. *The greatest girl in the world.* He'd been drinking, they all had, but Millie could tell he was serious when he begged her to give up Mark and be with him instead.

She'd been shocked, but flattered, too. Paul was exceptionally handsome, so much so that Millie had always been surprised at his lack of female company. Not that looks alone were the whole story but at that moment she realised she was drawn to him, too. But she was in love with Mark and nothing would change that. Of course, she said nothing to Mark. Paul seemed to accept the situation and for a while absented himself from group nights out, but he turned up at Millie and Mark's engagement party at the church hall.

Millie stuck like glue to Mark at first and Paul seemed happy, dancing with other girls and blending in with the crowd, although Millie noticed he was drinking heavily. Then later on, when Millie nipped out for a cigarette, he followed her, grabbed her hand, pulled her round the corner of the building and kissed her. She tried to resist but, with a few Dubonnets inside her and Paul quite drunk, it was well nigh impossible. He'd pressed her against the brickwork, kissing her unwilling mouth, his hands everywhere, and that was when Mark had appeared, dragged him away from her and landed him a blow to the face that

235

knocked him out cold for a minute and bloodied his nose.

Naturally there'd been repercussions. Paul put it about that Mark had attacked him for no reason and Mark refused to speak to or acknowledge Paul ever again. Millie and Mark argued about it for months and, although officially they were still engaged – at least the ring was still in place – their future seemed to be in jeopardy. Millie had given up apologising eventually; after all, she had done nothing wrong, not technically, though she felt that in some way she must have unintentionally led Paul on.

'I still don't see what it had to do with Karen,' Gus said. 'She wasn't even born then, was she?'

'No, but she didn't hang about. We patched things up, like you do, and the wedding went ahead – well, obviously – and I got pregnant on the honeymoon, possibly a bit before. Dates weren't so easy to pinpoint then. The doubt was always in Mark's mind that she might have been Paul's. It was nonsense, of course. Those kisses that night were all there ever was, but I had the feeling that Mark was never entirely convinced. Perhaps he sensed that the attraction wasn't all one-sided, I don't know.'

'But how could you marry him if he didn't trust you?'

'Love is never that simple, is it?'

No. Gus was beginning to learn that.

'And Karen?' he asked.

'Ah. Karen.' Millie's eyes were sad. They told of secrets Gus would never know. He felt suddenly, irrationally, jealous. 'Even before Mark met Irene, things hadn't been good between us. It was as if we'd kind of run out of steam and I did my best to keep it going but I seemed to be the only one trying. When we argued, that was the one thing Mark knew would get to me. Paul. He would find ways to bring him up and then accuse me of having cheated on him. That was his ultimate weapon in any disagreement, as if that incident haunted him and he couldn't let it go. Anyway, Karen must have overheard, more often than I realised, and made something of it – I had no idea at the time. Perhaps it all came back to her because of her turmoil over Jack, I don't know, she didn't say, but apparently she'd made up

236

her mind there was truth in Mark's accusations, and that Paul was her natural father.'

'And she never said anything before?'

'No, never. And now she's gone again, not like before, I know, but I wanted her back properly, Gus, not like this.'

Gus gave Millie's shoulder a squeeze. He didn't know what to say. He wished he could reassure her; he liked to think that Karen would do right by her mother but there was no guarantee of that. Guilt was marching in, telling him he should never have interfered, but how could he not, when Millie was plainly so unhappy?

'What did you say? Did you deny it, tell her she'd got it wrong?'

'Oh yes, but it wasn't easy. We were in the middle of a busy café, remember. It's going to take more than a few words of denial to sort this out, I can tell you that.'

She gave him a strained smile. She was close to tears, Gus could tell, but she wouldn't give way, not in front of him. If only he was as strong.

'Millie, I'm sorry…'

'No, don't. I know what you're going to say but you did absolutely the right thing in talking me round. I don't regret phoning her one bit. At least I've seen her and how well she looks. I just have to find a way through this, that's all.'

Gus had kept a number of his aunt's books, although he would never read most of them. They seemed too personal to give away, more so than her jewellery and the miniature china houses she was fond of collecting. The books resided in Augusta's small oak bookcase in the sitting room, and he had been idly picking them out at random and flicking through when he came across a small colour photograph tucked between *Pride and Prejudice* and *I Capture the Castle.*. It was of Augusta standing in the back garden. Although the sky was blue, it must have been winter or early spring because the shrubs in the background were scarcely in leaf and she was wearing a long grey coat, mannish in style, and sheepskin boots. With her tall, broad-shouldered frame and steel-grey hair pulled back tight into its customary bun, the overall effect was one of severity and Gus wondered who had taken the snap and under what circumstances, given the apparent lack of lightheartedness about the occasion. Even her smile had a grim edge to it, as if there had been no smile in place before or after.

And yet, although it wasn't a close-up, he could make out in her features a brisk kindliness and forbearance as well as determination, given away by the set of her chin. This was how he remembered her, how he wanted to remember her. He was beginning to realise he had done her a disservice by expecting her to be perfect, in nature, heart and deed, because he'd needed her to be, but how could she? She was human with human flaws just like everyone else.

She would never, though, have written her will without giving it careful consideration. What she chose to do with her property was her prerogative, as the solicitor had pointed out. It may have had nothing to do with stale disagreements and divided family loyalties. Perhaps she'd favoured him because he'd lost Clair, as simple as that. A tiny compensation, a kindness, to show she cared. She hadn't been effusive in her sympathy at the time but that wasn't her way.

He had left the photo out and every time he looked at it he felt a definite shift in his attitude towards his aunt, not a lightning bolt of understanding but a slow movement towards… towards what? Understanding, affection, even – he smiled at this – forgiveness.

He went to see Elspeth and explained cautiously, at great length, this new perspective.

'Told you,' she sang, when he'd finished.

Gus laughed. 'Told me what?'

'You were beating yourself up over nothing.'

She was laughing, too, but she knew, he could tell. Despite the banter, Elspeth knew this was important, that Gus was on the way towards a peace of mind he'd not experienced in a long time, and was glad for him.

He had brought the rug with him, the pink flowered one from Augusta's bedroom.

'Jenny will love this,' Elspeth said, as they went upstairs

and laid it over the cream carpet in Jenny's pink-painted room, next to the bed. 'It'll be a nice surprise for her when she gets back. Thanks, Gus.' She kissed him warmly on the cheek.

Gus stepped back. 'It's only a rug.'

Augusta's rug. All I can give because it's all you'll accept.

At once the room settled beneath the weight of a meaningful silence. Glances were exchanged and quickly discarded. Elspeth stooped to square up the already squared rug and straighten the valance on Jenny's bed, then stood up again and looked at Gus.

'It's all right for you to forgive Augusta, you know,' she said quietly. 'You don't need my permission. You must do what you feel, go with your heart, but I'm not sure I can do the same, forgive her on Robert's behalf, not yet. Perhaps in time, but without Rob's take on things, it's difficult. Do you see?'

Of course he did, he assured her. He felt sad, though, in a way; sad that Elspeth had felt the need to rebuff any new attempt by him to offer her money when it had been the last thing on his mind. Elspeth was wise and loyal but he wished she wasn't so fiercely protective of what, in her eyes, was the unshakeable truth. Sometimes you had to take a magnifying glass to the small print; he was beginning to discover that.

Downstairs again, he picked up a fat paperback with a drooping leather tongue.

'Any good?

'Not bad. Not your cup of tea, though,' Elspeth said. 'It's a romance.' Then, before he could reply: 'Talking of which, how's Millie?'

Gus's face turned into a furnace so fast and so intensely he had no hope of hiding it, nor from stopping his lips from stretching automatically into an inappropriate grin.

'She's fine. No, actually that's not quite true but it's a long story.'

'I'll take the potted version.'

Gus shook his head in mock exasperation and gave his sister-in-law what she wanted.

'Is that what's holding you back, the thought of taking on the daughter?'

'I'm not taking on anyone, the mother or the daughter, nor anyone else for that matter,' Gus said.

'Your trouble is you think too much, I've said so before.'

'Good thing I do. I might end up in all kinds of trouble otherwise.'

'I doubt it. You might find you have a much better time if you just go with the flow occasionally. You enjoy each other's company, don't you? And you haven't frightened her off so far. Must count for something.'

Gus blew out air. Elspeth was on a mission here and unlikely to be put off her stroke any time soon.

'Millie and I are just friends.'

'A good start,' Elspeth said, with an emphatic nod. 'You should bring her over one day, let me meet her.'

Gus was saved from answering by the honking of Jenny's taxi outside.

Chapter Thirty

Gus was attending to a sinkful of washing-up – last-night's supper dishes as well as this morning's breakfast things – when the phone rang. He rushed to answer it, drying his hands on the tea-towel as he went, then felt a dash of disappointment that the female caller wasn't Millie.

Ridiculous, really. If he wanted to talk to Millie, all he had to do was pick up the phone, but he'd resolved to wait a while longer, give his mind time to adjust to not having her occupy so much of it. Besides, she needed space in order to deal with the Karen problem and she could do without him cluttering it up.

'My name's Agnes,' the caller said. 'Agnes Williams, Punchard as was. You won't know me and I'm sorry to drop this on you but I saw the letter you sent.'

Punchard. The name had a familiar ring to it, although he couldn't work out why.

'Letter?' he said stupidly, rubbing a hand through his uncombed hair. He hadn't been up long, taking advantage of a free morning to catch up on his sleep.

'You wrote to my mother, Cecelia. I saw the letter when I went up there to visit.'

Cecelia. Cecelia was her *mother*? Gus's senses awoke suddenly as the defence mechanism kicked in. If this Agnes person was ringing to have a go at him…

'Feel free to send me packing right now,' she continued, her voice brisk but friendly, 'but I do hope you won't. We're cousins, more or less – there's another, by the way, my elder brother, Christopher. If you're agreeable, I'd like us to meet, just you and me. There are, shall we say, certain things I'd like to share with you.'

'Things? What things?'

'Family business, rather delicate. Not easy on the phone. I don't know if you ever get to London at all, only that's where I am, where I work. Do you think that's possible?'

A determined woman, Gus thought, this cousin of his who had sprung out of the woodwork. He didn't know why but he hadn't considered that Cecelia and the Dickensian Josiah might have offspring; Millie couldn't have gone that far in her research, otherwise she would have said. So he had cousins, two of them. Except they weren't, strictly speaking, not once he'd been adopted out of the family. What did she want from him? She must want something, surely. Perhaps it was to warn him off, stop him haring up to Newcastle and pitching up on Cecelia's unwelcoming doorstep. As if he had any intention.

'Can't you tell me now what it's about?'

'I'd rather not. As I said, it would be difficult on the phone. Look, I'm sorry to push this on you, Matthew – no, it's Gus, isn't it – but I'm in rather a hurry, due in court in half an hour. As the barrister, not the accused.'

She gave a deep-throated laugh. A sense of humour then, unlike her mother, his erstwhile Aunt Cecelia. Apart from Agnes's businesslike tone which he suspected owed more to her profession and being in a hurry than genetics, she sounded nothing like Cecelia at all. Despite his misgivings he began to warm to her.

'All right,' he said. 'I'll come.'

Thursday was the best day for her, Agnes had said, bringing Gus a superstitious sense of rightness for what he was about to do. It seemed strange, though, taking his usual train from his usual station, following the ritual of buying the *Guardian* to read on the way up then leaving it on the seat as he alighted at Victoria, but this time setting off purposefully in the direction of the agreed meeting place instead of dallying over coffee and taking pleasure in the randomness of it all.

Not that he expected today to be unpleasant – in fact, he was looking forward to it, he thought, surprised at himself, as his marching feet echoed with hundreds of others along tiled walkways and up and down escalators, until finally he surfaced with relief at Holborn and strolled down to Great Queen Street. It was only as he entered the elegant, modern foyer of the hotel that he felt a twinge of doubt. Had he not put all this behind him, stopped asking the questions to which there were never any answers? Yet here he was about to come face-to-face with a total stranger who claimed to be his cousin and who as such would be the only blood relation he had ever met.

He heard his name and, looking round, saw a striking, dark-haired woman in a white blouse, black skirt and high heels coming towards him. The heels made her almost as tall as he was. He visualised her in wig and gown, the lead player in the courtroom drama, the winner. She didn't look like an Agnes, nor like someone who could possibly be related to him. The mild shock caused him to lose momentary control of his movements and his feet scuffled a bit on the polished floor as he took the hand she extended and gave it an over-effusive squeeze to compensate for his gaucheness.

'Gus.'

'Yes.'

Swift smiles were exchanged, hers polite and assured, his uncertain, as she led the way to a corner where two vast white sofas conjoined to create a fairly private nook among the oversized pot plants. Agnes sat on one sofa and Gus sank gingerly onto the other as if his weight might cause him to be swallowed whole by cushions the size of a small dinghy. A pot of coffee, cups, and a selection of mini-muffins were arranged on a low glass table.

'I took the liberty,' Agnes said, 'but if you'd rather tea than coffee I can order some. Or would you like a proper drink? The sun's just about over the yard-arm.'

'Coffee's fine, thanks.'

'I'll be mother then.'

Agnes poured, passing Gus the milk and sugar. The cup rattled slightly against the saucer as he picked them up; seemingly his philosophical approach to the occasion had flown right out of the window.

'You read my letter.'

'Yes, do you mind?'

'No, of course not, if your… if you were shown it then it's fine.'

'Wasn't quite like that.' Agnes took a sip of coffee, leaving a rosy lip-print on the rim of the cup. 'I saw it on Mother's bedside table when I popped upstairs for something. Couldn't resist. It's hard-wired in, I'm afraid, the need to ferret out the truth.'

'I'm surprised she kept it,' Gus said, 'considering the reception I got when I rang. We didn't exactly part on the best of terms. I don't even know why I wrote. I knew she'd never change her mind and agree to talk to me about Catherine. Actually, I thought there was every chance she'd tear it up without reading it.'

Agnes smiled. 'My mother's mind works in mysterious ways.'

His letter, Gus remembered, had been brief, painstakingly courteous, almost distant. Agnes couldn't have gleaned much from it. Cecelia, apparently, had been reluctant at first to explain to her daughter about his phone call.

'I got it out of her, of course, and that's when I knew I had to speak to you. I felt you had the right to as much information as there was.'

Agnes put down her cup and saucer and sat forward a little. Gus found his attention drawn to her legs, long and slender in silky, flesh-coloured tights, as she tucked them neatly against the sofa, her skirt riding up just above her knees. She must be, what, forty or so? He peeled his gaze away from her lower half and focused on her face, finding there an imposing kind of beauty in the strong shape of her brow, the curve of her cheekbone, and the wide, full mouth. He tried to see something of himself in her but there was nothing, except the colour of her hair and her eyes which were the same shape and shade of brown as his.

Agnes looked back at him with some amusement.

'Sorry,' he said. 'I was staring.'

'You were looking to see if we were alike. So was I. Strange, isn't it? We live our lives by rules and conventions but at moments like this there aren't any, so we have to make up our own. I do have the headstart on you, of course, knowing you were out there somewhere.'

'You knew about me before you saw the letter, then?'

'Oh yes. Family secrets have a way of outing themselves, especially those of a salacious nature. I mean nothing derogatory by that, you understand.'

'I know.' Gus nodded.

'Some years ago I tried to find you, out of curiosity,' Agnes continued, 'but I wasn't successful. I had so little to go on, just your mother's name and your approximate birth-date.'

Agnes had always known her mother had a younger sister, she told him, and that she'd been banished from the family, having committed a sin against decent society and against God.

'Is it any wonder people turn against religion?' she said with sudden vehemence, interrupting her own story and echoing Gus's long-held sentiment. 'Such bigotry!'

She hadn't known what Catherine was supposed to have done, not until she was older, and then, through judicious questioning of various family members she found out about the baby, him. He had been born twelve years before Agnes, almost a generation's difference when you're that age. What had happened was separate, a rattle of the family skeleton, by the time she got to hear of it.

'Nobody I asked seemed to know who your father was. I got the impression she refused to say. I don't suppose you know?'

'No,' Gus said. 'She didn't name him on my birth certificate. He got off scot-free by the looks of it.'

'Does that bother you?'

'Funnily enough, it never has. In my mind it was some young lad who did a bunk as soon as he found out, if he ever did.' Gus shrugged. 'It happens. That's life.'

'Indeed,' Agnes said.

She poured them both more coffee. They sat in silence for a while, deep in their respective thoughts, until Gus spoke again.

'What do you know of her, my mother?' What else, he

245

meant.

'Very little. Left school at fifteen, apprenticed to a dressmaker, played the dutiful daughter, went to church on Sundays. No-one expected... well, there it is.'

'I found her birth certificate,' Gus said, 'then later there were some things in a bag, small personal things, tokens she appeared to have left for me. I couldn't understand why they were there, in the house.' He sketched in the story about Augusta and his inheritance. 'I'm afraid I got rather caught up in it all, a bit obsessive. I did some research, read about girls who got into trouble back then, so I knew how it must have been and why she had to give me up. What troubled me more, still does if I'm honest, was what happened afterwards, after she gave birth to me in the institution.'

'You were handed over to your new family after the statutory time, I imagine.'

'I was, yes.'

Gus fell silent. How much of his own family secrets, his inner feelings, was he meant to share with Agnes? He didn't want to talk about it, and yet they were here for a purpose and it wasn't just so that he could hear it confirmed that his birth mother had been sent away in disgrace. Agnes was gazing earnestly at him, as if she expected him to ask questions, yet how could he if he had none? What he wanted, or thought he wanted, from Cecelia – an insight into Catherine's state of mind, a reason for her to take her own life – simply wasn't there to be had. It was as Cecelia had stated; once her sister was out of the door, all ties were broken. He'd been clutching at the proverbial straw when he'd contacted her.

'That isn't what you meant, is it? What happened afterwards,' Agnes said quietly.

Gus shook his head. 'I meant what happened to my mother. It surprised me when Cecelia said she didn't know about it but perhaps her parents kept it from her. To them, suicide would have been the worst sin imaginable.'

'Yes.' For the first time Agnes seemed hesitant, a little distracted. 'Gus, when I was searching the records looking for you, I was sidetracked and I started to dig deeper. Like you, I felt there was more to be found.' She reached for the black handbag by her feet, opened it, and took out a folded oblong of cream paper. 'It might help if you look at this first, before we go on.'

Gus realised his hands were clenched, nails digging into his palms. He didn't want this. Whatever it was, he didn't want it. He wished he had never come. He looked longingly out of the window at the street as if by power of thought he could transport himself there but there was no escape. He looked back at Agnes, appealing silently for her to help him out but she simply held out the piece of paper towards him. He took it, opened it out. It was a certificate of some kind.

'I sent for it to corroborate the records I found on the internet. I'm sorry, it's going to come as a bit of a shock, I'm afraid.'

Gus took a deep breath, put on his glasses and looked down at the paper. *Certified Copy of an Entry of Marriage,* he read. *Hector Alan Parry, age 34, bachelor. Catherine Mary Harte, age 27, spinster. 2nd October 1965.*

No. Someone with the same name, it had to be. A mistake, an easy one to make; he should know, all the hours he'd spent trying to make sense of online records. Names you thought were unique were anything but, dates and places repeated and repeated countless times, life events so easily assigned to entirely the wrong family.

The garden at home. French cricket. His innocent question, its answer caught as lightly as the cricket ball and just as lightly tossed aside, into the long grass. A cigarette stump in his pocket waiting to be held between clandestine fingers and lit. And his father, head in hands, hunched on the old iron bench.

But why, if it wasn't true? *Why?*

Gus looked up, saw Agnes's expression, her fingers twisting and untwisting the chain of her necklace, and he knew there was no mistake.

Chapter Thirty-One

'Is this..?'

Even though he knew, he had to hear her say it.

'Yes, it's her.'

'She didn't die.' His voice was hardly above a whisper. '*She didn't die.*'

'No.'

'But I was told she had. My father told me she drowned. Why would he, if it wasn't true?'

'Presumably because he thought it was.'

'Has she… since?'

'No, no. She's still alive. She'll be seventy-two. No age at all.'

'But Cecelia, your mother…' Gus's voice caught in his throat.

'Has no idea. I never told her. No point.'

Gus nodded. He looked again at the certificate, at the parish of registration in the Newcastle district, at the name of Catherine's father – his own grandfather whom he'd never met – undeservedly inscribed on this document because the records required it, even though he had disowned his daughter years before. Then he looked again at the name of his natural mother. *Catherine Mary Harte.*

A surge of energy rose from the soles of his feet, spurred his muscles into action. He stood up, gazing at his surroundings as if it was the first time he'd clapped eyes on them. He wanted to run. He wanted to shout, to laugh out loud. He wanted to run along the street, turn his face to the sky, feel the breeze. Keep running, keep laughing…

'Are you all right?' Agnes was half standing, her hand on

his arm, her eyes anxious.

'What? Oh, yes.'

He sat down again. A long, slow smile began. He couldn't rein it in. And yet, and yet...

'I have more, census records, electoral register, that kind of thing,' Agnes said. 'I've been able to trace most of her movements. I didn't bring them in case it was too much for you to take in all at once but I have them at home. I could send them to you, or you could come up again.'

'I'm not sure,' Gus said after a moment.

She nodded. 'Shall we walk for a bit?'

How Gus managed to put one foot in front of the other he had no idea, but somehow he did, and somehow, without any memory of how they got there or what was said during the walk, he found himself sitting on a bench under a tree in a small park with Agnes beside him, her bag on her lap.

'I wasn't being entirely truthful when I said I'd brought nothing else today,' she said.

'Oh?'

'No. There's this.' She opened her bag and produced a black-and-white photo. 'If this is too much...'

'No, no.' He took the photo, fitting it into his palm as he fumbled in the pocket of his jacket for his glasses. 'It's her, isn't it? It's Catherine.'

'Yes. Taken when she was about sixteen or seventeen, I'd say. It was the only one I could find. It's yours now.'

It was a small snapshot, captured by a slightly unsteady hand. She was standing in front of a tall monument of some kind and there were trees in the background, a park. Her hair, darkish in the picture, was cut short and severe but her smile and the softness of her expression shone out through the fuzziness of the shot. She was wearing a flowered dress with short sleeves, the skirt fanning out from a nipped-in waist to just below the knee, and white shoes. She held a white handbag in front of her in both hands. A demure pose, behind it a spark of something, something that seemed ready to burst out.

'She was tiny,' Gus said.

'Yes.'

He felt his shoulders pulling him forwards as if they were attached to unseen weights. He closed his eyes, felt a rocking motion that came from deep inside. When he opened his eyes they were wet. He rubbed them, sat up straight.

'Sorry.'

'Don't be. I can't imagine what you're going through. I tried, knowing we were doing this today, but you can't, can you? Put yourself in someone's else's place. Not entirely.'

Gus turned to Agnes, surprised at this glimpse of her inner self. Perhaps he shouldn't be. 'Thank you. Thank you so much, Agnes.'

'I was right to tell you, wasn't I?'

'Oh yes, most definitely.'

When they parted in the street a while later – Gus, the photo in his pocket, headed for the tube, Agnes for her chambers – they hugged for a long moment. Agnes let go first.

'You must come and visit us, Adrian and me. I'll get Christopher down, too. We're out in Essex. An old farmhouse. You'd like it, I think.'

'I will,' he said.

Gus didn't look once at the photo on the way home in case he wasn't able to hold himself together. Instead he picked up an abandoned newspaper on the train and concentrated on its crumpled columns for most of the journey. Even when he arrived back at Prosperity Terrace he put off the moment, opening his mail, putting away the breakfast things he'd left on the draining board, showering and changing into his jeans, listening to an answerphone message from Tom and making some notes in his work diary for tomorrow.

When, eventually, he fetched the photo from his jacket that he'd left hanging in the hall and looked at it again, he wasn't overcome with sadness or anger or incomprehension. Instead he felt euphoric, much as he had with Agnes back at the hotel, but in a quieter sort of way, and deeply thankful that she hadn't died. He felt no urge to run or laugh or shout. In fact, all he wanted to do was sleep. For two pins he could stretch out on the sofa and fall into a coma, but he mustn't; he'd only be wide awake again at midnight. He made himself eat something, although he wasn't really hungry, then switched on the TV and sat back, his eyes on the screen, his mind elsewhere.

The question hit him full on. *What now?* What was he supposed to do? What did he *want* to do? In a couple of days he would have it all, the paper evidence of where Catherine had spent her life and where she was now. Not in Newcastle, Agnes said. Not anywhere north but down here, a spin around the coast from Brighton. Broadstairs. He had never been, at least he couldn't remember going. He visualised a windy promenade, a sandy bay, a pier, fishing boats, triangular white-sailed yachts, and a sea forever blue. They were all the same, these places, weren't they? Or was that a child's view? Picture-book heaven.

Had she known where he was, moved south in order to be closer to him? Stupid, stupid. Of course not. Had she *ever* known where he was? The law changed, he seemed to recall, allowed parents to find out where their adopted children had ended up. So why had she not looked for him? Did she despise him for being born, for changing her life, sending her off on a path she would not otherwise have taken? Now he was being melodramatic, letting his imagination run away with him. He must think logically, use his head. Except his heart kept getting in the way.

He understood she was dead, his father had said, that day in the garden. There were *certain signs*. Signs that she'd gone off the bridge after she disappeared from the institution. Gus had never forgotten the exact words. He'd packed them up and put them away, taken his own interpretation forward into his world. He had believed she was dead, believed it without question. Why wouldn't he? His father would never tell a deliberate lie about something of that magnitude. And had Gus not witnessed for himself his father's private distress not long after they'd had the conversation? He hadn't given it much credence at the time – if he'd felt anything it was embarrassment – but obviously his father had been feeling sad for the girl who had thrown away her life just because she had a baby.

Or perhaps he was distressed at having to tell Gus what had happened to his mother. Or he'd been upset about something entirely different and it was nothing to do with Gus and his damn-fool awkward questions. Anyway, people who adopted babies in those days didn't get to know the mothers, did they? So why, even if he thought she was dead, would he still be upset about it years later? And then there was Augusta and her part in it all, her possession of Catherine's birth certificate and the bag of belongings. That was a piece of the puzzle he'd never come close to solving.

The familiar quake of anxiety began to stir, making his forehead clammy, his stomach nauseous. He pushed away the feeling, took several deep breaths. He couldn't do this. He couldn't go there again, to the sleepless nights, the dark moments when every new thought gave rise to another and another until he truly believed he was losing his mind. He was a grown man; he had come this far, safe and well and relatively sane. He couldn't go back, rewrite history to fit what he now knew, demolish the store of grief as if it had never existed. It was too late. She didn't need him now, had never needed him, and he didn't need her. She wasn't his real mother. His real mother sang him German lullabies, baked him chocolate cake, made him a bag to keep his plimsolls in, and kissed away his nightmares. His real mother's name was Liesel Albourne, not Catherine Harte. This was not the beginning of a new story. It was the end of an old one.

On impulse he rose from the chair, went quickly upstairs and took from beneath the jumpers on the top shelf of his wardrobe the cotton drawstring bag embroidered on one side with a circle of flowers, leaves and birds, and within the circle the letter *M* in dark blue chain stitch with a row of small red hearts underneath. He shook the contents onto his bed: a leather-bound bible with her name inside the cover, a narrow silver bracelet engraved with a twining rose, a pair of grey kid gloves, quite worn through in places, a black poodle brooch with a red collar and a diamanté eye, and a plain white button attached to a frayed bit of material. Her things, and now his.

Remarkable things.

Or unremarkable.

Meaningless.

He spaced them out on the bed cover, then, touching each in turn just once, took the bag and placed everything back inside. Then he took the fuzzy black-and-white photograph of the girl from long ago and dropped that in the bag, too, before putting it back inside the wardrobe.

And then he slept.

Chapter Thirty-Two

Millie's mouth dried and her breath deserted her every time she answered the phone at home or at the shop but after a week had passed with no word from Karen, she made a concerted effort to behave normally. Charmaine, unusually for her, thought Millie should maintain a dignified silence and not even think of trying to contact Karen. After the way the girl had behaved, she could hardly expect her mother to go chasing after her. In her more rational moments Millie agreed with her friend, while at other times, times when she experienced afresh the aching sense of loss, not only of her daughter but of herself, she was tempted to march down to the vintage shop and give the girl a good shake, literally as well as metaphorically.

But she didn't, and neither did she try to ring her. Instead she channelled her energies into refreshing the stock in the shop, selling off as cheaply as she dared the items that had been slow to shift and bringing in a host of interesting new lines which Charmaine enthusiastically helped display to their fullest potential. She smartened up the window display and paid attention to publicity, too, persuading the little neighbourhood magazine to run a small feature and investing in a boxed ad in the local paper. All this effort paid off; the shop was busier than ever and Millie went home each evening physically exhausted but mentally satisfied.

'You work too hard,' Jet said, banging through the door one morning with a large take-out cappuccino in one hand and a dripping bunch of orange, yellow and white flowers in the other, still with the half-price sticker attached to the cellophane.

Millie kissed him on the cheek and met the full impact of a recent dousing of aftershave. 'They're lovely. Thank you. I'll stick them in a jug for now and take them home with me later.'

'Well, I wouldn't hang about. They go out of date at midnight.'

Jet lingered for a while, filling the small space behind the counter so that Millie had to squeeze past him, watching her drink her coffee, waiting while she served a customer and took an order on the phone. Not that she minded, but it was a tad unusual. Eventually Jet voiced what had clearly been on his mind from the moment he walked in.

'I've got a proposition for you,' he said, turning pink in the face and hopping from one large foot to the other.

Millie laughed. 'Now where have I heard that before?'

'Not that, although now you mention it...' Millie slapped him on the arm. 'No, what I was thinking, there's a caravan down in Wales. Tenby.'

'I imagine there are thousands,' Millie said.

'Yes, well, this one belongs to a mate of mine and he said I can have it, last week in August. How about you come with me?'

The man had tenacity, Millie gave him that. She just wished she didn't have to disappoint him so regularly.

'Jet, you know I can't,' she said, as kindly as she could.

Jet's eyes lowered briefly. He had beautiful eyes, blue-grey, with long, thick lashes. His eyes were the best part of him, aside from his sweet and generous nature. If only the spark was there, if only... But it wasn't, and never would be.

'Course you can. You could do with a break.'

'And I'm having one.' Millie lightened her tone, edging her way out from behind the counter to put a bit of space between them. 'I'm going to Malaga in September with Charmaine.'

'Malaga. Now there's posh,' Jet said, with a smile and no undertone.

'Not really. She and John have got a little apartment there. They've had it for years.'

Jet leaned his meaty forearms on the counter and regarded Millie with the most serious expression she'd possibly ever seen on him.

'Malaga's not the reason, though, is it?'

255

'No, it isn't,' Millie said, after a moment.

'It's that bloke, the one who comes and goes.'

Again there was no trace of self-pity or accusation. Jet was simply stating the facts, being truthful. If only she could do the same. She would, if only she knew what the truth was.

'You mean Gus, Gus Albourne. That's his name.'

'It's him you're thinking about when we're out and you go all distant on me,' Jet said.

Millie was back behind the counter in seconds. She put her arms round Jet, felt his ample warmth fold against her, his head drop to make contact with hers.

'I'm so sorry. I honestly don't know how I feel about him but I only know it's different from how I feel about you.'

Jet pulled gently away, rested his hands lightly on Millie's shoulders. 'It's all right. It's not a problem. I've always known we weren't going anywhere, you and me.' He smiled into Millie's eyes. It was a true Jet smile, open, genuine, and heartbreaking. 'Don't look so sad. Nothing to be sorry about. We're mates, aren't we? Lot to be said for that.'

Millie smiled back, wiped a hand beneath her eye. 'The very best. Always will be.'

Jet gave Millie a last, long, poignant look, then marched out to the middle of the shop, rubbing his hands together. 'Right then, that's me back to the grindstone. See yer later.'

'Yes, see you.'

When he'd gone, Millie went through to the back. On the formica top next to the sink the flowers leaned drunkenly to one side in their makeshift container. The sink itself was a mass of fallen petals. She didn't know whether to laugh or cry.

A compromise, Millie thought. That would be the answer. She wouldn't go on bended knee pleading with Karen to accept the truth about her father – she'd done and said all that, and look where it had got her – but neither would she give up on her entirely, not now she'd come this far. If Karen was too young, too naïve, too short-sighted to realise that she couldn't kick her mother out of her life and expect there to be no consequences then she would just have to be shown otherwise.

Putting the idea into practice, though, wasn't so easy. She began by ringing Karen's mobile and received only a rapid recorded response each time. After the fourth attempt, she left a short, businesslike message for Karen to call her back. Nothing. Her confidence already waning, she didn't want to go to Karen's flat and be left on the doorstep like an abandoned parcel, should she be denied entry. Neither did she want to turn up at the shop and risk public confrontation.

Another day passed while Millie kept a constant check on her mobile. Then she rang the shop.

'How Was It For You? Maxine speaking,' exclaimed a loud, confident voice, as if its owner was challenging the caller to disagree.

Millie took a slow inward breath and waited, forgetting that she hadn't actually spoken aloud. An undisguised sigh emitted from the other end.

'Yes? What can I do for you?'

Millie gathered her wits. 'Could I speak to Karen... Katya, please?'

'Hang on.' A few seconds of tapping and rustling, the screech of unoiled hinges, then: 'No, sorry. She's not here.'

Millie jumped in before Maxine could disconnect. 'Will she be in later?'

'I really couldn't say. Sorry.'

This second apology had a ring of triumph about it.

'Well I apologise for having disturbed you,' Millie said, with an irresistible but possibly unwise hint of sarcasm. 'Goodbye.'

Her new-found resolve already dwindling, she had to force herself to ring back an hour later. This time, the message from Maxine bore the marks of a very different scenario.

'I should have said earlier. When I told you Katya wasn't here, I meant she doesn't work here any more, so you see there's no point in you ringing back.'

Millie felt sick. Maxine was clearly acting under instruction but short of calling the girl a liar there wasn't much she could do about it.

'Where is she then? If she's not there, where is she?'

Millie flinched as the sound of her own voice with its hectoring tone resonated back to her, but she wasn't out to make a good impression. She rushed on.

'Look, if you do happen to see her I'd be grateful if you'd give her a message. Tell her that her mother rang and would she please get in touch.'

'No, I can't. I told you, she's gone. I didn't know that when you rang the first time but I do now, and I won't be seeing her. Sorry.' She rang off.

A smidgen of doubt crossed Millie's mind until she realised how stupid it was. Of course Karen hadn't gone. Maxine was her friend and she was part-owner of the place, wasn't she? She reconsidered going to the shop or waiting until this evening and trying to catch Karen at home, but those were the actions of a needy, desperate woman and she was neither. Karen could play all the silly games she liked but Millie was not about to join in.

At ten to five the shop phone rang.

'Preston Knits. Hello?'

'It's me,' Karen said indifferently.

Keeping the phone clamped to her ear, Millie walked to the door at a normal pace, turned the sign to *Closed* and walked all the way back again without speaking.

'Mum? Are you there?'

Satisfied, Millie sat down on the stood behind the counter. 'Yes, I'm here.'

'I'm sorry,' Karen said.

'Sorry for what, Karen? For running out on me the other day, for starting all that about your father, or for not answering my messages?'

'I rang, didn't I?' she snapped.

Millie held her breath but Karen was speaking again.

'Look, I'm sorry we got off on the wrong foot, and for… the other stuff. What do you want, anyway?'

Several replies suggested themselves, all too emotional, too close to Millie's heart. She stuck to the script.

'I wondered if you'd like to come over for lunch on Sunday? Roast beef and Yorkshires, I thought – unless you've turned vegetarian.'

'No, I'm not veggie.'

Millie sensed some amusement in the reply. 'How about it then?'

'Yes, all right, I'll come.'

What else was in that voice? Relief? Millie didn't dare to surmise.

'Good. We'll eat about one.' She rang off.

Karen ate a lot and spoke little, but even through the silences Millie sensed an acquiescence that gave her a warm, hopeful feeling inside. If the subject of her father was on Karen's mind, at least she had the good grace to keep it to herself and Millie concentrated on keeping what conversation there was to neutral subjects, as had been her intention all along. She chattered about the shop and her latest endeavours, then asked Karen about her new living arrangements. Yes, she liked her flat, she said. Not much more than that but it was a start.

Later, when Karen went upstairs to use the bathroom, Millie heard her go to her old bedroom and open the door. It was a few minutes before she closed it again. Millie smiled to herself.

The doorbell rang just after three. It was Gus. Millie glanced behind her, nodding towards the sitting room as she let him in. His surprise arrival and the presence of her daughter wrong-footed her, and she stood between the two of them not knowing quite what to say. But Gus, bless him, chatted to Karen quite naturally as if he'd fully expected to see her there.

Tea, Millie thought. The routine of boiling and pouring and stirring, the rescuer of all manner of awkward situations. The cure for all that ails. She was about to offer it when Karen stood up to leave.

'You don't have to go yet, surely?' Millie heard herself say, without meaning to.

The time had flown by. It hardly seemed five minutes since Karen had arrived but already she was opening the front door. As Millie and Gus stood on the step to see her off, Karen turned round, looked deliberately from one to the other and smiled knowingly before taking off up the street at a fast pace, long hair swinging. Millie could hardly look at Gus but he seemed not to notice her slight embarrassment. He went and sat down. Millie followed and sat next to him.

'How did it go?'

He meant with Karen, of course.

'Quite well, I think. I didn't mention the Mark thing and neither did she. Not that I was ever going to. She's had all the explanation she's going to get from me.'

'Good for you.' Gus seemed distracted, as if his own thought processes were running parallel to the conversation. 'At least she came, though. That must make you happy.'

'It does. I still haven't told her about the money Mark left, though. I wanted to, but the opportunity never came up. Probably me, not wanting to mention her father.'

'Sorry,' Gus said. 'I hope I didn't cause her to run off like that, before you'd had the chance.'

'No, not at all. She wouldn't have stayed long anyway. Actually, you turning up was the best thing. It gave her a get-out clause. There'll be other times, though. We've only just begun. That's how I feel, anyway.'

'Marvellous,' Gus said, clasping his hands together and looking down at the floor.

'Gus, has something happened?'

Millie stared at Gus, her hand over her mouth. She couldn't take it in. Catherine Harte, his natural mother, hadn't died, not then, not ever. Everything he'd been through – the guilt, the resentment, the soul-destroying sadness, the long, tired, lonely hours of wondering how and why – it was all visible in the mobility of his jaw, the twitching nerve in his temple, the over-brightness of his eyes.

'Oh. Oh, Gus.'

She moved closer, linked her arm through his. Immediately his hand closed over hers, holding on tight as if he needed her, really needed her.

'I know,' he said, with a rueful smile. 'You couldn't make it up.'

'No.'

'Thank you, Gus,' Millie said, after they'd sat for a while in contemplative silence.

He frowned. 'What for?'

'For coming to tell me. You didn't have to. It can't be easy for you to talk about it.'

'I wouldn't not have come, Millie. You were there at the beginning of the story. It's only right that you know the end. You listened. You listened, and you don't know how valuable that is.'

Oh, I do, Millie thought.

'Where do you go from here? You talk about the end of the story but it's not, is it?'

And again she sat in wide-eyed astonishment as she heard Gus describe, with calm and clarity, the sea-change in his heart.

But how could he not want to see her, his natural mother? She felt quite frantic, wanted to take him by the shoulders and make him realise how wrong this was for him, the regrets he would surely have if he didn't act now and Catherine moved on, away from the circumference of his life. Or she could die and then it would be too late for both of them. But she said nothing, because Gus knew precisely what she was thinking.

'I can't do it, Millie. We've managed without one another so far. I can't disrupt my life which I've only just got back on track and I can't disrupt hers. She's an old lady. It could kill her, hearing from me out of the blue.'

'I doubt that,' Millie said. 'But I'm not about to try and persuade you. It has to be how *you* feel, not me, not anyone else. Just one thing, though…'

'Go on.'

'It's what you said to me about family when we were talking about Karen. I know this is nothing like the same thing, nothing like it at all, but remember what you said about the blood ties of real family being important and how we mustn't lose sight of that, because if we do we lose the sense of who we are.'

Gus rubbed a hand across his head. He looked exhausted. 'Yes, well, I've changed my mind about that. Your parents are the people who brought you up. It's not fair on them otherwise.'

261

Millie nodded, understanding. She smiled, gave his arm a squeeze. He smiled back. It lit up his face. The nerves in Millie's stomach performed a little dance. She took her gaze away from his.

'Tea. I'll make some.'

She went to stand up but Gus still had hold of her hand.

'I'm going away for a while,' he said. 'That's the other thing I came to tell you.'

Millie blinked. For a moment she thought she might be going to cry.

'Not for long. Two or three weeks at most. I feel I need to give myself some space after all that's happened, take time out to clear my head.'

'Where are you going?'

'Devon. I've taken a cottage in the middle of nowhere. Nothing to do but walk and read and sleep.'

'And think?'

'Yes, and think. I told myself I wouldn't do that, think about it any more, but you've made me see that perhaps I should, because once I've made my decision it has to be final and I have to get it right. So I'll give it a little more time and then I'll let it go.'

'When do you leave?'

'Tomorrow. But, Millie…'

'Yes?'

'What I'd like, and I don't know what you think and I'm well aware that you might tell me in a minute, but when I get back I'd really like to see you, properly I mean.'

'I'd like that, too,' she said.

Chapter Thirty-Three

Gus paced through the long, brown hummocky grass, head bowed, counting out loud. Yes, it could be done, he was sure of it. He was in Elspeth's garden, right down at the end. Her wild garden, she called it. *If anyone turns their nose up I tell them it's a wildlife habitat.* Stepping round a virulent-looking clump of something prickly, he paced back, counting again, then turned and set off at a right angle, following the line of the fence, or rather the place where the fence would be had it not creaked its way to earth in the last gale.

He stood still and looked back at the house. One or two roof tiles looked a bit loose; he must remember to get up there and inspect them properly. Hopefully it would be a patch-up job, not an expensive wholesale replacement. He turned his attention back to the matter in hand. The gardens along here backed onto an unadopted road, not that wide but wide enough not to make access a problem. If the footprint of the new build was kept to a minimum he didn't see why planning permission should not be forthcoming.

'What *are* you doing?'

Elspeth was coming towards him, the tail of the lime-green scarf tying her hair back lifting in the breeze, her arms wrapped around herself against the chill that spoke of autumn.

'Build a house? What, here?'

She looked at him as if he'd gone mad when he told her what he had in mind.

'Not build it ourselves, just sell off a chunk of land with the architect's plans all in place and the council's permission. All done and dusted.'

'What if the neighbours object?'

'No reason why they should. You wouldn't be the only one to have done it. Four others along this road have done the same, haven't they?'

'And I'd get the money for the land?'

'You own it, don't you?'

'Yes, I know, but it sounds almost too good to be true. What about the expenses, beforehand I mean, of the architect and everything?'

'You can leave that to me. I'll cover everything until the sale goes through. I get mates' rates anyway.'

Gus hoped he had enough in savings to honour this promise; he thought so, but he would find a way, whatever it took, if Elspeth agreed. She could make a tidy profit if his estimation was correct. He would bring someone else over, though, to be certain before he went off at a tangent, and he'd contact the planning department for an up-to-date assessment on the permission side of things. Other than that, he could see no reason why this shouldn't work. Elspeth would still have a big enough garden for her, Jenny, and the dog to enjoy, of a much more manageable size, and he would make sure the plans included proper screening so they weren't too much overlooked by their new neighbours.

'You've really thought about this, haven't you?'

'I've burned a few brain cells, yes, but I didn't want to say anything until I had a proper plan.'

'Goodness,' Elspeth said, her green eyes alight. 'What a turn-up for the books.'

As they sat over supper in the kitchen later, Gus was tempted to tell Elspeth and Jenny of his other plans but keeping it a surprise would be much more fun. Gus was involving himself in something he had never done before nor imagined that he would – fundraising. After the accident, the day centre Jenny attended had eventually acquired another minibus but it had turned out to be a bad purchase. Nothing had gone right with it from the start and it spent more time at the garage than it did on the road, Elspeth had told him, besides which, the centre itself was expanding to take more young people like Jenny and when more of them wanted to go on an outing than the minibus could seat there was disappointment all round.

Had the centre not thought of trying to raise the money for a second bus, Gus had asked. But Elspeth said they'd decided against it for the foreseeable, thinking it unwise to ask people to dig into their pockets in such financially stretched times.

Gus had promptly arranged a meeting with the centre's managers and promised his practical and dedicated support if they were to reconsider. He'd wondered at times whether his enthusiasm had run away with him when the collection jar on the bar of the Dog and Trumpet and those in other local pubs and shops remained stubbornly a quarter full, but gradually, progress had been made, much of it down to Gus's cajoling.

It hadn't been easy to persuade Hangburton's residents to hold jumble sales, raffles and a dog show on the village green in aid of a cause that wasn't exactly on their doorstep, but he'd pressed on and gradually people had become as fired up with it as he was and the funds were swelling nicely.

In Elspeth's own neighbourhood, too, things were happening. An August bank holiday road race had brought in hundreds in sponsorship, local businesses had promised donations, and a barn dance held at the centre itself – which Gus had politely declined to attend, this being well outside the call of duty – had done well, too. Elspeth, of course, knew of the efforts that were being made; she just didn't know that he was behind it all.

It felt good, this new philanthropic side to himself. Perhaps it shouldn't, but he was not about to beat himself up over a little self-congratulatory moment. It would take months more before they had enough money to buy the bus, but when they had, that was when the second part of the surprise would come to fruition. The bus should be named after him, the managers at the centre had insisted. But Gus had refused. No, he'd told them. It would be named 'The Jenny Albourne bus'.

He watched Jenny now, her mouth – Robert's mouth – pursed in concentration as she twined spaghetti round her fork, and he could see the woman in her, the woman she was meant to be. He felt a rush of sadness, but Jenny looked at him and her face broke into a sudden, wide grin.

'You all right, Jenny?'

'I'm cool.'

'High five?'

'High five.'

Jenny dropped her fork with a clatter. Her hand came up and smacked into his. Elspeth raised her eyes.

Chapter Thirty-Four

The harvest was in, stubble was being burned off in the fields, and migrating birds climbed the blue rise of the Downs to sweep over the ridge in black, ragged formations. In the mornings, as always at this time of year, the air tasted of back-to-school and Gus felt again the raw rub of new shoes that were always slightly too big. In the evenings the subtle scent of furtive bonfires accompanied his walks – he tended to walk rather than run now – and windfall apples mouldered in plastic boxes outside garden gates with hopeful, felt-tipped notices: *Please help yourself.*

On one such evening he came across Grace and Gordon in the lane by Saint Saviour's, busily stripping blackberries from the bushes and flinging them haphazardly into an ancient wicker basket as big as a baby's cradle. He stopped and chatted to them for a while before wandering on, and the next day when he arrived home from work he found a blackberry and apple pie on his doorstep in an enamel dish like the one his mother had, the pastry still warm beneath the blue and white tea cloth that covered it. Not so long ago he would have panicked at such an offering, felt trapped as his mind rebelled against the implications. Now, for the first time since Clair died, he felt he had come home.

But settling down in Hangburton wasn't the only reason for the feeling.

The middle of September was somewhat late to be thinking about the beach, but the beach was where Millie wanted to be. It was a beautiful day, Gus conceded, as the two of them crunched over the pebbles to reach the perfect spot beside the groyne that Millie had her eye on.

The tide was coming in but was just far enough away to reveal a narrow strip of shiny brown sand festooned with oily flags of wrinkled seaweed. Gus rolled up his jersey as a pillow and sat back, feeling the warmth of the wall through his shirt as he watched the foam inch further up the beach until the sand had all but disappeared. He looked at Millie beside him, eyes closed, shoulders tinted pale gold by the sun, and wished he could preserve forever this moment of feeling completely at peace with himself, proof that he had made the right decision, not just about Millie but about everything his life had been about these past months.

'Goodness, I must have dropped off,' Millie said half an hour later, hoisting herself up and looking at her watch.

Gus smiled. 'My pleasure. You look beautiful when you're asleep. More than usual, I mean.'

'I should drop off more often then.'

She looked at him, those penetrating blue eyes smiling into his. He put his arm round her shoulders, leaning in. Millie leaned towards him in response, then twisted round so that she was half facing away from him. Gus let out the breath he'd been holding and kissed the top of her head. 'Make a move, then, shall we?'

They stood at Millie's window and watched the rain falling steadily from a navy-grey sky. It tumbled through the broad ray of the street-light, fractured and hard like particles of glass from a shattered windscreen.

'I rather like the way it changes, the weather,' Millie said. 'Clear skies one minute, monsoon the next.'

'I know,' he said. 'To think we were on the beach only, what, six hours ago?'

Millie whacked him on the arm. 'Yes, well the time just rattles by when I'm with you.'

The room was in semi-darkness but Gus sensed Millie's slight embarrassment at her own words.

'Same here, same here,' he said.

'Well you can't go out in this. You'll get a soaking. You'll have to hang on a minute.'

Gus's car was well in sight, just a few yards along the road. He smiled to himself.

'Suits me,' he said. 'Shall I put a light on?'

'No, leave it. I like it like this.'

They continued to stand in the bay, gazing out. Gus reached for Millie's hand, held it briefly to his lips. Taken by surprise, she giggled.

'I love your laugh,' he said. 'And I love you.'

Millie's breath whooshed inwards, loud in the quiet of the room.

'You do?'

'I do. I love you, Millie Hope.'

'That's good then,' she said, 'because I love you, too. Ever so much.'

Gus looked at Millie and a long, slow smile began. He couldn't pretend he wasn't scared, just a little. He knew she was, too – he'd heard the wobble in her voice – but that was what made it all the more right. He gathered her into his arms and kissed her, and Millie kissed him back as if her life depended on it.

Chapter Thirty-Five

'I'm sorry, Jess. I wasn't always very nice to you, I realise that. I'm a crass idiot at times but I never intended to hurt you, and I apologise if I did.'

He'd spotted her sitting alone in the window of a coffee shop in Haywards Heath where he'd gone in search of new kitchen taps. He hadn't realised how corroded his were until he saw Millie wrestling with the hot tap as she washed up the breakfast things on Sunday morning. Jessica had looked up in alarm as he stood hesitating on the pavement, then she'd recovered herself and beckoned him inside.

She held up a hand. 'No, don't, please. I'm embarrassed enough about the whole thing as it is.'

'There's no need,' Gus said, surprised, nodding his thanks at the waitress who had brought his hot chocolate.

'Oh, there's every need.' Jessica smiled, almost shyly, reminding him of the first time he'd met her among the group in the village hall. 'I was clingy and jealous and I behaved like a tart because it seemed the only way to get what I wanted. Which was you. Or rather I thought it was... *oh God*.' She covered her face with both hands and for a second Gus felt a bit apprehensive, but it was all right because the next moment she was smiling again.

'You'd have noticed,' Jessica continued, 'that my mother is a touch on the pushy side. Not that that's any excuse when you get to my age.'

They both laughed.

'I expect all mothers are. I know mine was. She was a bit more subtle about it, though.' Gus winked, remembering Sidonie's cross-examination of him in Rosemary's garden.

'Yes, well, it doesn't exactly help, especially when you live in a small village where everybody knows your business.'

'My thoughts exactly,' said Gus. 'I did wonder, for quite a long time, if I could ever settle there. There were other factors, of course, the way I came to have the cottage, the complications it threw up...' he waved a dismissive hand, 'but now, well, I wouldn't say I'll stay in Hangburton forever but it'll do me nicely for now. Anyway, you look very smart, I meant to say before. Not that you don't always.'

Jessica looked down at the sharp little grey suit she was wearing as if she'd forgotten she had it on. The jacket was nipped in at the waist and had wide, asymmetrical lapels. It looked expensive. Underneath she wore a modestly-buttoned cream silk shirt and her hair was swept up and fastened with a clip.

'I've been to Brighton, for an interview. Job interview,' she added, in case there was any mistake.

'*Have* you? What was the job?'

He hadn't meant to sound so surprised but Jess's face told him she'd taken it in good part.

'Receptionist in a health club. A very upmarket health club, full of professional types.'

'I should hope so, too, young lady,' Gus said, grinning.

This was fine, it was good and easy. Why couldn't it have been like this before? But that was partly his fault, the way he'd treated her.

'When will you know if you've got the job?'

'They said they'd phone this evening, after six, one way or another. It went pretty well, though. I think I'm in with a chance. If I get it, I'm moving to Brighton. A friend has a room going spare in her flat. It's high time I stopped moping about and started doing something useful with my life.'

For the first time since he'd arrived, Gus noticed a tinge of regret in her voice. It made him feel a little bit sad. He was about to wish her luck with the job and the flat when she leaned confidentially towards him.

'I need to get away from the village. It's taken me ages to realise it,' she said. 'Or perhaps I did realise but I was too

271

stubborn to do anything about it.'

Gus waited for more but Jessica had fallen into a pensive silence. He felt there was something he should be picking up on here.

'I met your friend, Dan. We got chatting in the pub one day,' he said.

Jessica's face told him he was on the right track. She hesitated for a moment, then she said: 'I don't want to be around when she, when *Anna*, comes.'

'Jess,' Gus said gently, 'are you in love with Dan?'

She smiled. 'Stupid, isn't it, after all this time? I wish it wasn't true but there you are, you can't help who you fall in love with. I tried, got myself a diversion…'

'Me.'

'Yes. Sorry, I used you a bit. Not that I understood that at the time. I'd convinced myself I was in love with you, but I don't think I was, not really. It was always Dan, you see. Still is.'

She shrugged. She wasn't looking for sympathy, he could tell; knowing that made him warm to her even more.

'Oh, Jess.' He reached for her hand across the table. It felt cold. Automatically he rubbed it.

After a moment she gave a quick smile and withdrew her hand. If she was upset she wasn't going to let him see. There didn't seem much he could say to her confession. It was true, you couldn't help who you fell in love with but, given time and distance, and especially if she kept herself busy, which by the sound of it was the plan, the fire would die down and hopefully she'd find somebody else to love, somebody to make her happy.

'Do you want a lift home?' Gus asked, when it became obvious the conversation was at an end.

'No, I'm fine, thanks. My car's over there, in the station car park.'

'Right then,' Gus said cheerfully. 'I'll see you.' He stood up to leave.

'Yes, see you.'

Gus picked up the framed photo from Elspeth's mantelpiece

and smiled. Jenny's bright smile beamed right back at him. It wasn't a close-up but he could tell how proud and excited she was by her posture as she stood beside the shiny, pale-blue minibus in which sat the driver and several of Jenny's friends, all giving the thumbs-up for the camera. Just below and to the right of Jenny were the words: 'The Jenny Albourne Minibus', in gold-edged navy-blue letters.

Still smiling, Gus replaced the photo but continued to gaze at it. Behind him, Elspeth was speaking. He hadn't heard her come in.

'I said, I wondered if you'd bring Millie with you. We got on so well last time.' Elspeth put the tea tray on the dining table and waved Gus to a chair.

The hint of wistfulness in her voice made him laugh. The first, and so far only, time he'd brought Millie here, he'd found it impossible to get a word in edgeways and in the end he'd sauntered out to the garden and left them to it.

'She's away,' he said, dunking a biscuit in his tea.

'Away? Where?' Elspeth looked up, her hand stilled halfway to the milk jug.

'Don't look so worried,' Gus said. 'She'll be back at the weekend. She's taken Karen to one of those luxury spa hotels. They've booked up for all sorts of wacky treatments, seaweed wraps and things. Millie texted last night, said she's thoroughly enjoying being pampered. I'm glad. She deserves it.'

'But you're missing her like crazy.'

Gus put his tea down and scrutinized his sister-in-law. 'How come you know so much about me and I know nothing?'

She laughed. 'Oh, I think you've picked up a few things. I wouldn't write yourself off just yet. She and Karen are getting along okay now, then?'

'Yep, and that's something else I'm glad about, honestly, for both their sakes. There are a few topics they're steering clear of, but other than that it's looking promising.'

Gus had been concerned about the renewed relationship for Millie's sake – he couldn't stand to see her hurt again – but Karen's reaction to the news of the legacy had cheered him. At first, in true Karen style, she'd refused to discuss it, let alone

273

have anything to do with it, but with Millie's kid-glove handling she'd come round to the idea of using some of it to support her through a training course in textile design.

At first, Gus had been surprised at Karen's insistence that she only take just what she needed with Millie keeping the rest, until he remembered that Karen was Millie's daughter as well as Mark's.

The clatter of scaffolding poles and a volley of shouts had them looking towards the new boundary fence halfway down the garden and the square, red-brick shell rising above it.

'It doesn't disturb Jenny, all this?'

'No, no,' Elspeth said. 'In fact she thinks it's all rather fun. Anyway they don't make a lot of noise, not usually. Gus, I'm so grateful for everything you did, coming up with the idea and organising it all, making it a reality. You can't *believe* how much easier my life is, having that extra money in the pot.' She glanced away, reddening slightly, then turned back to Gus and smiled, the moment's awkwardness gone. 'I've come to think of it as a gift from Robert. After all, he was the one who bought and paid for the house, after I stopped work when we had Jenny. He took pupils for private tuition for a while – do you remember? They came after school and Saturday mornings. It all helped, although it gave Rob hardly any time to himself. What he did have he spent with Jenny and me.'

'When he wasn't up a ladder,' Gus said.

'Quite.' Elspeth smiled indulgently.

They sat for a while without speaking, both lost in thought, while in the background the whine of a saw undulated into the autumn air.

Then Elspeth spoke. 'I could come with you if you like, when, you know… Jenny can go to Kieran's so it wouldn't be a problem.'

'I know, and thanks for the offer, but I think I have to go it alone on this one.'

Later, Elspeth stood at the door as Gus was leaving, wrapping her arms around herself against the autumnal chill. Woken by the sounds of activity, the Dalmatian came lumbering along the hall from the kitchen and flopped down across the step. Gus bent to rub his head and the dog gazed up longingly at him.

'There's no need to look like that. Gus has things to do,' Elspeth said, giving the dog a nudge with her foot.

'I could walk him before I go if you like, save you a job later,' Gus suggested.

'No, you're all right. I'll wait till Jenny gets home then we'll take him together. He doesn't need walking far these days. Gus...' Elspeth frowned, and tugged at the sleeves of her red cardigan. 'Don't...'

'...expect too much. I know.' He kissed her.

Chapter Thirty-Six

The woman who came to see me at Saint Christopher's didn't tell me her name, although she knew mine. She was tall, plainly dressed, and had her hair pulled tight in an old-fashioned bun. I couldn't guess her age. Not old, though.

A visitor, Matron announced with a knowing look, showing her into my room with a knuckle-tap on the door as if I was a paying guest. Visitors were rare; most girls didn't have them unless they were from the church or the welfare. Someone was sent up with tea and I realised then that Matron must be acquainted with the woman and she wasn't just a do-gooder, although doing good seemed the main purpose of her visit.

I remember thinking there was something about her that I couldn't quite catch hold of, as if I should know her, and yet I'd never met her before, I was sure of it. She looked quite sharply at me at first and I could tell she wanted to chastise me, call me all the names under the sun, but she didn't. All she said was that I wasn't at all what she expected. I should have challenged that, asked what indeed she had expected, but I was shy and innocent – not in every way, I grant you – and it didn't occur to me to ask questions.

She seemed much taken with the baby, standing over the cot making cooing sounds and stroking his little dark head. I asked if she wanted to pick him up but she said she'd better not, there'd be time enough for that, which was strange because she only stayed half an hour and I never saw her again.

I wasn't to worry, she told me. He would have a good home with the best family and be well taken care of. When people tell you not to worry it makes you worry more, I find, but I thanked her all the same without understanding exactly what I was thanking her for; it just seemed appropriate at the time. I spoke hardly at all while she was there, it was all one-sided, but I did assert myself at the end, for the baby's sake, not mine. I had given him a name, Matthew, I said, and I would like him to keep it, if it could be arranged. She nodded, then she left. She understood, I felt. For me it was over, but he had his whole life ahead and I wanted him to take something of me with him on that journey. Apart from a bundle of woollens and a handful of trifles, a name was all I could give.

Matthew was my favourite of the Gospels, the one with the Nativity; that was why I chose the name. And thank goodness I spoke up, otherwise I might not have made the connection with the story in the *Daily Express*. I would never have overlooked him, though, my first love. His dear face shone out at me as soon as I turned the page, changed hardly at all in the eight, almost nine, years since I had last seen him. I didn't look at her, his wife, not in any detail – I couldn't. At first I refused to believe that the lad sitting between the two of them was really Matthew. His name, his age, the intense expression so like his father's, the eyes so like mine – it all tied up. Yet it took a while for my brain to let in the joyful, impossible truth: the man who was never truly mine, but lent to me to love for such a brief time, had taken in his own son, our son, the child whom, as far as I was aware, he never knew existed.

It sealed off something in my mind, knowing they were together, put an end to the search that was only ever a part of my dreams.

The newspaper story itself alarmed me and I wished, oh how I wished, I could have been there to protect him. But that is the way of children. They get into scrapes, into danger. They make dens in crumbling sandy caves, places that aren't safe, no matter how many times they're told to stay away, then have to be rescued with shouts and shovels and scavenging hands. He was brave, the paper said. I'm not sure I would have been. I kept the cutting; it's over there, tucked among the books on the shelf.

I still have a fondness for the bible, for the stories it tells with such beauty, such conviction, but they are only stories. It wasn't God who rescued me from the bridge. A second's hesitation was all it took, a moment, and a man's arms were around me, containing my struggle, until he felt it safe to let me go. He'd been walking home from a nightshift at the railway. Stanley, his name was. His wife was called Ethel. Five children they had already, most grown up, off their hands. One more wouldn't make any difference.

I heard later that they thought I was dead at first, the people at Saint Christopher's, and I would have been, left to my own devices and devoid of the earthly compassion that dawned that morning, along with the rising sun and the mist on the river. The clues were there, it was true. My disappearance, a sighting of me walking by the Tyne, the wooden cross, too, perhaps. Stanley ripped it from around my neck, flung it into the grey water. *That'll do you no good.* I always thought it ironic that fate delivered me into a household of unbelievers.

I kept my promise, to myself and to a God I no longer had faith in, and made no attempt to contact my lover. I had let him go; one way or another, it was over. Then one day, after a year or so, I was sent across town on an errand and the bus chanced to pass the tailor's shop. It was closed, the windows were shuttered, an agent's board attached to the fascia, and I knew then that he'd gone. I wished him happiness.

There is so much that we as mortals don't know, and that's what allows us to believe that good things can come, no matter how far out of our reach they seem and how little we think we deserve them. Had I understood that then, I might not have been so convinced that my life without my child in it could not be lived. But there it is. Even hearts mend, in time, and I've found contentment that I never asked for or expected, and yet still it came. Luck, of course, plays a part – luck, fate, providence, whatever you choose to call it – that and human endeavour, human kindness, and a twist of time.

And now here I sit, my hands restless in my lap, watching the gulls arrow past the window, a bedazzle of white against a dreary November sky. We moved down here to Broadstairs when Hector retired, then last year when I lost him I changed the place round so my little sitting room is on the top floor. I like to look out at the sea and everything going on, and the light's marvellous for cross-stitch and reading. When I'm even more ancient than I am now, I might need a stairlift to get up here but so be it. It gives me a good view of the street so I'll know the minute he arrives. We didn't say a time – I didn't want that, looking at the clock, wondering if he's going to come.

We have written, spoken on the phone, too, and he doesn't know. He doesn't know that Henry was his natural father. Perhaps it is better that way. But we shall see. I only pray he can forgive me, all of us, for everything. It is all I hope for.

A tooting horn has me looking down. I see a car winding its way along the promenade. It won't be long now.

THE END